ENGLAND, SCOTLAND, WALES

THE SPIRITUAL TRAVELER

ENGLAND, SCOTLAND, WALES

THE GUIDE TO SACRED SITES AND PILGRIM ROUTES IN BRITAIN

MARTIN PALMER AND NIGEL PALMER

HiddenSpring

Illustrations and "strip" maps by Paul Saunders
Maps and city plans by Dick Vine
Art by Rebecca Hind
Picture research by Merilyn Thorold

© 2000 ICOREC

Parts of this book first appeared in *Sacred Britain: A Guide to the Sacred Sites and Pilgrim Routes of England, Scotland and Wales*, published in 1997 by Judy Piatkus (Publishers) Limited, 5 Windmill Street, London W1P 1HF, © 1997 ICOREC. This edition published by arrangement with Judy Piatkus (Publishers) Limited.

Palmer, Martin.
   The spiritual traveler : England, Scotland, Wales : the guide to sacred sites and pilgrim routes in Britain / by Martin Palmer and Nigel Palmer.
   p. cm.
Includes bibliographical references and index.
ISBN 1-58768-002-5 (alk. paper)
   1. Great Britain–Guidebooks. 2. Pilgrims and pilgrimages—Great Britain—Guidebooks. 3. Religious institutions—Great Britain—Guidebooks. 4. Christian antiquities—Great Britain—Guidebooks. 5. Historic sites—Great Britain—Guidebooks. 6. Sacred space— Great Britain—Guidebooks. 7. Shrines—Great Britain—Guidebooks. I. Palmer, Nigel, 1955-II. Title.

DA650 .P29 2000
914.104'86—dc21

00-031967

Published in North America by
HiddenSpring
An imprint of Paulist Press
997 Macarthur Boulevard
Mahwah, New Jersey 07430

www.hiddenspringbooks.com

Printed and bound in the United States of America

Front cover shows the Castlerigg stone circle, Cumbria, one of Britain's best preserved sets of standing stones.

Contents

THE SPIRITUAL TRAVELER

*S*acred journeys and sacred sites have been at the center of human-kind's spiritual life from the very beginning. The Spiritual Traveler series invites seekers of every faith and none to discover and connect with these ancient traditions and to find - either for the first time or anew - unique ways of pilgrimage in today's world.

PLEASE BE IN TOUCH

We have worked very hard to make this edition of The Spiritual Traveler as accurate and up to date as possible. However, any travel information could change at any time. If you think you have come across errors or omissions, please let us know. In addition, we would love to hear about your spiritual discoveries - any sacred spaces or peaceful places that you have found along the way, but not in this book. We will try to include them in upcoming editions. You can reach us at: thespiritualtraveler@hiddenspringbooks.com

LAST, BUT NOT LEAST

Please understand that the authors, editors, and publisher cannot accept responsibility for any errors in this book or adverse experiences you might encounter while traveling. We encourage you to stay alert and be aware of your environment while on your spiritual journey.

"I have seen many things in my travels, and I understand more than I can express." —Sirach (*Ecclesiasticus 34: 11/12*)

Our Authors

MARTIN PALMER is the Director of the International Consultancy on Religion, Education and Culture (ICOREC) and a religious advisor to the World Wide Fund for Nature. He is a frequent television and radio commentator and the author of numerous books on the spiritual traditions of East and West. He lives in Manchester. His brother NIGEL PALMER has collected guides to churches and other sacred sites for almost thirty years and has drawn upon his unique collection for this book. He lives in Blanbury, Oxfordshire.

Introduction

SACRED BRITAIN IS a reality. There are places in this land where Heaven and Earth have touched, changed lives and transformed landscapes. Some of these places are famous – great cathedrals, mighty stone circles; others are so personal that they may be known only to a few. Sacred Britain can mean the sites of antiquity – yew trees over five thousand years old – or places such as the Swaminarayan Hindu Temple in north London, which are so modern that the construction dust is still upon them. They can be places hallowed by centuries of prayer – churches, remains of medieval synagogues or shrines where pre-Christian and Christian veneration join hands; or they can be places scarred by suffering – Jews persecuted, villages destroyed by economic changes, sites associated with massacres, sacred to the lives lost and causes betrayed.

Discovering Sacred Britain

In searching for Sacred Britain, we need to listen for the stories which make places special to others as well as to honor those places which are special perhaps only to us as individuals or as members of a family. The more overtly historical ones – henges, churches, holy wells – we can find marked on ordnance survey maps. What are not marked are the sites on the spiritual and mental maps which are carried in people's heads.

Wherever you live, there are places which have meaning for you

The shrine of St Thomas at Canterbury was one of the most popular pilgrimage sites in England. The above badge, commemorating his return from exile, would have been bought and worn by pilgrims as a souvenir of their visit

because of what has happened there to you or to someone whom you care for. You have places where you go to heal yourself or to lick your wounds; places where you go to celebrate; places where you can think.

In broader historical terms, the sacred story of Britain is not an unbroken one. It is the story of upheavals as well as of long periods of calm. It is a narrative of invasion followed by annihilation, absorption or co-existence. As each new wave came, they brought their own beliefs and saw the same hills, the same forests, the same rivers through different eyes.

For much of human history in Britain, no one wrote anything down; we therefore have few conventional records of people's actual thoughts or beliefs. But they did write on something somewhat larger than a book or a papyrus scroll. They wrote on the very landscape which you now visit and travel through. Discovering how to read the sacred landscape is a journey into the past which helps prepare us for the future.

How Travel Becomes Pilgrimage

Exploring a sacred place involves two journeys – physical and metaphysical – running side by side. This is perhaps one of the most important things to remember when setting out to use this guide. While the places we shall take you to are often powerful in their sense of the divine, they require something from you as well. To arrive at a major religious site in a rush just before closing time, or to try and pack too much into a day, may mean you fail to arrive in a receptive frame of mind. The encounter with the sacred in our landscape is two-way: your response is what is needed to make the encounter happen. If you can use this guidebook to journey within as well as without, then you will

Little Gidding Church in Cambridgeshire where many pilgrims still go today to pray and meditate

have discovered a simple truth that every ancient traveler to sacred places knew: that the journey to the divine begins with the first step and begins within the pilgrim.

T. S. Eliot puts it better than we can ever say in his poem about one of the strangest of sacred places in the United Kingdom, the church and community at Little Gidding in Cambridgeshire (pictured above):

> *If you came this way,*
> *Taking any route, starting from anywhere,*
> *At any time or at any season,*
> *It would always be the same: you would have to put off*
> *Sense and notion. You are not here to verify,*
> *Instruct yourself, or inform curiosity*
> *Or to carry report. You are here to kneel*
> *Where prayer has been valid . . . .*

Rediscovering the Sacred Maps

There are two ways in which we can relate to a sacred landscape: we can be observers or participants. To illustrate this, here is an example from China, a country which has Buddhist and Taoist sacred mountains. Buddhism came to China from India two thousand years ago but it is still called a foreign religion. On its sacred mountains the upward Path links one great temple or monastery with another and you are encouraged to enjoy the scenery – you are an observer. On Taoist sacred mountains the temples and monasteries are tangential. In Chinese, *Tao* means Path and the Path is the purpose and meaning of the mountain. You stop not to admire the view but to hear stories which explain how a rock came to be that shape, or why a tree grows where it does. You, traveling the Path, become part of the narrative of the mountain.

So before we even begin to look at places, we need to realize that there are these two ways of entering and experiencing a sacred space or of discovering the sacred within and around a site. We can observe, or we can become a part of it.

The Sacred Land Project

This book has its origins in a unique project launched in the United Kingdom in 1997. The "Sacred Land Project" is a long-term commitment between environmental and conservation bodies such as World Wide Fund for Nature (WWF, UK), and the major religions of the United Kingdom. Very simply, "Sacred Land" seeks to enable local communities to recover, restore or create sacred sites in their own locale. Such sites may be places of great antiquity such as pilgrimage routes or holy wells. Or they may be the creation of sacred space – a garden or a place of quiet reflection – in urban inner city areas. "Sacred Land" now assists and inspires hundreds of local projects in the United Kingdom, projects which are designed by local communities and which are open to all regardless of faith. Similar projects and associated publications are springing up in Norway, Sweden, Ireland, France, Germany, Nepal and China.

PART ONE

THE EPIC OF SACRED BRITAIN

CHAPTER 1

The History of the Land

Here, I said: here where you stand
And stop, and let everything go still
Feeling your breath as you glance down
Is the ground that is everywhere –

nameless under our naming

As it ebbs to your feet like a sea
That your heart knows already, as it breathes
Through the soles of your feet, with relief.

THE EPIC OF Sacred Britain is the dramatic narrative of the formation of the landscape of this country over many thousands of years. The term "epic" has been used deliberately, for it is only if we can see the develop-ments – geological and human, physical and spiritual – as an unfolding drama that we shall be able to understand our crucial role in the possible denouement. All good epics are also about success and failure; about dan-ger and safety; about the sacred and about being scared; even at times about good and evil. They are about ambiguity as much as certainty, and loss as much as preservation. Epics sway back and forth across time, explor-ing issues that have a perennial significance even if they manifest them-selves in specific incidents at specific times. If an epic has to have an evil force, an external threat to stability, then in Britain's case it has been ice and cold in the past and today human exploitation and abuse of the land. From about 100,000 years ago until 12,000 years ago, much of the island was covered with ice and the environment was cold and harsh. While there is evidence of very early peoples living in Britain as far back as 450,000 years ago, the onset of the last ice age pushed them out of most parts of the island.

The Last Ice Age Ends

When the last great ice age ended the Mesolithic peoples began to infiltrate Britain, crossing over from continental Europe via a land bridge. We have virtually nothing from the Mesolithic peoples in Britain which could be described as religious or hinting at the sacred. What we do have, however, is the Gulf Stream; if ice and cold are among the evil forces of this epic, then the new presence of the Gulf Stream is one of the benign elements.

The warm air and waters of the Gulf Stream, pushing their way across the Atlantic from Mexico to Britain, have meant that our ancestors were able to develop agriculture. For Britain lies on the same latitude as Labrador in Canada. Were it not for the Gulf Stream, our ice ages would never have ended; even if they had, we would today be inhabiting a much colder land.

The first farmers, the Neolithic peoples who arrived c.4500 BC, were also the first to establish religious and spiritual centers in Britain. But we must beware of thinking that the epic is a straightforward story of gradual development and change. There have been periods throughout human history when the old sacred vision of the world has broken down and been replaced by the planning, exploitative and "objective" view. What is clear is that, with a warmer climate and the beginnings of agriculture, Britain witnessed a population explosion during the Neolithic period. This led to increased violence because of competition for scarce land, and to personal aggrandizement of the warrior aristocracy at the expense of others. Archaeological evidence seems to show early Neolithic settlements as being without defensive walls. The creation of fortified camps is seen as evidence of the growth of military groups and of increased violence between tribes.

The sacred land of the Neolithic peoples who inhabited the island from c.6500 years ago to c.4300 years ago is dominated by burial places, henges

PREHISTORY

- Paleolithic (Old Stone Age) from earliest human existence to end of last ice age, c.10,000 BC
- Mesolithic (Middle Stone Age) c.10,000 BC–c.4500 BC
- Neolithic (New Stone Age) c.4500 BC–c.2300 BC
- Bronze Age c.2300 BC–800 BC
- Iron Age c.800 BC to Roman times

and associated structures. We shall look at these in more detail in Chapter 2. There are also the remains of their villages and even of bridges and causeways, but these fall outside the scope of this book.

Burial Mounds and Stone Circles – Centers of Faith

Neolithic burial mounds – long barrows and megalithic tombs – were more than just burial places. Their position and surroundings clearly indicate that they were ritual centers of considerable importance.

These wonderful old tombs are almost always sited on a hillside, or sometimes right on the crest of a hill. For example, the weather-beaten chamber tombs of Minning Low Hill in south Derbyshire (3 miles S of Pikehall, off A5012). These tombs, on top of the highest hill for miles around, are a clear sign that the hill itself was sacred. Yet on chalk hills, while the barrows are often well situated for a good view they rarely dominate the landscape; the many burial mounds around Avebury in Wiltshire are a good example. But, being created from chalk, they originally stood out brightly against the green and brown of the landscape.

The same is true of stone circles or henges, and the strange embankments which often accompany them. Many of these structures are found on low-lying land. Stonehenge, for instance, stands in a flat plain. Admittedly it is visible for many miles, but there seems to have been little attempt to use natural features to heighten its drama.

But perhaps this is to miss the point. Many of the great tombs, stone circles and henges were approached down ritual pathways – the avenues of standing stones still clearly visible at Avebury and at Callanish on the Isle of Lewis, or, in the case of tree-lined avenues, to be sensed at Belas Knap in Gloucestershire. At many sites there are causeways – banks of earth which have no defensive purpose but seem to have been ritual walkways. From the evidence of the tombs themselves, processing along pathways or corridors was important to Neolithic people. Rather than take to the hilltops for spectacular effect, they seem to have made their pathways, which lay along the edge of valleys or ran across broad plains, the center of their ritual life. It is worth recalling that by the time many of the great henges and mounds were being built, c.3000 BC–2000 BC, much of the accessible land on the lower hills had already been cleared of forest and was being cultivated.

Neolithic Faith

We know very little of Neolithic religion or how it related to the envi-

The Neolithic site of Stonehenge in Wiltshire

ronment. The Neolithic peoples were certainly the first to leave their mark upon it, through tombs, henges and cultivation, but what they believed as they did so is largely beyond our grasp. Women seem to have had equality with men, not least in the sphere of religion. Tantalizing hints of goddess figures carved on stone entrances to tombs and of astrological and astronomical alignment of the henges to the moon or sun can be discerned. What is important to stress is that the druids, who first appear c.400 BC, had nothing to do with Stonehenge, Avebury or any of the other Neolithic sites. They seem to have shunned such places, as will be seen later.

Of the architecture in Britain of which we have any record, the stone circles and henges are the first which go against the lie of the land. Far from blending in, they were meant to stand out in contrast to their surroundings. Something within Neolithic culture at its highest, most developed end wanted to say, "Here we are," and did so through the megaliths.

The Bronze Age Transformation

With the coming of the Bronze Age, c.2300 BC–800 BC, Britain was transformed almost as radically as it was later under Roman rule. Metal

TOMBS AND RITUALS

Most megalithic chambered tombs (some 250 in England and Wales, 600 in Scotland) seem to have been almost parish centers, for they developed over the centuries and were obviously places of feasting and celebration. The area in front of the tomb entrance was used for gatherings and rituals. The tombs have been found to contain many bones, the oldest often brushed aside to allow new bodies to be accommodated.

These tombs seem to have been communal burial places, perhaps only later being covered over. But then something interesting begins to emerge. The great long barrows (of which some two hundred survive, primarily in southern England along the chalk hills, but with a number in Lincolnshire and Yorkshire) seem to have been status symbol burial places reserved for great chiefs. Here ostentatious burial goods were deposited and the corporate burial mound is dwarfed by what appear to be family or even individual burials. Increasingly also, the people buried in such special tombs are warriors. It seems that late Neolithic cultures initiated the warrior cult which has lasted until the present day.

technology came from Europe, together with peoples who could use this technology to conquer the stone-using farming inhabitants. The impact of bronze weapons and tools was to speed up the destruction of the forests, begun by Neolithic peoples, and the final clearance of many lowland areas for agriculture. The first discernible roadways, such as the Icknield Way (running from East Anglia to the coast) and the Ridgeway (running across north Wiltshire and through Berkshire), appeared; it seems likely that Britain was criss-crossed by such routes, many now lost to sight or built over by the Romans. Trade had begun with other parts of Europe, explaining the presence of Aegean-style daggers carved on to the stones of Stonehenge during the rebuilding in the mid-sixteenth century BC. The most distinctive remains of the Bronze Age are its round burial mounds, of which it is still not known how many exist in the UK; the estimate is between fifteen thousand and twenty thousand. These occur primarily in the western half of Britain, with the greatest concentration in the south of England.

The Bronze Age, particularly from c.1500 BC onward, also left its mark on the fields. While the question of dating field systems is a fraught one – there seems to have been no discernible change in peasant farming from

Bronze Age to post-Roman – it appears that many so-called Celtic fields pre-date the Celts by a thousand years or more. The Bronze Age system of plowing produced squared fields. Centuries of such plowing and the clearing of stones from the fields have created the field walls known as lynchets. They can still be seen on the chalk downs of Wiltshire (especially at Ogbourne St George) or on the chalk hills of Dorset (around Abbotsbury and Portesham). One definitively dated Bronze Age field system is at Plumpton Plain near Brighton in Sussex.

Over the long period of its existence, but increasingly in the last four to five hundred years (c.1200 BC–c.800 BC), Bronze Age culture was therefore transforming the landscape and leaving its mark. It was also hunting to extinction various species. We know that the cave bear, lion, hippopotamus, woolly rhinoceros and reindeer were all wiped out at some time from about thirty thousand years ago, and from the remains of hunters' fires and rubbish tips on Neolithic and Bronze Age sites we know that human activity contributed to their demise. In fact, with the exception of the wolf and the aurochs (European bison), by the Iron Age all the earlier large land animals were extinct; the range of medium-size wildlife which we have today – badgers, foxes, wildcats, deer and so forth – was all that was left, along with wild pigs.

Ecological and Religious Collapse – c.1000 BC

However, while human activity certainly helped to push many species to the brink, a major climatic change also had its effect. Around 1050 BC a massive volcano erupted in Iceland and the resulting ash created a long dark winter in which the sunlight could not penetrate the ash layers in the atmosphere. Agriculture seems to have collapsed in many parts of the country. The damp, dark climate caused the decay of the existing plant life and the creation of peat bogs. In many places in Ireland, where excavations have taken place, you can see the stone walls of the Neolithic and early Bronze Age lying underneath the peat bogs. Britain underwent a similar collapse of agriculture, though less dramatic.

This was the first major ecological disaster that Britain had to face after the ice ages. It seems to have led to a rejection of the old egalitarian beliefs and systems, for at about this time there is evidence of a move toward increased patriarchy and a great rise in the status of the warrior class. At the same time the majority of the ancient sites such as stone circles were abandoned. Essentially, the deities had failed. Darkness and death had descended upon the landscape. New ways were to be sought.

The Revolutionary Iron Age

The Iron Age had an even greater impact than the Bronze Age. Iron was introduced from Europe around 750 BC, and its additional strength for fashioning implements enabled more land to be used for agriculture. This and the resultant rise in population pushed wild Britain even further to the edge.

Perhaps the most distinctive feature of our landscape left by the Iron Age is the hill fort. In some areas it is impossible to look at any hilltop or ridgeway running along a top contour without seeing one. Even today, after some 2500 years of British weather and neglect, the earth ramparts can be seen clearly against the sky from 10 miles away and more. Yet these ramparts, when built, would have been possibly a third higher than they are now, and gleaming white when cut into chalk.

Over 1300 hill forts have been identified in southern Britain, a massive effort which changed the skyline dramatically. They are a further sign that society was becoming more violent as a result of the growth of a warrior hierarchy. The disruption of the volcanic ash, followed by waves of new invaders and technology, caused over-population, scarcity of resources and the collapse of society, as evidenced by the abandonment of the old sacred sites. To this day, relics of the fear of these new iron-working tribes remain in British folklore. The smithy, the blacksmith and those who work with iron are still in legend associated with the devil, with dwarfs and elves and with the darker forces of life. The arrival of the Iron Age was a traumatic time for many. And foremost among these new warrior tribes were the Celts.

The Coming of the Celts

We know far more about the religious life of the Celts than we do about that of any earlier inhabitants of Britain. Foreign writers such as Julius Caesar and some of the Greek geographers comment upon them. Now for the first time a distinct concept of the sacredness of nature is evident. One indication of the Celtic understanding of the shift in values is the orientation of their round houses – communal homes, places for storytelling and possibly even ritual. All Neolithic and Bronze Age round houses had their entrance facing west, the direction of the dead, but the Celtic ones faced east, to the rising sun and new life.

With the Celts, a different cultural emphasis appears. While farming, the building of hill forts and trading continued and developed, Celtic religion focused on natural features such as forests, groves, sacred lakes and holy wells. There is a visible retreat from the plains and the old ritual centers such as Stonehenge.

Although southern British tribes such as the Trinovantes founded towns like Camulodunum (Colchester), the priesthood and most of the tribespeople lived in the forests and hills. For the druids it was the woodlands that were sacred – not the spaces cleared in them, but the mighty and divine oaks, yews and ashes and the parasitical mistletoe. It was to streams and lakes that the priests and worshipers came. For example, a druid "prince" was sacrificed some 15 miles south of modern Manchester, apparently willingly, by being thrown into a boggy swamp in some ritual of repentance or supplication. Over two thousand years later his body was found, preserved in the peat at Lindow Moss near Wilmslow in Cheshire.

Was all this a reaction against the cleared lands and their stone circles, remnants of the earlier failed cultures? Or were the Celts, in their long journey from their origins in the Russian steppes, bringing with them a love and fear of nature which the Bronze Age and earlier settlers of Britain had either never possessed or lost? It is impossible to tell. All that is clear is that for whatever reason the Celts left the traditional places of worship – Stonehenge shows no signs of use during this period, nor do Avebury or indeed any of the major stone circles – and centered their religion on the forests.

Sacred Groves

By their very nature, the sacred yew groves of the druids have left virtually no mark. There are remnants of probably two sacred groves in Surrey – we visit one on the route to Canterbury from Winchester. Certainly those remaining yews over two thousand years old, often now enclosed within ancient churchyards in remote areas, might be taken as fragmentary evidence of the former presence of sacred groves. Most fascinating are the yews, the ruined church and the Bronze Age bank and ditch at Knowlton near Wimborne St Giles in Dorset (see also p. 62).

Nor do we have much idea where the Celtic sacred oak groves were, for oaks live only a few hundred years. However, the place-name Derry seems to indicate an oak grove. We know that there was a great forest sanctuary known as the Medionemeton in lowland Scotland; it is possible that this site is celebrated in the name Holywood, near Dumfries.

The evidence for Celtic worship and ritual sites comes, not from buildings or standing stones, but from sacrifice lakes such as the one at Llyn Cerrig Bach on Anglesey – one of the greatest centers of druid training –

and from the stone heads found in high places such as the Pennines of Yorkshire (see p. 39). But all that changed, as did so much else, under the Romans.

Ruined church, henge monuments and yew trees at Knowlton, near Wimborne St Giles, Dorset

The Impact of Rome

Many people know that the excessive farming techniques of the Romans, striving to feed the vast metropolitan centers of Rome, Alexandria and Constantinople, turned the rich arable land of Egypt and North Africa into the deserts of today. Yet few realize that massive, impersonal agro-business in Britain deforested vast areas such as the hill ranges of Yorkshire; caused the build-up of silt in the Wash (East Anglia); and made most of England, especially the south, such a ruined agricultural waste-land, devoid of trees and topsoil, that it was incapable of supporting the towns and cities that the Romans had founded. Putting it simply, England's first major ecological crisis caused by humanity of which we have clear evidence was produced by the Romans. By the late fifth centu-ry AD it had left England looking like many regions of the environmen-tally devastated "developing world" today.

Before that time, for some four hundred years since the full invasion of Britain in AD 43, the Romans had developed the landscape of England, Wales and southern Scotland in ways that had never been experienced there before. In particular, they had transformed the southern half of Britain into a semi-urban agricultural landscape. With the Romans appeared the first true towns and cities. Roads rather than tracks were carved across the landscape, and they are still famous for being as straight as possible, regardless of the terrain (though we have always enjoyed the fact that the Roman road which passes by Silbury Hill in Wiltshire, the largest humanly constructed prehistoric hill in Europe, has to do a dog-leg to get round it!).

Many of the temple sites from this period were built to house Celtic deities: after the power of the druids was destroyed and the Celtic tribes settled around and within towns and cities, their religion came out of the forests and woods. It is from this time that many of the Celtic temples which later transformed into Christian churches originate – for example Old St Pancras in London (see p. 40).

Britain, as part of the huge Roman Empire, was exploited as thoroughly as many third world or developing countries have been exploited by more recent foreign powers. Britain also benefited in many ways, but in terms of landscape the legacy of the Romans is secular rather than religious – indeed, given the damage to the natural environment it harmed much of the innate sacredness of the land.

Roman Ecological Collapse Leads to Invasion

By the end of the Roman period, c.AD 450, many parts of England had been farmed out and consisted of vast areas of scrubland. But in those parts of the country where the Romans had had only marginal impact – most of Scotland and Wales – the landscape was not affected.

With the collapse of the Roman Empire and the withdrawal of Roman troops to defend their homeland against invaders from the east, Britain itself lay open to invasion. From about AD 450 to 550 the Celts were driven to the west and north as new tribes from across the North Sea came in to take their lands. At first the newcomers lived by raiding, but soon they began to settle. However, because the land was not in a good state agriculture was not the only or best way to sustain themselves; warfare and raiding was. This state of affairs continued until the re-emergence of Christianity in the sixth century.

Christianity Rises Again

Since at least AD 180, probably much earlier, there has been Christianity in Britain. It was an urban phenomenon, or linked to great Romano-

British estates and their houses. We know of churches such as St Martin's in Canterbury which date from c.AD 320. There were also great Christian settlements such as that at Bangor-on-the-Dee/Bangor-is-y-coed in Clwyd, which from c.AD 180 until its destruction by the Saxons in AD 607 was the greatest Celtic Christian community. But in 397 a new form of Christianity appeared; within 150 years it was ready to claim the whole island and, in so doing, to solve the environmental crisis left by the Romans.

In Whithorn, Dumfries and Galloway, St Ninian built the first monastery in Britain (see p. 252). Reputedly a Roman citizen, Ninian chose to build his monastery on the beautiful but wild shores of the Solway Firth, outside Roman control. Here he founded a simple way of life centered on prayer and working the land by sustainable means.

As will be revealed in the relevant pilgrimage sections in this book, soon monks and nuns were criss-crossing Britain and bringing with them a new form of agriculture: replanting forests; cutting new waterways to irrigate parched land; creating ponds and lakes, and, most importantly, building upon the old Celtic sacred vision of the land, of all nature, to revive the very land and spirit of Britain. By doing so they helped the incomers, the Anglo-Saxons, to settle and to become better neighbors to the remaining Romano-British peoples. In this way the Celtic and Christian traditions restored the sacred to the landscape and refounded settled life in Britain. (For more details, see pages 100-102, 129-130, 142-145, 256-257.)

The Christian Vision of a Sacred Land

At this time the great pilgrimage routes were created, taking people into the landscape on new sacred journeys. The pioneers were the Benedictines, one of the earliest of religious orders, who combined practical work with a love of all creation because it spoke to them of God. Like generations of Christians since, they saw the whole of the landscape as an expression of God's love and of love returned to God. This led to their developing agricultural methods which increased both the fertility and diversity of plant and animal species on their land. Until very recently even our towns and cities were built to express this vision and the built human environment was perceived as being charged with spiritual powers and forces, as will be seen in Chapter 4.

The Coming of the Scientists

Now the epic comes to another momentous shift in ideas. The concept of a rationalist and reductionist way of looking at life arose with the early scientists, who believed that if you could reduce something to its component parts you could fully understand it. The trouble is that it is not as separate parts that something works or makes sense, but as a whole.

Nevertheless for three hundred years and more, all aspects of creation have been reduced to what constitutes them and how much they are worth. The famous challenge of the rationalists, "Show me where in the body the soul is to be found," was a death knell to the sacred in the landscape. If you cannot "find" the soul in a human body, how can you find the sacred in earth, rocks and rivers?

So the path was cleared for a mechanical view of nature and of human beings, and as a result we have now discovered much about how things are made and how they work. Industrialization arose from this mechanistic and exploratory world view. Consumerism also emerged from a cultural perspective which knows the price of everything and the value of nothing. What has so often been missing is an answer to the question: why? There was, of course, some reaction against this – by the Romantics, for instance. But the driving force was reductionism.

Britain became the first industrial country in the world, the first to have a greater urban than rural population. Now it is among the first to have to deal with the aftermath in terms of pressure on the land and strain on human life. Landscapes, especially sacred ones, can only "carry" so many people. Already places such as Stonehenge, Callanish and Avebury are overloaded and the landscape is being punished by the sheer numbers. Yet we need to escape from the urban world that we have created, and we have so mechanized the countryside that it is only the old wild places which offer sanctuary.

Today our land is besieged with chemical fertilizers and machines and there is an increasing absence of people in the countryside except as visitors. Hedgerows that took centuries to grow are being uprooted. Ancient woodlands have shrunk drastically since the 1940s. Urbanization has spread and destroyed so much of the beautiful landscape around our towns and cities. We are in a state of cultural, religious and spiritual crisis.

Today and Tomorrow – the Sacred Pathways to the Future

Nevertheless we are capable of recovery, for we have been this way before. But today we have better information than at any previous time, together with a diversity of religions encompassing a multitude of ideas to draw upon. But first we need to understand that the landscapes around us are not a blank sheet on which we can write as we choose; nor are they all a mistake which we have to wipe clean. What we must do is make contact with the sacred landscapes which surround us. We need to learn to see again, to make the familiar unfamiliar so that we are excited and challenged by what we see.

PART TWO

THE SACRED
LANDSCAPE

--- ✍ ---

CHAPTER 2

Stone Circles and Tombs

Sacred, sacrosanct, sanctuary
In the ruins of what was sacred space that we need back:

These monoliths to moon and sun remind us
That we abandoned the stars for ourselves, only to find
That we have no rite for being human

But now as the breeze stirs, and we slow our steps
Where stone breathes we can receive its whispered gift again

THERE IS AN inescapable romance in ruins. To wander among piles of stones, discovering a carving here, a doorway there, and trying to imagine yourself in the lives of those who once lived here, has a perennial fascination. Whether the ruins are ancient, such as those of Rome or Greece, or modern, as in the case of a ruined Welsh slate port, time is less significant than atmosphere.

A Sense of Atmosphere

It is this sense of atmosphere which draws us inexorably to the great remains of the Neolithic, Bronze Age and Iron Age cultures. For most of us it is not necessary to know exactly when or by whom such places were raised; more important is the knowledge that at some point in the past others came here to marvel at their environment, to mourn the dead, to feast and to celebrate, perhaps to ward off deep fears. As many of these issues – death and life, celebration and fear – still affect us today, these sites give us the opportunity to release our imagination and to sense something bigger, older, deeper than just ourselves and our age.

What place do sites whose faith is lost to us have in a book on Sacred Britain – a book primarily concerned with living faiths? After all, we know next to nothing of the beliefs, myths or language of those who built these stone monuments. Our reason for including them is that, in order to understand our present and to envisage our potentially sacred future, we need to see what the sacred past can tell us. For example, it is important to appreciate that Britain has already been through two ecological disasters – c.1000 BC and after the fall of the Roman Empire – and that each time the result was a shift in religious thought. The past is not continuous; it exists in leaps and bounds, pitfalls and retrenchment, and from this we have come to be who we are. Attempts to re-create the past are often nothing more than nostalgia and retreat from today. Ours is an urban culture. Rural imagery is helpful in defining what we have lost and what we have deliberately chosen to leave behind. Rural retreat, however, can be a retreat from the present reality of the human condition. Any spirituality worth its name is going to have something to offer to this new reality. If it cannot, then it will eventually dry up and perish.

This is why religious sites die once their role has begun to change. They still retain their power, of course. They are still, in Eliot's words, places where prayer has been made valid. They are still symbols of the quest for something beyond just ourselves. But they no longer provide the lens through which we define reality.

So in looking at these wonderful Neolithic, Bronze and Iron Age sites we shall try to combine archaeological information and insight, scientific study and a sense of awe and wonder. By drawing upon archaeology, we can start with what is known or possibly known. This frees us to go beyond, each in our own way. But we should try to do so with the same integrity as that which drove people four or five thousand years ago to build and then abandon these extraordinary edifices. We need to see not just what brought those people here to construct such places, but also what led them to forsake their creations. Both hold the key to our future.

When today we look at stone circles or old churches and see them as essentially historical monuments which no longer speak to us of faith, we are part of the same kind of movement which left behind the stone circles. Perhaps we can now begin to observe the signs of newer ways and places which will feed the spiritual needs of Sacred Britain in the future. All this is fed by looking at abandoned sacred sites and asking, not just why were they built and what went on, but why they were left.

Why Were They Built?

These sites were built for both practical and religious reasons. They seem to have been ways in which a tribe or tribes could learn to work together and forge bonds of mutual support. Also, after the harvest had been gathered in the autumn there was little to do in the long winter months other than hunt; so building great ditches, circles and so forth kept the people occupied and warm. From the religious viewpoint, it is clear that some places were different in association and use from the run-of-the-mill fortified hilltop or settlement – they were places of obvious power. For example, building defensive ditches is a common feature of late Neolithic and Bronze Age cultures. Most of these were dug simply to keep wolves, foxes and human predators out. But when a ditch was dug around the stones of Avebury, it was built in such a way as to try and keep something in. Whatever was here was perceived as having much greater potency than just a few stones. Such inward defensive ditches can be seen at many sites, for instance the remarkable triple stone ditches of Thornborough Circles, Yorkshire (see p. 145).

When burial centers, often containing a score or more bodies, were covered over and "housed" in elaborate mounds, with walls of dressed stone and dance areas before them, it was not just a convenient way of disposing of the dead. This was communication with the threat or possibly promise of death itself.

When stones were set up to indicate the midwinter or midsummer sun, or, in the earlier phases of many stone circles such as Stonehenge, to indicate the moon's movements, they were probably practical – important ways of keeping track of time and telling people when to start preparing for the coming of spring. But they also served a major psychological and spiritual role, giving a sense of time moving on and warmth returning, even in the depths of winter. Thus they were timepieces and festival centers, combining practical need to know with symbolic and ritual ways of getting through the winter.

Why Were They Abandoned?

It was precisely because they were functional places as well as sites of mystery and ritual that they fell silent. Once they ceased to be effective and no longer ensured the return of the summer heat and crops, they were abandoned. The cataclysmic failure of agriculture c.1000 BC meant that, despite the rituals and the careful alignment of the stones, the timepieces and invokers of divine natural powers had failed.

But such places also have a beauty born of antiquity and their setting in old landscapes. Because the rings of stone and mounds of earth were respected for what they had once been, the areas around them were, until comparatively recently, untouched. Modern farming has destroyed many, but it is still possible to stand beside some of them and see a landscape shaped over four thousand years ago and then left. Cairnholy, near Kirkcudbright in Dumfries and Galloway (see p. 251), and Arbor Low in Derbyshire (see p. 138) are good examples. Others have been desecrated and have lost something of their power: the Nine Ladies circle in Derbyshire (see p. 25) has had a quarry carved into the hillside next to it and is now so heavily visited that the immediate surroundings have been badly eroded.

The Historical Background

Tombs raised above the ground and housing more than one person are a distinctive development of Neolithic culture (c.4000 BC–2400 BC). Earlier, the dead were buried in single tombs or holes in the ground. What caused the Neolithic people to erect the great megalithic and long barrow tombs is unknown. But it may be that, as they invaded the lands of the hunger-gatherer Mesolithic peoples, their collective tombs were used as land markers, setting the dead to protect the living and scare away the dispossessed.

The building of henges come later. The earliest seem to date from c.3000 BC, and the addition of stone came a few hundred years later. New knowledge which the Neolithic peoples acquired led to the development of these sites, for nothing like them had existed before. The key to them seems to be astronomical, since they are usually oriented to the moon and, in the later examples of c.2800 BC, to the sun.

There is now considerable evidence that at least some of the henges were platforms for the dead, who were brought here and left to the elements and the ravages of crows, foxes and wolves. Once the bones were picked clean, they were buried: Stonehenge has given up hundreds of bodies, laid out to the four compass points and buried four to a hole in fifty-six or more pits. Perhaps the most famous evidence to support the idea of the mortuary platform is the causeway enclosures on Hambledon Hill in Hampshire. Here the central enclosure is clearly a mortuary, for remains of the dead were placed in the ditches surrounding the enclosure and hill. The links between the moon and death seem to be strongly signaled, which explains the lunar orientation of a site such as Stonehenge.

The interest in the sun indicates a change in values and beliefs, and a definite shift in religious use of the henges – from funeral parlor to cosmic

THE TERMINOLOGY OF
STONE CIRCLES

These can be of stone or earth (see henge) or even wood. Here is a list of the most commonly used terms which should help you define what you are looking at.

Avenue Leading to and from the henges there are often avenues, either marked by embankments (see cursus) or indicated by standing stones set out down either side of the route. These appear to have been ceremonial walkways, and it is likely that rituals began at the entrance to the avenue. They date from *c*.2800 BC, though the stone-lined ones tend to have been constructed *c*.2000 BC.

Boulder circle A circle of small rounded stones. They date from the Bronze Age and may mark a hut foundation rather than any religious center.

Cairn A burial mound of any shape.

Causeway camp Defensive area, usually for sheltering cattle and ringed by earth ramparts.

Circles These can be of stone or earth (see henge) and even wood. The use of circles for religious purposes indicates completeness and containment. They would probably have been walked round in a clockwise direction.

Cist A stone-lined tomb covered by another stone slab. One of the most dramatic is in Wales, at Rug in Gwynedd, 1½ miles west of Corwen. It is preserved in a medieval castle mound and inside a chamber tomb.

Cove Either the remains of a small megalithic tomb with the central chamber stones left while the mound has gone or never existed, or a later imitation of these early tombs by late Neolithic builders, *c*.2200 BC. These often form the center of stone circles.

Cursus Long parallel banks of earth with outside ditches, often with a square end. The greatest of them is at Stonehenge (see p. 28). They are not defensive, for they indicate rather than enclose. The Greater Cursus at Stonehenge is 3000 yards long and 33 yards wide. Their precise use is unclear, though they may have been some form of raised processional way related to avenues. They are early, often contemporary with the original earthen henge of *c*.2800 BC or a little later.

Dolmen A basic megalithic tomb with a small chamber topped by a large overhanging capping stone.

Henge An earthen rampart circle usually enclosing wooden or stone circles, though these are often later additions. The oldest type has one entrance. Good examples can be seen at Gorsey Bibbury, 6 miles north of Cheddar near Charterhouse on Mendip in Somerset, and at Woodhenge near Amesbury in Wiltshire. Later ones had two entrances. Henges date from *c*.2800 BC and are usually the first development on a site. A very large one is Durrington

Walls outside Amesbury, while the scale of the earthworks can be seen at the henge at Dorchester in Dorset, which the Romans reused as an amphitheater. The earlier existence of earthen henges is clearly illustrated by the later terms which define their rebuilding: Stonehenge and Woodhenge.

Long barrow   Earliest form of burial mound, dating from c.4000 BC to 1800 BC. They usually contain fragments of six to seven bodies and are built of blocks of chalk, not stone or earth. They are higher at the ceremonial east end, tapering down to ground level when they finish, often some 30–90 yards further. They are flanked by earthen ditches, which sometimes meet up. Especially fine examples can be seen at Capel Garmon, just off the A5 near Betws-y-coed in Gwynedd; Carn Glas, just south of Inverness, near Torbreck; Cashtal yn Ard, south of Ramsey on the Isle of Man; Grimston, south of Gilling Castle in Yorkshire; Spellow Hills, off the A16, just south of Ulceby Cross in Lincolnshire; and, most famous of all, West Kennet, just off the A4, south of Avebury in Wiltshire (see p. 23).

Megalithic tombs   As the name indicates, these are built from large stones and have stones of this size at the entrance to the tombs. They have been likened to parish churches in that they grew and changed over time, sometimes over a period of two thousand years. Built from c.4000 BC, they were for large-scale burial of up to sixty bodies and appear to have had status significance, being clearly visible for miles around.

Megalithic tombs fall into two broad groups. Passage tombs have a central chamber from which side chambers run off and which is reached via a passage from the entrance. Gallery tombs have rooms or galleries which all run from the central long passageway.

The tombs contain vast amounts of stone which forms the mound. One archaeologist has estimated that an average megalithic tomb in Caithness has enough stone piled upon it to build five average-size parish churches. It seems that such tombs were used over long periods of time; usually only the last skeleton remains complete while the others show signs of having been moved to make way for the next burial. This seems to indicate a rather pragmatic view of bones – no religious qualms about shifting skeletons.

Good examples are Wayland's Smithy on the Ridgeway, 1½ miles west of the Uffington White Horse in Berkshire (see p. 71); Lligwy, just off the A5025 south of Moelfre on Anglesey; the Grey Mare and Her Colts, 1½ miles north of Abbotsbury in Dorset (see p. 71); and Irefigneth near Holyhead on Anglesey.

Outlier   A standing stone some way from the main circle of stones. Outstanding examples are at the Rollright Stones in Oxfordshire (see p. 26) and at Stanton Drew in Somerset (see p. 27).

Trilithon   Three stones, comprising two upright capped by the third. Stonehenge provides the best examples.

center, we might say. Why the change? Perhaps there was a new priesthood, a new level of religious control and thus a new form of religion. A similar shift can be observed in fifteenth-century BC Egypt when the older gods, centered on death, were for a while displaced by sun worship and a form of monotheism. Something changed in Britain between c.2800 BC and 2000 BC which broke the older pattern and created a new one.

The answer, at least in part, is the coming of the Bronze Age. Life became a little easier. Tools were stronger. Foes, animal as well as human, were more easily overcome. Trees could be cut down more swiftly. There was a mini-industrial revolution which seems to be reflected by the shift in religious focus.

Once the orientation had become predominantly the sun, from c.2300 BC onward, little changed except at sites such as Stonehenge with its capped stones – of which more later. Essentially the henges continued in ritual use until c.1000 BC at the very latest, when they ceased to be used for reasons given earlier.

In the realm of tombs, sites became simpler. Small round barrows for the collective dead became common from the Bronze Age to the Iron Age. Nevertheless the evidence suggests that they were still used as ritual centers. Nor should we make the mistake of thinking that a tomb was used only for religious rituals associated with death. These barrows were the most visible sites on the ancient landscape after the enclosures and henges. Henges are today nowhere near as common as barrows, so perhaps the barrows served as local ritual centers for families, while the henges were the scene of larger gatherings.

Sites

The following list contains details of some of the most important and interesting stone circles and tombs in England, Wales and Scotland. Others which form part of a pilgrimage route are described in Part Three.

ENGLAND

ARBOR LOW, MIDDLETON · DERBYSHIRE
5 miles SW of Bakewell

This circle, situated in one of the finest sacred landscapes anywhere in Europe, is described in detail and set in its wider context on the pilgrimage from Lichfield to Mam Tor (see p. 138).

AVEBURY · WILTSHIRE
1 mile N of A4 and A4361 junction – 10 miles S of Swindon

Stonehenge has most of the fame, but Avebury has most of the atmosphere. When we were teenagers in the sixties we often cycled to Avebury from our home in Bristol; usually we were the only people looking round. Today there are tourist facilities and a car park and Avebury is achieving the fame it deserves. But will it go the way of Stonehenge? Will tourism destroy its wonder? Let's hope not.

The first site was an earthen henge, built *c*.3000 BC. But the site, or rather the immediate area, had already been occupied for a long time. At **Windmill Hill** to the north-north-west there is an earlier henge and causeway camp. To the south-south-east is **West Kennet long barrow**, which was finally sealed *c*.3300 BC. A distinct era seems to have come to a close then.

What forces brought about the shift in emphasis which created the first lunar-oriented henge here? And, even more to the point, what brought about the development of this, the most extensive sacred landscape in Britain, over a period from *c*.2700 BC to 2400 BC?

One thing can be fairly certain: there was a considerable population in this area. The area just north of Avebury down to Salisbury in Wiltshire

Inside the West Kennet long barrow, Avebury, Wiltshire. This site would probably have been a communal burial place

shows signs of having been more densely populated in the Bronze Age than it was, say, a hundred years ago.

The henge at Avebury is vast and contains three circles: an outer ring and two smaller inner rings, known as the north and south rings. To gain some idea of what the original, undamaged stones looked like, look at the vast Swindon Stone or Diamond Stone which hangs dramatically over the road. Many of its companions were broken up for commercial use in the eighteenth century when the circles were mined for building stones. In fact destruction and reuse of the materials seem to have been going on since Roman times.

Of the two smaller circles the southern one is more complete, though only one quarter remains intact. Of the northern circle just two stones around the perimeter are still standing. At the center of the northern circle are two stones remaining from a cove. There is evidence of an attempt to build a third circle near the Diamond Stone, but this was abandoned. The circles seem to be aligned to the moonrise. It is even possible that the northern circle was not a full circle but a horseshoe shape, as combinations of circle and horseshoe have been found elsewhere. It is reminiscent of the horseshoe ditches around long barrows. The south circle had a tall pillar stone at its heart, and here there is evidence of offering pits, votive foods and sacrifices.

The avenue is one of the finest that survive, and its long line of stones stretches off into the distance toward the River Kennet. The size and shape of the stones varies and this is thought to be symbolic, perhaps sexual, for long, thin stones are followed by shorter, squatter ones. But this is all speculation. It seems to indicate that many visitors came to attend ceremonies; perhaps many of the dead who were brought for exposure and then burial arrived by water and were carried up the avenue.

Finally, go to **Silbury Hill.** This is the highest prehistoric construction in Europe, built c.2400 BC, and no one has a clue why it is there! Excavations, including one undertaken by the BBC, have found nothing that might have been expected. There was no body or gold at its center, but only a smaller,

The mysterious Silbury Hill, Avebury, Wiltshire

older mound of banded clays and chalks. Perhaps there were ritually impure people who had to stand away from the celebrations and needed a viewing platform. Or perhaps it was meant to imitate some sacred mountain. What we do know is that it adds to the sacred landscape of Avebury something totally unique in Europe.

Yet again, it had been abandoned by c.1000 BC. All the energy, enthusiasm, beliefs and hopes poured into it for some fifteen hundred years or so have vanished. Despite its importance and scale, there is still much to be discovered about Avebury. What little we have leaves us wondering – and that, perhaps, is how it should be.

CASTLERIGG · CUMBRIA
1¹/₂ miles E of Keswick

Visually one of the greatest stone circles, set in spectacular mountain scenery and still in a fine state of preservation (see front cover). This is thought to be early, dating to c.3200 BC. Thirty-eight stones out of forty-two, all in local metamorphic slate, survive. Although not tall compared with other stone circles, their setting gives them a sense of stature. Just within them is an earthen henge, not very prominent. To the side of the circle is an unusual rectangle of smaller stones whose function is not known, except that the tall radial pillar is in line with the sunrise at the midwinter festival of Samain (the Celtic New Year which fell on October 31). Within the circle are a number of cairns, so it can safely be assumed that this was a place for the dead. However, it is also thought that it was a trading center, especially for fine stone axes – one was found here. This is surprising, as it seems clearer that the place had a funeral role. But perhaps trading started at funerals and then developed a life of its own. After all, saint's day celebrations often gave rise to riotous fairs with only tenuous links to their spiritual origins.

THE NINE LADIES, BIRCHOVER · DERBYSHIRE
3¹/₂ miles SE of Bakewell

The Nine Ladies stand in what remains of a major Neolithic landscape, now much damaged by quarrying, changing land use and wear and tear by visitors. The stones are set in a copse in an area of burial mounds and cairns, close by the site of another stone circle now gone.

The circle is a small one with low stones dating from the Bronze Age, so it is c.2000 BC. In the center is an older burial mound – presumably one reason for its construction. The nine stones are enclosed by the remains of a basic earth henge, while an outlier seems to be a more recent addition. Sadly there is often evidence of vandalism such as daubings or fires, and the site can at times look a little sorry. But on a crisp, cold day it retains some magic.

A report prepared by the *Women's Environmental Network* talks about the stones' orientation and its implications:

> The main stones of the circle are aligned north-north-east and west-south-west to the sun at the winter solstice. Many monuments in Britain and Ireland appear to be aligned on the midsummer or midwinter solstices and the festivals we celebrate today in the Christian calendar are derived from old festivals of the sun and moon. The most obvious is Christmas where we celebrate the birth of Christ – at the Nine Ladies Stone Circle the midwinter sun at the solstice represents the birth of the sun, since after the solstice the days gradually become longer once again.

ROLLRIGHT STONES, CHIPPING NORTON
OXFORDSHIRE
2¹/₂ miles NNW of Chipping Norton, 1¹/₂ miles W of Great Rollright by lane to Little Rollright

A late Neolithic site and so c.2800 BC, this is one of the finest and most precise of all the stone circles: the seventy-seven stones form an almost perfect circle. The name is a corruption of the Anglo-Saxon *hrolla-landri-ht*, meaning the land of Hrolla. The site started out as an earthen henge into which the stones – originally eighty – were set, with just one entrance. This is one way of defining that it is Neolithic and late. To the north-north-east is an outlier, much damaged by people chipping bits off for good luck. It is known as the King Stone. The outlier is perhaps much younger than the ring as it marks a tomb – a couple of cairns were found beside it containing Bronze Age burials of c.1800 BC. A little way off can be seen the stones of a now exposed megalithic tomb, known by the picturesque name of the Whispering Knights as they lean toward each other. The circle is clearly oriented toward the moon at midsummer, inferring that this place is possibly a cemetery henge where the dead were laid out.

The stones are famous for their mythology, in particular the belief that they are a king and his army turned into stone for crossing a witch. Indeed their old name was the King's Stones. It is said that no one can ever count them twice and arrive at the same number.

STANTON DREW · SOMERSET

Off B3130, 1½ miles E of Chew Magna, 2 miles W of Pensford. At edge of village near church

This major site is still comparatively unknown. It dates from the late Neolithic, c.3000 BC–2600 BC, and is set in an outstanding sacred landscape, still visible despite changes in land use over the millennia. The core is the Great Circle, 112 yards across and containing thirty-six stones, which makes it the largest stone circle in Britain after Avebury. Running from the Great Circle are the remains of a stone avenue. To the north-east is a second, much smaller circle, which ironically was made with the largest stones. Perhaps this is a later addition in the manner of Stonehenge. From this a second avenue of stones runs off. To the south-west lie the badly damaged remains of a third circle.

To the south-east is the Cove, a megalithic tomb with three stones still standing. At least this is what it looks like, but it may have been built as an imitation of the megalithic tombs, perhaps because even by this period they were the standard sign of a sacred site. The Cove is thought to be earlier than the rings and is constructed from stones of a different kind. It seems to be oriented to the most southerly moon rising. The large outlier to the north-north-east of the circles is known as Hautville's Quoit and was supposedly thrown there by a local medieval knight.

The legend about the stones is that they represent the dancers at a Saturday wedding. The guests were having such a good time that they did not want to stop at midnight when the musicians left, and were delighted when a fiddler came down the road and agreed to play on into the Sabbath for them. Little did they realize that he was the devil. Once they started dancing to his music they could not stop, no matter how much they begged him. At sunrise they were all transformed into stones: the bride, groom and vicar form the three stones of the Cove.

Recent archaeological excavations have revealed a remarkable find – c.3000 BC the largest wooden building of British prehistory stood here – one third the size of the Millenium Dome in London. What was the wooden building for? It consisted of hundreds of pillars and contained five ritual pits at its center. Was this a palace or a temple? Was it raised by some megalomaniac ruler and destroyed when he was overthrown? The site is even more important than previously thought and further archaeology may reveal more about why a magnificent wooden building was replaced by crude stones.

STONEHENGE · WILTSHIRE
2 miles W of Amesbury, just N of A303 at junction with A360

When seen in the right light from the right angle, the world's most famous stone circle is still capable of sending a chill of excitement down the spine. Proposed changes may soon return some sense of majesty to the site. The problem for the owners, English Heritage, is that some people treat these stones as a means of gaining cheap publicity by daubing statements on them. Some who do so claim to be "pagans" exerting their "rights." But no self-respecting pagan would dream of harming these stones, ruins long before the cults that modern pagans claim to follow had arrived in Britain. The future of Stonehenge is an uncertain one. This is ironic given that the site has stood here for over five thousand years; Stonehenge is a classic case of gradual and shifting development.

At first there was a large earthen henge with a central hut and an out-lier. The orientation of the henge is toward lunar worship, so it was prob-ably a funeral site where bodies were exposed. The so-called Aubrey Pits contained sets of four bodies in the fifty-six holes, as already mentioned. Their layout within the holes suggests some ritual use of the skeletons, as they were orientated to the four main compass points. This stage dates from *c.*3200 BC.

Next came the building of two incomplete circles within the henge, *c.*2200 BC, of Welsh bluestone. Much has been made of these stones. Were they brought by boat from the Preseli Mountains of south-west Wales? If so, why? As Aubrey Burl has pointed out in his book *A Guide to Stone Circles of Britain, Ireland and Brittany*, stone circles beside the Preseli Mountains do not make much use of the local bluestone, so it does not appear to have any religious significance. It now seems increasingly likely that the bluestones arrived on Salisbury Plain millennia earlier by means of glaciers. However, the debate continues and it has been shown that the transport systems of Bronze Age culture could have moved the stones here. The question is: why? For by stage three the stones had been discarded, which does not argue much for their inherent sacredness! The two circles continued to be moon-oriented, using the Heel Stone which was erected at this time.

The third stage dates from *c.*2000 BC. The bluestone circles were demolished and the stones discarded. Local sarsen stones were now used to build the distinctive trilithons – a major achievement. The stones were grooved and slotted as if they were wood, showing that the builders were probably carpenters. For the first time, the orientation was toward the midwinter sun.

The fourth stage, c.1600 BC, involved the re-erecting of the bluestones to form a crude horseshoe shape inside the sarsen stone circle. The Altar Stone was erected at the same time, along with two other outliers including the famous Slaughter Stone which adds emphasis to the rising of the midsummer sun as it shines directly between them. At about this time, the first carvings were made on the stones; the type of dagger carved seems to indicate a link with the Bronze Age cultures of ancient Greece. Certainly some new impetus had come to Stonehenge which transformed it from a great lunar temple to the key solar temple. Finally, around 1100 BC, the avenue began to be expanded but was soon abandoned. Shortly after that, the whole complex was deserted.

What traumas caused these shifts, this abandonment? This is, at one level, the importance of Stonehenge for today. Crises, dramas, change, loss, destruction and collapse are all part of the cycle of human existence. The permanence of these stones actually speaks of the impermanence of the beliefs – first lunar, then solar, then abandoned – which caused the henge to be built and developed over two thousand years. This, at a very profound level, is the message of Stonehenge – transience.

SWINSIDE, SWINSIDE FELL · CUMBRIA
5 miles N of Millom off A595, 3 miles W of Broughton in Furness. Follow road to Cragg Hall. Accessible along farm track

This circle once had about sixty stones of which fifty-five remain, making it one of the best-preserved circles. The alignment stone is a tall thin pillar at the north end. The ceremonial entrance in the south-east is still marked by two portal stones just outside the true circle. As with Long Meg (see below), the alignment seems to relate to the midwinter sunset. Legend says these stones fell from a church which the devil tried to destroy by flying away with it.

OTHER SITES IN ENGLAND

Cumbria contains a number of significant sites. At Burn Moor, Eskdale (6½ miles NE of Ravenglass and ¼ mile from Boot) are five stone circles. They comprise two pairs of two – **Low Longrigg** and **Brat's Hill**, **White Mon** and one large circle with three outliers. Cairns are to be found inside all five rings.

The evocatively named **Long Meg and Her Daughters** (Little Salkeld, 6 miles NE of Penrith, follow signposts out of village) and the much disturbed

One of the "daughter" stones at the site of Long Meg and Her Daughters, Cumbria

Little Meg are two interesting circles. Little Meg has been broken up by plowing but has carvings of concentric circles on the slab lying beneath the tallest upright stone. Long Meg is so called because one elongated stone stands among more rounded shorter stones. It is a large circle – the sixth largest in the Western world – and the size suggests that this was a site for assemblies. Seventy stones remain. Long Meg is in fact an outlier carved with rings and spirals. Its alignment is with the midwinter sunset.

Derbyshire contains many fine stone circles. Apart from Arbor Low and the Nine Ladies, sites worth visiting in this county include Barbrook I, II, and III. **Barbrook I** is 4¹/₂ miles SE of Hathersage and 2¹/₂ miles NE of Baslow; follow footpath signs. **Barbrook II** is 2¹/₂ miles NE of Baslow and lies NNW of Barbrook I. **Barbrook III** is 2¹/₄ miles WNW of Froggatt down a footpath off the A621. It lies 200 yards E of the reservoir, clustered on the NE side of the village of Baslow. Each is small but focused upon cairns, and at Barbrook III eleven stones with carvings have been found. **Nine Stone Close**, Harthill Moor (1¹/₂ miles SE of Youlgreave to E of lane from Elton to Alport), has only four stones left but they are of impressive dimensions.

WALES

CERRIG DUON · POWYS
Off B4067, 3 miles S of Cray Reservoir

A circle of twenty stones from an original group of between twenty-eight and thirty, in a remote and dramatic spot surrounded by mountains. The highest stones are about 20 inches high. The circle is in fact an oval, tapering to the north where a large standing stone is found and close by two smaller stones further north. Quite what this alignment, unique in Wales, signifies is difficult to say.

Some 10–12 yards to the east of the top of the oval are two rows of stones marking a classic avenue – wider at the far end than at the end nearest the oval. The setting is dramatic, with hills and mountains surrounding. This was quite a complex site for such an apparently remote place.

DRUIDS' CIRCLE, PENMAENMAWR · GWYNEDD
4 miles WSW of Conwy via A55. In village of Penmaenmawr turn S into Fernbrook Rd. Take the second turning right into Merton Park. At T-junction turn left and then right into Mountain Lane

This complex site, dating from c.3000 BC, is described on the Chester to Bardsey Island pilgrimage route (see p. 222), and is well covered by local guidebooks and a Historic Trail.

SCOTLAND

CALLANISH, ISLE OF LEWIS · WESTERN ISLES

This magnificent and complex site is comparable with Avebury and Stonehenge. The core is a ring of thirteen stones, not a perfect circle but an ellipse, with a large single stone lying just off center, and a mock cairn which seems to have been added last. From this ellipse run rows of stones, five each to the east, west and south, and a much more substantial avenue running north. Nearby are three other circles. The whole landscape is one of immense sacred significance, deliberately using the most visually stimulating sites. This is one of the few circles that lie above land which had previously been farmed. Someone took a major decision to take agricultural land out of use and make it a sacred site.

Here it is possible to understand the scale of the environmental disaster which afflicted Britain when volcanic ash cut out the sunlight and killed agriculture c.1000 BC. The stones were for a long time thought to be quite small – they are in fact almost 15 feet high at some points. Only in 1857 did excavators realize that they were half buried in peat, formed during the Iron Age and symptomatic of the climatic changes which brought these great circles to their religious end. The fact that no one had cleared the peat bog debris from the stones gives a clear indication that, with the coming of the peat following the collapse of the ecosystem, these stones were abandoned. The peat had risen nearly 5 feet up the stones, reducing them to little more than average-height stones. Now we can see them in their proper scale.

The north avenue is extensive – over 83 yards long, with nineteen of the original thirty-nine stones still standing. Due to their thinness and elongated shape they can look like specters in the mist – sentinels on duty which give a very distinctive feel to the site. Interestingly, the avenue narrows down as it approaches the stone circle, presumably as part of the concentration of forces upon the circle. It could also be an early example of the use of optical illusion, in the same way that landscape gardeners create an impression of greater distance and greater size. This avenue is roughly on line with the setting of the southern moon, while the other three shorter directional rows align as follows: the eastern one (actually east-north-east) seems to lead to the Pleiades star cluster; the western row leads to the equinox sunset; while the southern row seems to be an exact north–south line, with no other focus.

These four alignments offer three valid reasons for considering that Neolithic and early Bronze Age people used these sites for differing purposes. The moon orientation is probably the earliest, associated with death. Callanish looks out to the setting sun – the direction of death for most cultures. Then comes the shift to the sunset. Finally, at least as far as we can see, comes the interest in the Pleiades and in directional focus. This fits with the archaeological evidence. The circle dates from c.2200 BC and represents the last gasp of the Neolithic fused with the earliest Bronze Age. The avenue comes next, and the three other rows are later still.

Interesting external evidence of the continuing knowledge and perhaps worship of all three aspects, lunar, solar and stellar, is provided by a most unusual source – the Greek historian Diodorus Siculus, who described an elliptical site in Britain. Writing about a "spherical temple" he said, "[the moon] dances continuously the night through from the vernal equinox until the rising of the Pleiades." In the past, as Aubrey Burl points out, this was thought to be Stonehenge. But the alignments do not add up. They do at Callanish, however, and it is far more likely that a Greek would know of a site on the coast than one inland, as Greek and Phoenician ships traded through these waters.

Callanish contains many enigmas. None of the avenues orientates to the center of the ellipse. The burial chamber in the ring is odd, too – a much later addition, disturbed and ransacked and then used again, which bears no resemblance to anything known elsewhere in the region. Something intruded and desecrated this site over three thousand years ago. Repairs were undertaken, but then the whole place was suddenly abandoned.

Is this evidence of the rise of the aristocracy? Some commentators believe that these grandiose schemes, including Stonehenge, came to be personal expressions of power and wealth, taking over from the older henge with its communal funeral role. These monuments then become the gaudy and extravagant displays of the *nouveaux riches* of the Bronze Age, showing off their wealth and the size of the teams of laborers which they could put together. Yet again, the site itself remains virtually silent. Ancient tales affirm that the stones must be respected or trouble will ensue, and until very recently the stones were regularly "visited" by local farmers to pay their respects. There is also a fascinating legend that the stones were erected by a high priest and "black men." But which stones, when and by whom it is impossible to know.

TORHOUSEKIE · DUMFRIES AND GALLOWAY
3 miles W of Wigtown beside B733 on route to Kirkcowan

In this wonderful setting stands a circle with nineteen remaining stones which reach their greatest height in the south-east. To the north-west is an unusual earth bank, while to the east are the Three Stones which are aligned to the midwinter sun. Again we find the moon orientation in the circle and the sun in a later addition. At the center of the circle are three

The Ring of Brodgar, Orkney, known in legends as the sun temple

rounded boulders whose purpose is unclear, while to the east is another
outlier with a deep bowl worn into it. This is a place of peace now, but who
knows what scenes it used to behold, of ceremonies for the dead and the
moon and the midwinter sun and the coming of new life.

OTHER SITES IN SCOTLAND

The Highlands and Islands contain numerous circles. One of the most
famous is the **Ring of Brodgar** (see preceding page) on Orkney ($3^1/2$ miles
NE of Stromness and W of B9055). Just a mile to the south-east is the
equally huge **Ring of Stenness**, with the large **Ring of Bookan** one mile
north-west of Brodgar. Despite their size, the three rings defy easy explanation. Legend called Brodgar the sun temple and Stenness the moon
temple, but there is nothing to confirm this. Likewise, excavations have
indicated a Bronze Age date but nothing firmer.

The three rings need to be seen in the context of local ancient villages
such as **Skara Brae**. These enormous assembly areas, so close together,
hint tantalizingly at a great cult center – the greatest in the UK. But hints
are all that we have.

CHAPTER 3

⟶ ⟨⟩ ⟵

$\mathcal{H}$oly Wells

Dig under:
Where the well is depth, is other
Is the underworld, the otherworld, the Earth's and Hers –
What do you want? What have you brought here?

And as the gold coin of your asking sinks like a sun
Into the slippery moist mirror of its blackness
You may find the Source, and the cure
That to dry up is to die

$\mathcal{W}$ATER HAS ALWAYS been associated with the giving of life. We are
largely composed of water ourselves, and anyone who has been dehydrat-
ed on a hot day or through sickness knows how the body can crave this
precious commodity. Most of the world's major religions arose in regions
where water was scarce and therefore treasured – a relationship which has
transformed water's earthbound life-giving qualities into eternal life-giving. In St John's Gospel, when Jesus asks the Samaritan woman at the well
for water he then moves on very easily to discuss spiritual refreshment, saying: "Whosoever drinketh shall never thirst again."

It is hardly surprising, then, to find that wells, springs, streams, rivers
and lakes have always been regarded as special, indeed often as holy. Apart
from churches and burial mounds, the most common landscape feature
with a specific holiness or sacredness attached to it is the holy well. There
are thousands of them, many lost to sight and buried, while others are
known only locally.

The healing properties of certain waters have added to their mystery
and power. Many saints' wells are also renowned as healing wells, and their
waters have often been found to contain valuable minerals. Some wells

formerly associated with images, saints and miracles later became famous as health spas. Rational humanity in the eighteenth century found a new reason for doing what medieval Catholics, early Christian Celtic society and pre-Christian peoples had done for religious reasons: enjoying fresh water *au naturel*.

Water can, of course, also take life away. It can crash through villages and towns, leaving destruction in its wake. Water is one of the oldest symbols for the Other, for that which is opposed to order, and must therefore be propitiated or at the very least treated with respect. This is why places such as St George's Well in St George's parish, Denbigh, or in Roman times the wells of hot water at Bath, have been considered evil places, capable of bringing down a curse on those whose names are cited in prayers or desires for revenge. So water is ambiguous, and therefore mysterious.

Pre-Christian Holy Wells

It is uncertain what significance wells, springs and rivers had in pre-Celtic Britain. There are no obvious signs of water worship, and because the Celts overwhelmed the previous culture there are no linguistic traces in place-names. But there is clear evidence of Celtic lake worship, during which precious objects were cast into the waters. The discovery in Anglesey of a sacred lake and its treasures was mentioned on p. 9. Similarly, rivers such as the Thames and Severn have yielded major works of art in bronze or iron, which indicates that rivers too were venerated. Some authorities have tried to prove that such rivers were believed to be deities. For example, a report by the *Women's Environmental Network* (WEN) contains an interesting hypothesis concerning the River Ouse in Yorkshire:

> The river name is, like many river names, associated with the goddess – its original name Usa/Isa may relate to the Egyptian goddess Isis. The etymological root is the Sanskrit word "Ud," meaning water (Udan – a well). There seems to be some evidence then for the river's sacredness, and, though speculative, it provides us with fresh thinking about how we might see one of our most important resources – clean water.

It is, however, more likely that lakes and rivers were seen as ways in which prayers could be carried to the deities. The waters were sacred messengers.

Whereas lakes and rivers pour your supplications away and therefore calmed the gods and goddesses or alerted them to your problem, the benefits of wells are usually depicted as being given freely to all. This is reflected in the saints' stories associated with so many wells in Britain. Wells are often believed to have appeared at the request of a saint – for example Pistyll Dewi, Gweslan and Eliud in and around St David's Cathedral in Pembrokeshire are said to be the result of prayers uttered by the saint. Others arose to signify that a miracle had taken place at the site. Best-known of these are St Withburga's Well at East Dereham, Norfolk (see p. 115), and St Winifrid's Well at Holywell, Flintshire (see pp. 44 and 218).

At East Dereham the well in the church grounds is supposed to have appeared when St Withburga's body was removed from its original burial place and found to be uncorrupted. The empty burial place filled with water, which has flowed ever since. At St Winifrid's shrine, just below the ancient parish church, the water is supposed to have appeared at the spot where her head fell after she was attacked and beheaded by a frustrated suitor.

Similar stories exist in connection with many places. They indicate that the waters of wells are viewed as a gift of God, the saints or the deities. This is important, because they represent a breaking through into the world of powers beyond.

There is strong evidence that many pre-Christian wells passed from one faith to another as the people themselves embraced Christianity. This is what we should expect. If the waters are viewed as a gift of the divine, even if the understanding of who or what constitutes the divine changes, the gift remains. This is especially true of healing wells, whose medicinal effects add to the sense of the water being a gift.

There are, of course, some key pre-Christian wells and holy water sites whose deities we know something of. The most important are the hot springs of Bath in Somerset and Buxton in Derbyshire.

BATH

The Roman name for Bath was Aquae Sulis – the Waters of Sulis. The name Sulis is that of a Celtic deity worshiped here before the arrival of the Romans, who identified her with their goddess Minerva. The waters were therefore seen as very

The famous Roman baths, Bath, Somerset

directly and explicitly linked to a deity. Some very interesting work, in parts very convincing, has been done by the WEN on the sacred landscape of Bath and its surroundings. Their report says:

> The City of Bath was supposed to have been founded by King Bladud. Bladud was a leper, cast out by his family, who became a swineherd. . . . Bladud's pigs were cured of their own scabs and ailments in the hot muddy springs at Bath, so Bladud followed their example and was himself cured. Bladud was also said to have founded a temple on Solsbury Hill dedicated to Apollo, the sun god. . . .
>
> Solsbury Hill [near Bath] is directly related to the goddess Sulis, known to be the principal deity of the hot springs in Bath. . . .

BUXTON · DERBYSHIRE

The town called Buxton today was known to the Romans as Aquae Arnemetiae – the Waters of Arnemetia. This name seems to combine two pre-Roman motifs. The first part may be a form of An or Ana, the name of a major goddess, while "nemetiae" is clearly Nemeta, meaning a sacred grove. So here we have a sacred grove, holy waters and a goddess.

This is what the WEN report says about the name and its links to the many St Ann's or Anne's wells: "St Anne is linked with a number of holy wells and appears to be a Christianization of the pagan goddess 'Anu' or 'Ana' mentioned in the old chronicles of Ireland. Anu, Danu or Ana was the mother goddess of the original Irish. Close by Killarney in Ireland are two mountains known as the 'pap' (breasts) of Anu. . . ."

Here again there seems to be a clear link: today the holy well at Buxton is called St Anne's. The linking of Ana/Anu/Danu to water is also very clear. As the Celts traveled across Europe from c.1000 BC until they arrived in Britain c.500 BC, they bestowed the name of their goddess on various rivers. This is why we still call one mighty river the Danube and another the Don; both are derived from the name Danu/Anu.

But while there may indeed be links between older deities and the saints' names given, we do need to be a little careful. After all, the name "St Anne" could come from an actual local saint.

OTHER PRE-CHRISTIAN WELLS

Wookey Hole in Somerset is not only a prehistoric cave and the source of the River Axe, but also a former Celtic burial ground. Here there are signs

THE CELTIC HEAD CULT

Throughout areas where Celtic peoples settled, carved stone heads can be found at key sacred sites. The stone heads replaced or represented actual heads taken from those whom Celtic warriors slew in battle or from executed slaves. The reasons for the Head Cult are vigorously debated. Some claim that taking a head represented total power over not just the individual, but the enemy itself. Others see it as part of the human sacrifice culture of the Celtic world as evidenced by ritually executed corpses such as Lindow Fold man from Wilmslow, Cheshire or as recorded by Roman writers such as Julius Caesar. A very fine collection of Romano-Celtic stone heads can be seen at the Roman museum, Ribchester, Lancashire, 1 mile N of A59, 6 miles E of Preston.

Stone severed head from Corbridge, Northumberland

of the Celtic head cult so often associated with holy wells, for fourteen bodyless heads were found in the outer caves. Recent excavations, such as those at Milton Keynes, have revealed Celtic and Romano-Celtic holy wells. Here, a temple beside an Iron Age village centered on a circular post found to contain a sun-wheel (see p. 49), a statue and sacrificed animals and fowl. At Carrawburgh in Northumberland excavations have revealed a holy well dedicated to the goddess Coventina. Southwark Cathedral in London is built over a Roman holy well (see p. 93).

A good example of a pre-Christian well that became Christian is St Helen's Well at Burnsall in North Yorkshire. This well, paired with St Margaret's Well a few hundred yards away, is also known as Thorskeld – almost certainly a reference to an earlier dedication to the Norse god Thor. But it is also clear that many wells seem to have acquired their sacredness because some saint lived beside them, baptized in them or had a miraculous encounter there.

Names in the Landscape

Holy wells have left a deep mark on the place-names of Britain. The most famous and most complete medieval well shrine in Britain is at Holywell in Flintshire (see p. 44). There are many other Holywell towns and villages, all of which refer to some ancient shrine. Holywell-cum-Needingworth in Cambridgeshire – a well used for baptism – is one and Holwell in Oxford another. But there are many other less obvious names which indicate sacred wells. In London, Clerkenwell means the Clerk's Well, while Muswell Hill derives from the Mossy Well; Willesden (meaning a spring or well at the foot of a hill) is another (see p. 279).

While saints' names are the most common, many well names are tree-linked: sacred wells often had a sacred tree growing beside them. Ashwell in Glastonbury, Somerset, for instance, which seems to be the earliest formal well in the area, is named after a sacred ash. Yew trees also often feature near or above wells. The standard image of a holy well is that it arises beneath the roots of a tree, such as the one at Llanfyllin, Powys. St Myllin's Well on a hillside just above the town, has been splendidly restored with sensitive landscaping and good access to the well waters. Here, so the plaque says, St Myllin baptized in the sixth century.

The Dying of the Waters

If we bury the living waters, covering them to avoid seeing the mess and smelling the pollution which we pour into them, we are in danger of losing sight of how essential water – clean water – is for life. And we do not need to believe that they are literally holy in order to respect them and to realize that using streams, rivers and well springs as sewers is violation of the most profound kind. Under all our towns and cities, ancient streams and rivers have been hidden so that we cannot see what we are doing to their waters or because they got in the way of building works. Perhaps the most famous is the Fleet River in London, which gave its name to Fleet Street. Few people today would think of the area around King's Cross in north London as holy. Yet once the area from Old St Pancras church to St Chad's Well, which stood beside the ancient Battle Bridge in what is now Gray's Inn Road, was called Paradise Valley or Holy Valley because of the holy waters – the Fleet and a holy well – which flowed through it.

Today, many wells are running dry because we take too much water from the land and have denuded the hills of trees, so the water is no longer slowly filtering into the ground to emerge again as springs. Many have dried up completely. Southam in Warwickshire, for instance, has a very ancient holy well which has given its name to an area of the town called Haliwell. Only a decade or so ago, the well was restored and baptisms and processions took place here. But now it is dry and the surroundings have lost their religious and cultural purpose. We would do well to look to our wells as living – or dying – indicators of the overall health of our environment.

Rediscovering Holy Wells

For clues, look at place and street names: Holywell, Hotwells Rd, Well St, Spring Gardens and so on. In some towns and cities, wells can be traced from the surveys of water supplies undertaken in the late 1840s after bad cholera epidemics; make enquiries in the first instance at your local public library.

Books, booklets and articles on wells throughout the UK range from major studies such as Francis Jones's *The Holy Wells of Wales*, through the somewhat quixotic *The Living Stream: Holy Wells in Historical Context* by James Rattue, to local studies such as R. W. Morrell's *St Ann's Well and Other Medieval and Holy Wells of Nottingham* and J. Taylor Page's *Cumbrian Holy Wells*. A good bibliography is provided in Rattue's book. Jones gives a very full list of wells in Wales and some indication as to where they are. However, Rattue's list of wells in English counties is far from comprehensive and gives few directions. For these details local guides are more useful.

If you are looking at the landscape to find holy wells, the best place to start is beside churches built before the Norman Conquest of 1066. Throughout Britain, early churches and monasteries were built beside wells which were holy or became so. These wells, like the sacred rivers and streams which feature so greatly in early Christian sites, were used for ritual as well as practical purposes. Today, few holy wells have survived with their sanctity intact. In many country areas, even within living memory people visited certain wells to make offerings of metal, usually pins; this was surely a relic of the old Celtic offering sites, at which metal objects were left for reasons still not fully understood. At other places rags were tied to branches above wells in the hope of having a wish granted. The origin of the use of rags has been much debated. Were they once items of clothing from a sick person, left there to "wash away" the illness? Or are they symbolic of clothes that used to be left as offerings? Today the tradition has degenerated into throwing a coin into a wishing well. Yet most such wells were once holy, and the offering was made in gratitude for the gift of clean water from God and the saints. Is it possible that one day we shall return to a respect for these wells?

Holy well hunting is a combination of good detective work, research and intuition. Even when you find the well, it may be on private land and

WELL-DRESSING

By the end of the nineteenth century, the art and custom of well-dressing had virtually died out. In earlier times most holy wells were decorated with flowers on their saint's day, and processions took place. For example, at Bristol all the major wells which supplied conduited water to the city were visited in a formal procession by the Lord Mayor and Council until the mid-sixteenth century. Their waters were supposed to be especially efficacious on the saint's own day.

But in the nineteenth century antiquarians in Derbyshire began to revive well-dressing in the Peak District. In part it was a romantic escape from the horrors of the surrounding industrial cities such as Manchester and Sheffield, and in part it was a celebration of pure water and of the gospel. For it has long been the tradition that wells are decorated with large and complex flower pictures of biblical scenes, often with a watery theme.

Today well-dressings are a major feature in spring and early summer in the Peak District. The High Peaks Tourist Authority can tell you when these ceremonies take place; the best ones are at Tideswell, Tissington and Youlgreave. The revival of this ancient custom has helped to preserve the wells and has ensured that the waters are kept as clean as possible. Could this be undertaken elsewhere too?

The ancient custom of well-dressing, Tissington, Derbyshire

being obliterated (as is the case with the Anchorites' Well at Kendal in Cumbria), or locked and inaccessible (as with the well at Llanaelhaearn in Gwynedd, p. 226). But sometimes an unknown treasure can be rediscovered, and then brought once again into public and even ritual use.

Sites

There are thousands of holy wells in Britain, and the ones listed below are just a selection of the better or more interesting ones. Some are only mentioned in passing in this chapter as they are included in the various pilgrimage routes and described there in greater detail.

ENGLAND

The most famous sites are the Romano-Celtic wells at **Bath** (see p. 37) and **Wells** in Somerset, and at **Buxton** in Derbyshire (see p. 38). **Glastonbury** also has famous wells (see pp. 202–204).

In **Bristol**, there is a very famous holy well at **Brislington**. **St Anne's Well** originally stood in a forest and may have pre-Christian origins, but in the Middle Ages it was a pilgrimage destination almost as popular as Canterbury. It had fallen into disrepair and recently *Source,* a group dedicated to reopening or restoring wells, restored it. Unfortunately local people were not involved, and the well was quickly vandalized.

Also in Bristol, the oldest Jewish mikvah in Britain has been discovered at **Jacob's Wells**, in Jacob's Well Road, just west of Cabot Tower on Brandon Hill. The mikvah is a ritual bath for Jewish women and this one, fed by a spring, was in use until 1290 when the Jews were expelled from the city. Only through the accidental discovery of the well buried under the road, and in particular the discovery of a Hebrew text on the stonework, was its role recognized. Now plans are in hand to restore it.

Sometimes holy wells are very small and simple. **Whitchurch Canonicorum**, near Bridport in Dorset, contains one of the very few intact medieval shrines to St Wite. Nearby on **Chardown Hill, Morcombelake**, is the remains of **St Wite's Well**. This has been allowed to decay and its waters now appear only in a stone cattle trough.

A once great and famous well, now neglected, is **St Madron's at Madron**, Cornwall, beside an ancient chapel. The chapel and well are about 2 miles north of Penzance. The water flows through the baptismal font/well in the church and this is, despite its neglect, one of the clearest sacred water sites in England.

St Martin's Well, in the **Cathedral Close at Exeter**, Devon, is a Roman well given an early Christian dedication. **St Augustine's Well, Cerne Abbey**, Dorset, beside the church and close to the abbey ruins, lies at the foot of the chalk-cut figure of the Cerne Abbas giant, possibly a Roman figure of Hercules or a Celtic fertility deity renowned for his enormous genitals. The site was originally known as Silver Well, which may be pre-Christian. Its later name is associated with a legend that St Augustine struck the ground and the well appeared at the spot. **St Bartholomew's Well, Cowley, Oxford** stands in the churchyard and was a very special well which brought forty days' grace in Purgatory, thus shortening your time there before going on to Heaven. Scenes of drunken behavior put it out of favor, but it was purified in the seventeenth century. **St Chad's Well, Stowe,** Staffordshire has ancient associations with the saint; restored in 1923, it is an ecumenical site used by all Churches (see p. 133). **St Richard's Well, Droitwich,** Hereford and Worcester still feeds the spa and gave Droitwich its fame as a salt town by bringing the salt to the surface.

WALES

Wales is richly endowed with holy wells. **St Winifrid's Well at Holywell,** Flintshire (just N of A55, 15 miles NW of Chester) is the greatest holy well in the United Kingdom. Cut into the hillside, just below the medieval parish church, the well is completely encased in a late fifteenth-century shrine. Above the well is an exquisite chapel. Below, the waters bubble up into an octagonal well into which steps descend. A covered cloister-like pilgrims' path circles the well, and outside the well itself is a large bathing pool. The site is in the care of Roman Catholic nuns and the atmosphere is one of quiet reverence and reflection. Coming here you feel as if you have stepped back five hundred years in time (see also p. 218).

The interior of St Winifrid's Well, Holywell, Flintshire

Gwydelfaen Well at **Llandyfan** near Llandeilo, Pembrokeshire, was a medieval holy well and then became a Baptist Church baptismal pool. A classic holy stream runs beside **Nevern** church in Pembrokeshire. **St David's** in Pembrokeshire abounds with wells, the best preserved of which is **St Non's** (see p. 242). **St Beri's Well,** a quarter of a mile north-east of **Llanberis** church in Gwynedd, was famous as a healing well and once contained sacred fish.

St Seiriol's Well at **Penmon** in the Isle of Anglesey is framed by a monastic cell and a hermit's cave. The local church is dedicated to St Seiriol, who lived and preached nearby and is buried on Puffin Island, visible from the well. **St Trillo's Well**, just outside **Colwyn Bay** in Conwy, is a delightful ancient chapel, possibly twelfth-century, built over a holy well which rises beneath the altar. To visit this humble little place and then the magnificence of Holywell is to enter the world of medieval holy wells in a way that is almost impossible anywhere else in Britain.

SCOTLAND

In Scotland, almost all churches built before AD 800 have either holy wells or holy streams beside the original church enclosure; these were used for baptism. Examples include **St Finian's Well, Chapel Finian**, beside the seashore; a small ruined church 5 miles south of **Auchenmaig** on the side of the B747 in Dumfries and Galloway; **St Drostan's Well** at **Aberdour Bay** near New Aberdour and 3 miles west of Rosehearty, Fife; **St Fillian's Pool**, a healing well beside the ruins of Strathfillan Priory, 3 miles from **Crianlarich**, Perth and Kinross; the island of **Iona**, Argyll and Bute; and **Lismore**, also in Argyll and Bute (see Chapter 17).

CHAPTER 4

⁓

Sacred Cities

Deep in sun-bright memory and longing
And around on the ground invisibly at our feet
Lies the Other City, that is home – glimpsed
In the light between our eyes that lifts our exile:
So we say: put the heart back where we live
In this Babylon of bondage raise it to the sky
So we can feel a haven around us again –
Bring our city back to the Divine.

SACRED LANDSCAPES, sacred sites, sacred waters – yes, we expect these. But sacred cities? It seems impossible to conceive of the city as a place of holiness. This is partly because over the last two hundred years our culture has tended to romanticize the countryside in contrast to the brutality and ugliness of the city. Since the time of Wordsworth, Cobden and Blake we have seen the city as a place of evil or at least of disfigurement. But it was not always so.

Powerful figures in medieval society built churches and monasteries to express their love of God, themselves, wealth and those in need – not necessarily always in that order. They represented biblical stories and classical legends on artifacts from humble pots to precious chalices. They embroidered similar scenes on tapestries, altar frontals and banners. Their castles and manor houses had chapels and, when they could afford it, stained glass depictions of religious events. They went on pilgrimages and fought in the Crusades against the Muslims, and they died paying for priests to chant prayers to bring them safe through Purgatory. Even the poorest named their children after figures in the scriptures, while the year was dictated by the feasts and fasts of the Church and time was marked off by saints' days. Holidays were originally holy days.

But if present-day historians of our towns and cities are to be believed, there was no religious element in the actual building of these places. In fact there was, but because economic and social history has had the ascendancy for so long we have lost the art of reading such places religiously. This chapter tries to rediscover this vision by "reading" certain towns and cities and providing some basic clues to help you find the sacred in your own town or city.

Sacred City Planning in China and Russia

The idea of cities being designed according to religious precepts is not a novel one, and most cultures have at some time built in this way. Best known for this in the West is China, where the laws of the art of feng shui or geomancy have determined the shape and even the color of cities for two thousand years and more. Beijing is a classic example of a feng shui city, and despite the ravages of this century its plan is still clearly visible (see next page). The core is the Forbidden City, which straddles the meridian line of Beijing and thus placed the emperor on his throne in the chief audience hall on the center line in the middle of the city. Everything radiated out from him.

The city is divided into the northern sector dominated by the Temple of Earth and the southern sector dominated by the much more famous Temple of Heaven. West is the site of the Temple of the Moon, while on the east is the Temple of the Sun. The reasons for this arrangement are theological and cosmological. North is the direction of yin, the dark, winter, female, cool force of the universe; and Earth is yin. South is the direction of the yang force, hot, fiery, male, active, summer; and Heaven is yang. The West is the direction of death and demise, but also of spirituality – hence the moon; while the East is the direction of the sunrise – hence

FENG SHUI

Feng shui means literally "wind-water," and refers to the need to position all buildings, especially tombs, in such a way as to be in harmony with the natural forces that surround them and lie beneath. Humanity ignores these natural forces at its peril – given time, they can undo any work done by human hands. Feng shui is therefore about finding the right place to build, making sure that it is the right height, and ensuring that its proportions are correct and in balance with the scale of the site and the existing landscape features.

the sun. With these four temples Beijing is balanced cosmologically and the emperor was protected and guarded, but he also guarded the balance of nature, of yin and yang, of Heaven and Earth, sun and moon.

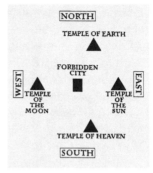

Beijing – a cosmologically balanced city

Christian Russia is exactly the same. The ground plans of all the great medieval cities – Moscow, Novgorod, Zagorsk, Arkangelsk and Kiev – are designs in theology, embodying the circle of God's completeness: the triangle of the Trinity; the narrative of the cross; and the outline of the Heavenly City which St John the Divine describes in the Book of Revelation as descending to Earth at the End of Days. Thus the main church or monastery of St John the Divine is outside the city walls, for he bears witness to the city. The Kremlin in Moscow contains churches dedicated to the Mother of God, the Archangel Michael and the twelve Apostles; most ancient Russian cities have kremlins (citadels) of a similar nature at their heart. The positions occupied by the other churches and monasteries depend upon a theological cosmology which has to be replicated here in the city. The city wall usually has twelve gates to correspond with the twelve gates of the city described in Chapter 21 of Revelation. To a devout member of the Russian Orthodox Church, his or her home city is as capable of being the Heavenly City, Jerusalem the New, as any place in the Holy Land itself.

Once Britain had a similar sacred cosmology. Is it really conceivable that Saxon kings and queens, so many of whom became saints, should have put everything at the service of God except the cities and towns of their new Christian world? Of course not: they built as cosmologically as the Russian Christians or the Chinese Taoists and Confucianists.

Saints, Hills, Towers and Protection

ST CATHERINE

Churches dedicated to St Catherine of Alexandria and St Michael the Archangel are often found on top of hills or mountains. There are two reasons for this, both theologically cosmological. St Catherine's symbol is the wheel upon which, according to legend, she was tortured; after it broke she was beheaded and supposedly buried on Mount Sinai. Yet most authorities believe that she never existed – so why is this mythical woman linked with hills and wheels?

The answer is that the wheel is a very ancient symbol for death. Many Iron Age tombs across Europe contain wheels to accompany the dead into the afterworld. But the wheel is also associated with the sky god of the interface between Roman and Celtic culture – again, found throughout Europe. The sky god is usually described as a male figure such as Jupiter, but there were also female forms. Indeed, the twelfth-century heretical sect known as the Cathars were so called because they believed that St Catherine was a sky goddess, the equal of God. Thus the Catherine myth is one of death and wheels, high places and sky deities. This is why prominent hills were so often crowned with a chapel dedicated to St Catherine – for example, beside Abbotsbury in Dorset or outside Winchester, Hampshire, both very ancient landscapes. For other examples see St Catherine's Tor outside Hartland in Devon and St Catherine's Hill outside Guildford in Surrey (p. 85).

ST MICHAEL

This saint is also associated with hills and high places – see, for example, St Michael's Mount, Cornwall, on p. 205. Behind Glastonbury Abbey in Somerset stands the Tor, on top of which is St Michael's church tower. Outside Bristol's old city walls stands a church known as St Michael on the Mount Without, meaning without (beyond) the walls. Islands with steep rocks upon them are also often dedicated to St Michael: Steep Holm in the Bristol Channel, Looe Island in Cornwall and Drake's Island in Plymouth Sound were all topped by churches dedicated to St Michael. But there is one extra point to note about the St Michael churches outside important places: both the Tor and St Michael on the Mount Without are north of the abbey and town respectively. They are there to protect these places, just as the Archangel protects Heaven from attack. In traditional Christian cosmology the evil ones come from the north. This idea is derived partly from the Norsemen, the invaders who attacked Britain after the fall of Rome, but also picks up on prophetic texts in the Old Testament, especially Jeremiah and Isaiah, who predicted the invasion of Israel and Judah from the north.

ST HELEN

Churches dedicated to St Helen often stand close to a greater church, abbey or monastery which once supposedly held a fragment of the True Cross. A good example is St Helen's in Abingdon, Oxfordshire, just down the road from the abbey which held a piece of the True Cross (see p. 185). According to legend, when the True Cross was found, it was St Helen who directed the excavators because she was sure she knew where it was. No other relic was as powerful as a fragment of the True Cross. On medieval maps the center of the world is Jerusalem, and the center of Jerusalem in Christian iconography, geography and thought was the church of the Holy Sepulchre. Here was the site of Jesus's crucifixion, burial and resurrection, so a piece of the True Cross brought Christian cosmology and geography home to wherever it was housed. If you come across an old St Helen's church, find the nearest bigger church or site of a great monastery. Dig into the records, and you will almost certainly discover that it once held a piece of the True Cross.

Saints and Castles

ST MARTIN AND ST PETER

These are the two most popular dedications for churches within castle walls or next door. St Martin was a soldier who left the army when he converted, saying that as a Christian he could not fight. By dedicating a castle church or one nearby to St Martin, the Church was making a very pointed comment about the whole business of warfare. A dedication to St Peter is often found next to or within castles, which contained dungeons for holding prisoners, to make a similar point. In Rome there is a lovely little church called San Pietro in Vincoli, which means St Peter in Chains. St Peter was imprisoned in the dungeon over which this church was built, but was freed by an angel. Here the Church, which used to provide sanctuary to those accused of wrongdoing, is again making a point. By juxtaposing the spirits and powers of the ex-soldier and ex-prisoner with the harsh walls of the castle and prison, physical force was being counteracted by spiritual force.

ST GILES AND OTHER SAINTS

A church or hospital dedicated to St Giles will almost always be found well outside the original walls or boundaries of a town or city; a good example is at Shrewsbury in Shropshire. St Giles was the patron saint of lepers, and leper hospitals had to be sited outside the city boundaries for health reasons. Churches dedicated to other saints with specific patronage will also be found in appropriate places: St Nicholas at ports, such as Ipswich and Bristol, and All Saints or All Hallows often in the central area, representing those saints beyond number who protect a city. Churches of St John are often placed outside a city or on a city wall, for he observes the city of the future. Thus St John's church and hospital lay just outside old Lichfield in Staffordshire; Norwich has its St John on the Wall, as does Bristol; while Chester's St John's lay just outside the old walls.

Marking the Sacred City

Various concepts of what constituted a divine ground plan can be found in British towns and cities. Where there was a clear site upon which a ground plan could be laid, the pattern is quite simple. The basic form was a circle or ellipse, symbolizing the unity of the place, reflecting the circle of existence and the Oneness of God – as seen, for example, in the use of three circles to express the Trinity – and expressing the fascination with circles found in all Celtic and Anglo-Saxon art. Within this circle, if the land allowed, there would be a Celtic cross in the form of the four main streets running north, south, east and west. Many of the towns founded by Alfred the Great demonstrate this plan, for example Wallingford in Oxfordshire and Chichester in Sussex, whose street names at the central cross are East Street, West Street and so on. Anglo-Saxon foundations such as Ipswich in Suffolk and Bristol exhibit the same kind of structure. Many smaller settlements follow a similar pattern but without the defensive walls.

THE OMPHALOS

At the center of such crosses, and indeed at the center of all towns and cities, there would have been what the Celts called an omphalos – Greek for "navel." This was usually a pillar, reflecting the phallic nature of its role. Here was the center point of generation of the town or city, and from here the powers radiated outward. Most old towns and cities therefore had a market cross, set above steps and pointing to Heaven. This was the case even where the Celtic cross

An example of a Celtic cross design – St Brynach's Cross, Nevern, Pembrokeshire

pattern was not fully developed due to underlying older street plans such as those of Roman cities. York, Chester and Canterbury all had what was called a high cross, as did newer towns and cities; again, Bristol and Ipswich are classic examples. Indeed, when Bristol's high cross was taken down in the eighteenth century to allow more traffic to pass, it caused great unrest as if people sensed that something central was being taken from them. It was later restored and re-erected

The omphalos at St David's, Pembrokeshire

at Stourhead in Wiltshire, and there is now some pressure to have it returned to Bristol.

Smaller towns and villages such as Dunster in Somerset, Fettercairn in Aberdeenshire and Clearwell in Gloucestershire also have examples of an omphalos. Indeed, if you investigate most old towns and villages you will find that there was once an omphalos standing in the main market square. It was not uncommon for conduited holy well water to be brought to troughs beside the omphalos – Bristol, Wells, Ipswich and Bath are good examples. Today, many of the sites once occupied by the old high crosses have been taken over by war memorials. And it is always interesting to note, when traveling through such places, that it is on the steps of the omphalos that the young people gather at night!

Postmedieval Sacred Planning – or the Lack of It

It might be thought that postmedieval town planning left the sphere of theological and cosmological design entirely. It certainly dropped much of the Christian geometry and geomancy, but it took on a version of Greek cosmology. The idea of a grid plan of streets, a structure of curves and squares, is a reflection of a more mechanistic post-Newtonian vision of the cosmos as order and pattern, immutable and fixed. The cross of medieval city cosmology gave way to the formal squares and straight rows and crescents of Georgian cities. But the notion that what man imposed upon the ground should reflect the greater reality of what was imposed on the universe still held.

The Victorians appear to have been the first to break completely from the notion of sacred geography. Ironically, they filled their new estates with mock-medieval churches and schools, but missed the point that these only make overall sense within a bigger picture.

If the Middle Ages saw the city as divine geography, the twentieth century seems to have sold any soul it had to the devil. The destruction of old street patterns and city centers, and the intrusion of buildings quite out of scale, have destroyed so much of the pattern of the past. In modern times we have built and redeveloped without paying due consideration to theological and cosmological needs. Our new "cathedrals" are the vast out-of-town shopping centers where we "worship" on Sundays. These shopping centers have become our new sacred sites, albeit without the structures or cosmology which underpinned the old centers. As a result our cities are dying: we cannot tear out their hearts and expect them to live.

The shopping center is modern society's walled city. Many actually do have an omphalos – a fountain, pillar or statue – which acts as a focal point. These centers are walled against invasion and offer security through enclosure. They are divided up into spheres of influence, as were the old cities. But they are ultimately soulless, for their purpose is not cosmological, nor theological, nor even dramatic. They reflect such a narrow understanding of what it means to be human that it leaves one alarmed for the future.

However, we should not be against all new developments per se. After all, people have always disliked change. The concern is that in our modern rebuilding we have left out spaces for quiet, for running water, for worship, for ritual, for ceremony and for nature. Unless we can find a balance, these secular temples will crash through an inherent inability to handle the cosmology which we have now displaced from the decaying city centers.

Nevertheless it is to be hoped that as we leave behind the arrogance of recent town planning, especially that of the sixties, we will be able to use the best of modern technology and design to recover a sense of the sacred in our cities. Perhaps we can produce again a sense of being part of the cosmos, and find once more the vision of the human city as the earthly counterpart of the heavenly city, which St John portrays so movingly in his Book of Revelation:

And I, John, saw the holy city, the new Jerusalem, coming down from God out of heaven, prepared as a bride adorned for her husband.

And I heard a great voice out of heaven saying, Behold, the tabernacle of God is with the people and he shall dwell with them and they shall be his people, and God himself shall be with them, and be their God.

And God shall wipe away all tears from their eyes; and there shall be no more death, neither sorrow, nor crying, neither shall there be any more pain; for the former things are passed away.

Sites

The following are just a few examples of the many towns and cities which were originally laid out or later developed to express Christian geomancy.

ENGLAND

BRISTOL

As indicated above, Bristol is one of the most classic examples of a sacred city. It was built upon untouched land in the eighth and ninth centuries, and by the time of St Wulfstan (c.1009–95), who as Bishop of Worcester had Bristol under his care, it was the most important city in the region. During the Middle Ages it was the second city of England.

As a new site, it had the opportunity of starting from scratch, although the rivers Frome and Avon had to be taken into account. The city was originally confined to the north bank of the Avon; the suburb of Redcliffe grew up from the eleventh century, and was not originally part of the sacred geography. The earliest city was therefore able to have an elliptical wall running around it which followed the course of the Frome as it curved in from the north-east and ran round to the south to meet the Avon beside St Nicholas's church. Later the Frome was extended to the west, so the old curve to join the Avon became redundant.

The circles of the walls enclosed a perfect Celtic cross formed by the four main roads, at the center of which stood the omphalos of the high cross (see next page). The high cross was faced by three or possibly four churches, one each in the nub of the four quarters of the city, being All Saints, Holy Trinity (now called Christ Church), St Ewens and a possible fourth one of which no details have been found. The first two of these dedications are classic city center names emphasizing all the saints and the core of the Christian faith – the Trinity – at the heart of the city. This is remarkably similar to Russian Orthodox tradition. Very close to the central crossroads is the church of St Mary le Port. Theologically, the Mother of God is standing close to, but a little apart from, the Trinity at the cross-

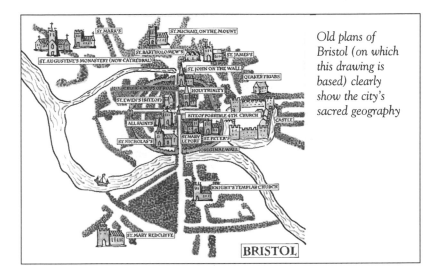

Old plans of Bristol (on which this drawing is based) clearly show the city's sacred geography

roads. To the north of the city stands its guardian angel in the form of the church of St Michael on the Mount Without. St John the Divine keeps watch from the city wall. St Nicholas's church still stands above the old port. St Peter's looks out toward where the castle once stood, bearing witness to the saint in chains.

Around the edges of old Bristol are still to be found traces of monasteries. St Augustine's is now the cathedral and St Mark's the Lord Mayor's chapel. Remains can also be seen of St Bartholomew's, of which a lovely old doorway survives; St James's; and the quaintly named Quaker Friars, the site of a friary which was later taken over by the Quakers.

To the south was the church of the Knights Templar and then the magnificent St Mary Redcliffe. Redcliffe was in Somerset, Bristol in Gloucestershire, until in 1373 Bristol was created a county in its own right. Rivalry between Bristol proper and Redcliffe was considerable. St Mary's, rising up on a bluff above the Avon, was endowed by the merchants of Redcliffe as a sign of their independence and wealth. Not every church was built just for theological reasons!

BURY ST EDMUNDS · SUFFOLK

At Bury St Edmunds, the layout chosen by the Abbot Baldwin in the twelfth century emphasized, by the direction of the main road and the placing of a major square before it, the pivotal role of the abbey and its relics of St Edmund.

CANTERBURY · KENT

Town and city building with a theological emphasis ranges from the entire layout of cities such as Bristol (see p. 54) to the refocusing of existing layouts toward new religious centers. Canterbury is a good example of the latter. Here was a Roman town, still in use in some form when St Augustine arrived in Britain, with his message of Christianity, in 597. But by the thirteenth century Canterbury had had a Christian geomantic pattern laid over it. It had elliptical walls from the Roman period which conformed well to sacred geometry. It was then rather crudely quartered, using Roman roads but slightly deviating from them in order to create the cross at the center.

Many of the church dedications indicate the sacred geography. All Saints' church once stood in the center, and St Helen's, also gone, bore witness to Holy Cross church and the relics at the cathedral. St John's church and hospital outside the city walls by the north gate bore witness to the Heavenly City. St Martin's was the original Roman Christian church outside the walls, where it had developed away from the prying eyes of the Roman authorities. St Sepulchre's church – commemorating a non-existent saint, and in fact referring to its being built on a Roman cemetery – also stood outside the walls, for the Romans never buried their dead inside cities.

The cathedral quarter, the Close, lies in the eastern quarter, the direction of Jerusalem and of prayer. The castle lies to the south, with the market and living quarters filling the rest. The whole city was also served by holy wells linked to churches, including the oldest, St Martin's Well, and St Augustine's Well.

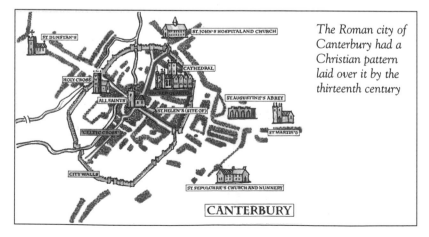

The Roman city of Canterbury had a Christian pattern laid over it by the thirteenth century

As discussed in the Canterbury pilgrimage route (see p. 97), the cathedral itself is a classic example of sacred topography, rising to form a hill inside the building where the high altar stands – a model of Golgotha hill, with chapels underneath reflecting the topography of the church of the Holy Sepulchre in Jerusalem. One distinct geomantic element to Canterbury is that where one might expect to find a St Michael on the Mount Without, as at Bristol, there is a St Dunstan's. This much-loved archbishop seems to have become the protector of Canterbury and to have taken the place of St Michael.

LANGPORT · SOMERSET

A smaller but clear example of the focusing observed at Bury St Edmunds can be seen at Langport near Minehead in Somerset. Here the focal point is the hill upon which stands the church of All Saints. From here the small town radiates out in one street which then splits into two, taking into account the layout of the land.

NORWICH · NORFOLK

It was traditional in Celtic planning to lay out a city with the four quarters serving distinctly different functions. One of the best examples of this, albeit undertaken by the Normans, is Norwich. Unusually, there are two center points. One is the castle on the natural high point of its mound.

THE CATHEDRAL CLOSE

The area around a cathedral is known as the Close, which is a Celtic concept and term. Traditionally, in Celtic places the Close encompassed within a wall the church; the ossuary, where bones were placed after the flesh had decayed in the earth; and the calvary, a place built to resemble the hill of crucifixion. Today the Close will contain the church, graveyard and dwellings for the clergy. In their own way, these Closes keep alive the original spirit of the enclosed city and the notion of a sacred space. **Norwich** provides one of the most vivid examples, along with **Peterborough** in Cambridgeshire. Outstanding Closes which date back to Celtic Christianity or Anglo-Saxon foundations can be seen at **Lichfield** in Staffordshire, **St Asaph's** in Denbighshire and **Wells** in Somerset.

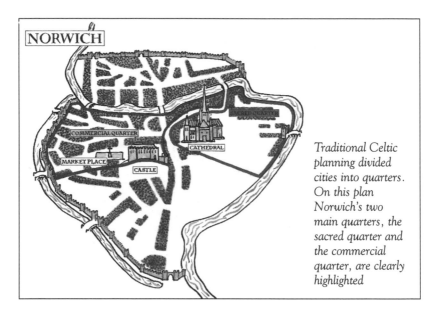

Traditional Celtic planning divided cities into quarters. On this plan Norwich's two main quarters, the sacred quarter and the commercial quarter, are clearly highlighted

The other is the marketplace with its high cross. From these two centers the city was roughly quartered, allowing for the river which sliced through the north in a curve. To the west lay the commercial area, while to the east was the vast religious area of the cathedral and associated buildings such as the hospital; east, of course, because that way lies Jerusalem, the direction of prayer and spiritual matters.

WALES

ST DAVID'S · PEMBROKESHIRE

The layout of the city of St David's is the opposite of that found at Bury St Edmunds. The holy site at St David's is in a hollow by a river with high land surrounding it. The streets therefore radiate toward the high cross, from where one road leads down to the cathedral itself.

SCOTLAND

ST ANDREWS · FIFE

Natural features and religious objects were another way of defining a town or city layout. St Andrews is an excellent example. The town owes its present shape to the relics of St Andrew, which were brought here in the tenth century. The cathedral in which his relics were kept was built on the high point, the bluff overlooking the harbor in one direction and the hinterland in another. The two main streets run toward this high point, with a third radiating out from the cathedral. All eyes are drawn to the mystery at the heart of the city – the relics. (See also p. 266).

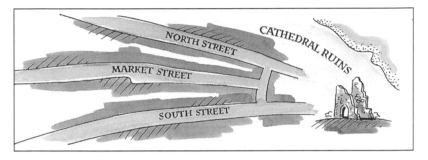

The main streets of St Andrews lead to the cathedral and therefore drew pilgrims to the relics which lay at the heart of the city

CHAPTER 5

Sacred Plant and Animal Life

And outside, in the depth of a timeless wood
– where you drive under trees as the sunlight dapples –
Is the green heart of magic, the other world
Where everything is written, alive in silence
And you can become the unknown one you are again,
The creature, the dreamer, the witness . . . till you emerge

And you will not harm with eye or hand,
And you will greet and grieve the wild ones as your friends

IT IS NOT just the natural features such as hills, rivers and mounds that have been considered sacred in our landscape: we also inhabit a world of plants, trees, animals and birds. This chapter takes us into the sacred groves to the oldest living thing in Britain, possibly in the world. It asks us to see the plants and wildlife around us, in Christian terminology, as the Second Book of God, the natural Book, which complements the Written and Revealed Book, the Bible.

Trees

THE YEW

The oldest living things in Britain are sacred trees: three yews over five thousand years old. In **Fortingall** churchyard, Perth and Kinross, Scotland, (8 miles W of Aberfeldy, 1¹/₂ miles N of Fearnam which is on the A827) stands what is possibly the oldest yew, which may even be eight thousand years old (see right). All the important history of Britain, from Neolithic peoples to the present day, has occurred during the lifetime of this tree. The nearby remains of stone circles may be contemporary with its planting, or the tree may already have been up to three thousand years old at the time the stones were erected. This is an obviously holy place – a feeling which has continued into the Christian era not just with the building of the church beside the yew, but through an extraordinary story claiming that Pontius Pilate was born here (see p. 265). The legend is very unlikely to be true, but that is not what mat-

The Fortingall yew, believed to be the oldest tree in Britain

ters. What it appears to be attempting is to link this most ancient of sites to the most significant of religious events. The story seems to be saying that this tree and its surrounding area, sacred for so long, were not bypassed or made redundant some sixteen hundred years ago by the coming of Christianity to the area.

The desire to forge a link between the tree and Christ is extraordinary evidence of the symbolic significance of the yew in pre-Christian Britain. This is clearly demonstrated by the results of work done by the *Conservation Foundation*, who have directed a survey of yew trees across the UK in order to establish their dates. David Manning of the *Church and Conservation Project* is busy collecting further details from churches, and it is hoped that a full account of the range and age of these sacred trees will soon be available. Some of the *Conservation Foundation's* information is included on the maps of sacred sites at the back of this book. We have marked all those yew trees which are over fifteen hundred years old; the vast majority stand in churchyards, and in most cases the churches do not pre-date the yews.

So what are we looking at in this extraordinary juxtaposition of yew trees and churches? What in particular are we to make of the fact that

AN ANCIENT TRADITION

The common yew (*Taxus baccata*) is indigenous to the British Isles and the earliest fossil record of one here (a species known as *Taxus jurassica*) dates from 140 million years ago. It is also indigenous to Scandinavia, where it is almost certainly the cosmic tree Yggdrasil, the tree of knowledge and life and the pillar of the universe. The traditional Christmas Yule log is the yew tree. The Magna Carta of 1215 was, it is claimed, signed under a giant yew tree on Runnymede, 1 mile north-west of Egham, Surrey. The tree still stands today.

many of these churchyards and trees also have standing stones or stone circles within a very short distance – even within the churchyard itself? For example, at **Kennington** in Kent (on the outskirts of Ashford on A28 N) the yew tree is thought to be two thousand years old and stands opposite the church on an ancient burial mound. At the famous site in **Knowlton**, Dorset (on B3078 8 miles N of Wimborne Minster), the church sits within the banks of a henge and the yew trees there are two and a half to three thousand years old. Again, at **Llanerfyl** in Powys the yew tree in the churchyard is some sixteen hundred years old – probably contemporary with or a little earlier than the church itself – and there is a fifth- to sixth-century pre-Christian burial stone beside the church.

It is clear that the yew was the most sacred of trees not just to the Celts but also to earlier peoples. It has continued to be associated with sacredness, which is why it is so common in churchyards. But just why was the yew so sacred? The answer lies in its ability to survive – it is a symbol of eternity. The yew can stop growing when conditions are unsuitable, and then, decades or even centuries later, come back to life and continue growing as if nothing had happened. Often yews have been destroyed by humans who, seeing no new growth for some time, assume that the tree is dead. But in churchyards little changes over time, so yews have survived better there.

Archaeological evidence from barrows where yew branches were laid to rest alongside the dead seems to show that the yew was sacred to Neolithic peoples – as might be assumed from the presence of trees four and five thousand years old on major Neolithic sites. The persistence of the yew through centuries of change must have had a major psychological impact on Neolithic and Bronze Age societies. People have noted outstandingly ancient yew trees almost since written records began in this country. It is fair to assume that stories passed on from one generation to another in pre-literate Britain would have done the same.

The yew tree therefore has roots deep in our culture, and its survival and well-being are as clear an indicator of the physical and spiritual well-being of the country as you could wish to find. Indeed, it now seems as if this oldest being in Britain may help save lives. Dried yew tree clippings contain chemicals which can be used to combat cancer, and organizations such as *Friendship Estates* in South Yorkshire are now harvesting the tree in ecologically sensitive ways.

DRUIDIC RITUAL

The yew is almost certainly the tree which formed the sacred groves of the druids. When a yew tree spreads, it can do so by moving out in a circle from its original trunk and creates a ring of off-shoots with a clear space in the center. These natural tree rings were used by the druids as ritual centers. Some of the pilgrimage routes include the remains of druidic yew tree groves – see, for example, p. 85 of the Canterbury route.

THE OAK, ASH, HOLLY AND ELM

Other trees were sacred apart from the yew. The oak, ash and probably holly all have sacred connotations, reflected in the latter case in the popular Christmas carol "The Holly and the Ivy." But none of these trees survives more than six to seven hundred years at most, so there are few left which we can claim had sacred status, though one or two stumps exist.

Carmarthen has the battered remains of **Merlin's Oak** beside the Town Hall, which it is said will fall only when Carmarthen falls (see p. 236). The tree probably dates from 1660 when it was planted to celebrate King Charles II's return and coronation. There is a particular association between this king and oak trees. While escaping from the Parliamentarian forces after his defeat at the battle of Worcester in 1651 he took refuge in a vast oak, whose branches concealed him from his enemies. For many years May 29 was celebrated by royalists as Oak-apple Day, and oak leaves were worn to commemorate his "miraculous" escape. This cult seems to echo earlier veneration for the tree, almost as if the oak had voluntarily cared for Charles and had performed a sacred rite in preserving him.

The oak was sacred to the sky god, who in Britain often went under the name Penneos Jupiter, combining the Celtic god with the Roman one. Oak trees are often found alone and thus provide a perfect target for lightning, which adds to their drama and to their links with the sky god. Mistletoe was considered especially blessed because it was believed to grow on oak trees as a result of lightning strikes. The oak tree thus became the wand of the sky god, and its twisted shape is the reason for the traditional twisting shape of a druid's staff.

The ash too seems to have great powers. Many holy wells include the name "ash" and their original sacredness seems inextricably linked to the tree itself. The oldest well at **Glastonbury** is **Ashwell**. At **Ashover** in Derbyshire, the holy well was originally covered by an ash tree. At **Ashstead** in Surrey, **Ashtead Well** was originally known simply as Ash Well; and at **Myddle** in Shropshire there is **Astwell**. No doubt before the re-baptizing of the wells with Christian names there were many other "ash wells."

Finally, elm trees also were sacred, and there is some evidence of their still being a focus of worship in areas which had become Christianized. An example is the strange story of the elm tree at Stow which is recounted on the Lincoln to Crowland pilgrimage route (see p. 124).

Holy Plants and Gardens

While little of the sacredness of these trees, with the exception of the yew and to some extent the oak, has persisted into modern times, other smaller species continue to exhibit their special nature and relationship with sacred matters. Many plants bear the names of saints or of the Virgin Mary, and until this century were used for a range of medicinal and quasi-magical purposes. White and yellow archangel, for instance, are two forms of nettle which were used to make a medicinal broth; while lady's fingers or lady's mantle were named from popular stories of the Virgin Mary.

Perhaps more importantly, the medicinal qualities of many plants were seen as a sign of the sacred. In the past, monasteries grew medicinal herbs in their gardens, for one of the chief functions of the monks was to provide an infirmary and free medicine for the poor. Growing their own meant that the herbs were within the Close, the sacred space enclosed by walls which marked the holiest and most special part of a town or city (see p. 57). The plants grown in monastic sacred gardens included sage, rue, fennel, horehound, wormwood, lovage, white lilies, poppies, mint, catmint, mandrake, parsley, coriander, lettuce, onions, shallots, daffodils, beetroot,

A monastic herb garden which has been re-created at Jedburgh Abbey, Scotland

sorrel, marigolds, peonies, celandine, rosemary, acanthus, orache, smallage and clary (see next page). Fascinating details about this aspect of monastic life can be found at the Brother Cadfael Centre in Shrewsbury, Shropshire, named after the fictional medieval monk detective created by Ellis Peters.

A typical monastic garden was subdivided into areas for specific uses, such as the physician's garden, the cook's garden and so forth. The notion of sacred flowers is again found in the *Gardini Sacristi,* areas of monastery grounds and churchyards where wild flowers grew and were used to decorate the church at festivals and events such as weddings. Among the plants found in these sacred gardens were old roses such as *Alba maxima,* Maiden's Blush, Blush Damask, *Rosa x alba* (White Rose of York), *Rosa gallica officinalis* known as the Apothecary's Rose, *Rosa mundi, Rosa eglanteria* and *Rosa phoenicia.* Records of monastic gardens by writers such as Benedict of Aniome (Capitulare de Villis) and Walahfrid Strabo (Hortulus) give a vivid picture not just of the application of herbs and flowers but of their symbolism in medieval times. For example, roses represented the blood of Christ while white lilies signified the purity of the Virgin Mary.

PLANTS TRADITIONALLY FOUND IN
Gardini Sacristi INCLUDE:

Alchemilla vulgaris (Lady's Mantle)
Allium schoenoprasum (Chives)
Allium sativum (Garlic)
Anethum graveolens (Dill)
Arnica montana (Arnica)
Artemesia abrotanum (Southernwood)
Anthriscus cerefolium (Chervil)
Borago officinalis (Borage)
Coriandrum sativum (Coriander)
Foeniculum vulgare (Fennel)
Helleborus niger (Christmas Rose)
Hyssopus officinalis (Hyssop)
Lavandula spica (Lavender)
Levisticum officinale (Lovage)
Melissa officinalis (Lemon Balm)
Mentha spicata (Spearmint)
Mentha suaveolens (Apple Mint)
Lonicera periclymenum "Belgica"
    (Honeysuckle)
Nepeta cataria (Catmint)
Paeonia officinalis "Rubra Plena" (Peony)
Papaver Rhoeas (Field Poppy)
Petroselinum crispum (Parsley)
Primula vulgaris (Primrose)
Ruta graveolens (Rue)
Salvia officinalis (Sage)
Sempervivum tectorium (Houseleek)
Rosa x alba (White Rose of York)
Rosa gallica officinalis (Apothecary's
    Rose/Red Rose of Lancaster)
Rosemarinus officinalis (Rosemary)
Viola odorataa (Sweet Violet)
Vitis vinifera "Purpurea" (Grape Vine)

Borage

Field Poppy

Lemon Balm

All this went when the monasteries were dissolved by Henry VIII in the sixteenth century. However, a number of them became cathedrals or parish churches. The monastery gardens had been planted in raised beds, and it is still possible to see traces of them in some cathedral and church grounds. Good examples of sacred gardens can be seen today in the churchyards of St Mary's, at **Stoneleigh** in Warwickshire, St Lawrence with St Mary's at **South Walsham** in Norfolk and Holy Trinity, **Beckenham**, Kent.

LIVING CHURCHYARDS

In recent years much attention has been focused upon the environmental significance of churchyards, which are important sacred sites within villages, towns and cities. Their walls mark the boundary between religious and secular, and they have not been farmed, built upon or, until recently, sprayed or affected by modern agricultural methods. They preserve the old meadowlands from which they were carved. In the separation of the churchyard from the outside world one can see still the delincation that a medieval town or city builder was making. The town or city was the refuge, the sanctuary, the place of civilization and the place of religious expectation, marked off by walls or boundaries from the rest of the world.

The *Living Churchyards Project* has been set up as a way of creating sacred space and protecting sacred plants by offering a sanctuary for rare and endangered species. Over a thousand churches have committed themselves to cutting some part of their grounds only once or twice a year, thus enabling plants to grow and flower. Others have planted local native species. Yet others, having surveyed their grounds and found hundreds of plants, insects and animals, encourage these through protected areas, the creation of ponds or wet areas and limited mowing.

These Living Churchyards are the most recent expression of the notion that inside a church, shrine or temple walls everything is protected and holy before God. This scheme, originally aimed mostly at Anglican rural parishes, is now spreading to other faiths – for example, in Leicester Muslim and Hindu communities are working along similar lines – and into urban areas and sites such as municipal cemeteries. The work being undertaken, often by voluntary labor, in these precious green spaces is highly impressive and speaks volumes for a surviving sense of the sacred in our natural surroundings which we might be recovering just in time.

Sites

The following list gives a number of excellent churchyards that are worth visiting. Other non-churchyard sites have already been mentioned in the text of this chapter. For cemeteries, **York** provides one of the best examples and offers conducted walks as well as first-class do-it-yourself walk guides and details. This is a major site and well worth visiting. In **Bristol**, the sprawling and semi-derelict Arnos Vale cemetery is also well worth visiting, not least because new species are still being found there. In **London**, Highgate cemetery is the best to visit because of the range of habitat and the excellent guided walks.

All these sites below are in their way retaining or restating a link between the sacred and the natural. Small though they are, they are important flickering lights in a world of ecological darkness. They are also the sort of scheme that any parish, any school with grounds or any public building with gardens could undertake almost anywhere.

CHESHIRE
St Thomas's, Mellor (3 miles N of New Mills, close to B6101); St Mary's, Acton (2 miles W of Nantwich on A534).

CORNWALL
Kenwyn church (1 mile N of Truro); the United Benefice of St Genny's church, St Genny's; St James's, Jacobstow; St Werburgh's, Warbstow; St Gregory's, Treneglos (all 10–14 miles S of Bude, off A39).

CUMBRIA
St Cuthbert's, Kirkby-in-Furness; St Aidan's, Barrow-in-Furness.

ESSEX
In Essex, the diocese of Chelmsford has gone further than most in encouraging such work. The churchyard at Witham (8 miles NE of Chelmsford, off A12) is especially fine; the vicar at the time of writing, the Rev Nigel Cooper, is also a botanist who has written extensively and taught nationwide about the vital role of such sacred sites for nature conservation.

GLOUCESTERSHIRE
Lydney parish church (14 miles NE of Chepstow on A48).

HEREFORD AND WORCESTER

Colwall Green parish church (5 miles SW of Great Malvern off A449).

LANCASHIRE

St Peter's, Bolton; St John's, Great Marsden, Nelson.

LINCOLNSHIRE

St Giles's, Lincoln; St Peter and St Lawrence's, Wickenby (11 miles NE of Lincoln, off A46).

NORFOLK

Sisland parish church; South Walsham parish church (9 miles E of Norwich on B1140).

OXFORDSHIRE

Stanford-in-the-Vale parish church (5 miles E of Faringdon, off A417).

SHROPSHIRE

Hope Bagot parish church (5 miles E of Ludlow off A4117); Westbury parish church (9 miles E of Ludlow, 1 mile W of B4214); Hopesay parish church (6 miles W of Craven Arms off B4368).

SOMERSET

Aisholt parish church (6 miles S of Nether Stowey).

SUSSEX

Holy Trinity, Hurstpierpoint, West Sussex; and St Pancras, Arlington (6 miles SW of Hailsham, East Sussex).

WARWICKSHIRE

Stoneleigh parish church; Brailes parish church (3 miles E of Shipton-on-Stour on B4035); Hillmorton parish church, Rugby; Great Wolford parish church (4 miles E of Moreton-in-Marsh, and N of A44).

YORKSHIRE

Parish churches at Sheriff Hutton, North Yorkshire (9 miles SW of Malton, off A64); Low Moor, Bradford; and Mirfield, Kirkless (3 miles W of Dewsbury on A644) and Hutton Buscel, North Yorkshire (5 miles SW of Scarborough on A170).

Animals

THE HARE OF PENNANT MELANGELL
2 miles W of Llangynog, on B4391

Hidden away at the end of a secret valley in North Powys, lies a twelfth-century church that contains the shrine (c.1164) in which lie the relics of Saint Melangell (c.607). This was taken down during the Reformation. In 1720 the pieces of carved stone were built into the outer walls of the church where they remained until 1957 when experts removed them. They were later restored to their proper place. A gravestone in the apse is thought to be the original grave site of Saint Melangell.

Pilgrims now come daily to this place of peace and beauty. Since the death of the priest who committed himself to the restoration along with a committee of experts and parishioners, his widow, now ordained, ministers at the church and runs the center for the sick and those who are suffering with cancer. This is a holy and healing place, but how did the little church and shrine come to be on a Bronze Age site with yew trees dating back 2000 years?

The story goes that in the sixth or seventh century a woman hermit named Melangell lived here. One day a local nobleman, Brochwel Ysgythrog, was out hunting hares when a particularly fine one was flushed from cover and the hunters gave chase. The terrified creature ran straight to Melangell and hid beneath her robes. When the prince arrived and demanded his hare, Melangell refused and the hare

The hare was the symbol of the Celtic goddess Eostre and is still considered sacred today

was saved. From that day on hares in her valley were considered sacred and never hunted.

This story is interesting for many reasons. The hare has long been considered a sacred animal. In Celtic culture the hare is the symbol of Eostre, the goddess of the spring moon. Hares, of course, are famous for going "mad" in March – the time of the vernal equinox. The hare is thus associated with the moon, as indeed it is in places as far away as China and Tibet. In pre-Roman Britain, the hare was considered sacred and rarely eaten.

Then the Romans came, and one of the sports which they introduced was hare coursing. It seems to have caught on in Britain – there are Roman mosaics which depict greyhounds chasing hares and probably destroying them, and certainly overriding the older reverence shown to these animals.

When Christianity arrived, it reinstated the sacredness of the hare. The name for the greatest of Christian festivals is Easter, taken from the name of the goddess Eostre, whose festival fell in March or April at the time of the full moon after the spring equinox – the same time as the celebration of Christ's resurrection, which itself is fixed to this full moon by reference to the date of the Jewish Passover. With the adoption of her name came her sacred animal: hence the Easter bunny – really an Easter hare. And hence, too, the need for the St Melangell story, which gave a Christian justification for the protection of the hare. Sadly, however, the Roman hunting tradition has continued, despite the best efforts of those who stressed the sacredness of hares.

SACRED HORSES

High on the Berkshire Downs above the village of Uffington lies the **Uffington White Horse**. This extraordinary elongated outline of a horse, cut into the white chalk, has attracted many theories over the years. Some believe that it is Saxon and marks the victory of the Saxons against the Danes under Alfred the Great in the 890s. Others believe it to be a pre-Christian Celtic tribal "banner," proclaiming to all who encroached on the area that it was already occupied. The Celtic pre-Christian dating now seems to be widely accepted, making this the oldest hill figure in Britain; the famous Giant of Cerne Abbas in Dorset is the second oldest, possibly Roman.

What we have, therefore, is a tribe identifying itself by its sacred totem animal, the horse. This fits with what little is known of the animal associations of both the Celts and earlier Neolithic and Bronze Age peoples. The horse was seen as sacred from India to Europe. The *Rig Veda* and other early Sanskrit texts talk of sacred horses and of their sacrifice, for the fate of such horses was to be sacrificed to bring fertility or blessings.

In Britain traces of the horse cult remain. For example, on the hills above Portesham in Dorset is a megalithic burial mound known as the Old Grey Mare and her Colts, in front of which used to be the large, crudely carved head of a horse. The name seems to indicate a folk memory of horse worship here. The number of existing chalk carvings of horses is also interesting, though few are more than a couple of hundred years old; nevertheless, there is no reason to believe that the Uffington Horse was the only early one.

The Uffington White Horse on the Berkshire Downs is believed to have been a pre-Christian Celtic tribal "banner"

In the past bulls, wild boar and bears were venerated. Today, virtually nothing remains. We have moved beyond the few remaining wild animals of our land to adopt other creatures as symbolic animals whose future we feel responsible for, or who evoke within us some deeper sense of spirituality or reverence. The whale and the dolphin are perhaps the two most potent modern sacred animals; others include the rhinoceros, elephant and giant panda. We judge the spiritual, environmental and moral wellbeing of our world by the way we treat these creatures.

Some people equate talking about the sacred in animals with worshiping them. But that is not true, and our relationship with animals has always been complex. A major feature of the horse cult, after all, was the sacrifice of a horse each year. Yet by respecting and honoring its death as a life-bringer to the people, the early tribes in Britain understood that we are interconnected. We cannot unstitch one part of the web of life and not expect the rest to unravel. By rediscovering a respect for animals, even a sense of their sacredness, we might be able to stop ourselves from unraveling the web of life – and ourselves and our world in the process.

PART THREE

PILGRIM
ROUTES
THROUGH
SACRED
BRITAIN

THE THIRTEEN
PILGRIM ROUTES

FINDHORN

IONA

GLASGOW

EDINBURGH

LINDISFARNE

GRETNA

ASPATRIA

NEWCASTLE • JARROW

CARTMEL

RIPON

LEEDS

MANCHESTER

MAMTOR

LINCOLN

CHESTER

WALSINGHAM

BARDSEY ISLAND

LICHFIELD

CROWLAND

BIRMINGHAM •

ELY

WORCESTER

ST. DAVID'S

DORCHESTER-ON-THAMES

WESTMINSTER

LLANDAFF

LONDON

CARDIFF

BRISTOL

WOKING

CANTERBURY

GLASTONBURY

STONEHENGE

WINCHESTER

SOUTHAMPTON

TINTAGEL

PLYMOUTH

ST. MICHAEL'S MOUNT

——— PILGRIMAGE ROUTE
••••••••• MUTI-FAITH ROUTE

$\mathscr{T}$HE CONCEPT OF sacred land and sacred sites is inextricably inter-twined with pilgrimages. Whether it is Benares or Jerusalem, Makka or Glastonbury, sacred cities draw pilgrims and so pilgrim routes are created.

The earliest sacred sites in Britain, the great henges and stone circles three to four thousand years old, show that pilgrimage was a part of reli-gious ritual even then. Sacred avenues led the worshiper to the site, and their broken remains stand to this day. The Judaeo-Christian tradition is steeped in pilgrimage. The Old Testament/Hebrew Bible records places of special sacred significance, such as the tomb of Rachel or the shrine raised

THE SACRED WAY

Jay Ramsay, whose poem "The Sacred Way" appears in sections at the beginning of each chapter, has devised seven stages of pilgrim age which run from Chapters 10 to 18 (stage seven runs from Chapters 16–18). These stages are based on his own experience and you may find them helpful in understanding the nature of pilgrimage, though the stages should be seen as ideas rather than rules.

The first stage involves feeling what it means to be a pilgrim and how different this is from just traveling between A and B.

The second stage has to do with reading the signs, seeing that journeys are entities and that they take on a life of their own.

The third stage is becoming aware of our companions and why we are in the company we are. This isn't always easy!

The fourth stage relates to the history, the "story" we are witnessing, and its social, spiritual and political implications.

The fifth stage is about losing our role as observer and becoming part of the landscape, part of the story.

The sixth stage leads into a more visionary appreciation of the land, see-ing it as a place where Heaven and Earth touch. Here we are seeing with the eyes of spirit.

The seventh and final stage is an affirmation that we are all God's peo-ple, whatever we understand by that phrase. We are a spiritual people, and pilgrimage is a way of opening ourselves up to that in a way which is both confronting and revealing.

by Jacob at Bethel, the place where he had his dream of a ladder to Heaven. These were recorded and given locations because they were places of pilgrimage and veneration, and at one level the Bible is an early guidebook to the sacred topography of Palestine.

By the time of Jesus, Judaism had a long tradition of pilgrimage to the Temple at Jerusalem. In the *Lives of the Prophets*, written about AD 50, there are lists of tombs of Jewish prophets and sages which can be visited. In the Christian world pilgrimage began very early, and the faithful were visiting sacred Christian sites by the beginning of the second century. By the fourth century pilgrimage was big business and the first pilgrimage guide to the Holy Land, the *Itinerary of the Pilgrim of Bordeaux*, dates from AD 333.

The concept of pilgrimage in Britain seems to have passed from the pre-Christian Celtic sites to the Christian ones with little difficulty. Some sites were shared – places which had been holy in the older religion retained this status through association with a saint. Many of the sacred sites and churches of Cornwall and Wales fall into this category. Although local saints attracted local pilgrims, and much pilgrimage was therefore on a local rather than a national basis, some places soon achieved international status. For example, the relics at St Andrews in Fife were drawing pilgrims from all over northern Europe by the eleventh century. The pilgrims' route to Bardsey Island off the coast of North Wales was frequented by thousands from Ireland as well as Britain. St Etheldreda's at Ely was popular with pilgrims from across the British Isles and wider afield. And of course the cult of St Thomas à Becket at Canterbury, which began in the late twelfth century, attracted pilgrims from great distances. Pilgrims also left the British Isles to travel to the great sacred sites of Christianity in Rome and the Holy Land; we know of British pilgrims in Syria by the fifth century.

But pilgrimage was not all about religion. For some it was also an escape from reality, a means of avoiding their family, a way out of the constraints of medieval life. It is still the same today. Any group of modern pilgrims will have a whole spectrum of reasons for being on the road. So if you set off on these routes for other than religious reasons, don't feel you are not a pilgrim. However, you may find that you are surprised by joy or that such a journey touches places of pain or uncertainty within yourself.

Today most of us will never walk entire pilgrimage routes, nor can we travel with the beliefs that drove medieval pilgrims to take to the road. Modern transport makes visiting most places easy: in a single day we can speed along a route which pilgrims in the past spent weeks covering. So does this mean that pilgrimage is beyond us? We would argue not. Jay

Ramsay's seven steps can take weeks to come to fruition, or just a couple of days. We may have speeded up the process, but the basic ingredients are the same. We are all human beings with sorrows and joys, pains and delights, certainties and doubts. The crucial issue is still how open we are to what we might find both externally and within ourselves.

Although most people today make their own journeys to sacred places, there are growing numbers of organized pilgrimages. These range from two- or three-week walks to places such as Iona, Lindisfarne or St David's, to one-day pilgrimages such as the one described at Dorchester-on-Thames (see p. 186) or the Hindu pilgrimages to Bhaktivedanta Manor in Hertfordshire (see p. 280). Pilgrimage groups, magazines and organizations are constantly being set up. Just as the focus for many people's spiritual life is now the retreat center because of the depth of experience it offers, so increasingly is the pilgrimage becoming part of the way that Christians and others explore the idea of being a believer today. So welcome to Sacred Britain, explored and revealed through pilgrimage routes. Let us explain how these routes have been selected.

First of all we sought ancient ways which have been trodden for centuries and where local knowledge has kept alive the traditional route. These time-honored journeys underlie the Winchester and London to Canterbury routes, the Saints' Way in North Wales, parts of the South Wales route and elements of the Scottish route. Secondly, we adapted old routes and added our own ideas of how to get from one interesting place to another. This is how the Lincoln to Crowland route and the Stonehenge to Glastonbury route were devised. Thirdly, we have created totally new routes which enabled us to explore important sites and issues. These include in particular the multi-faith pilgrimage, the Lichfield to Mam Tor route and the Cumbrian route.

In preparing the general routes, we have combined old routes with new. The Reformation spelled the end for virtually all pilgrimage routes. Many of the original routes have been all but lost. Others now lie under tarmac or even motorways. Therefore the routes have been developed to be practical, to link a wide range of sites and where possible to follow known ancient routes such as the ones to Canterbury or probable ones such as that from Lincoln to Crowland. But it is important to stress that new routes are as valid as old ones. Pilgrimage routes go to places of spiritual and often environmental power. Many of our old destinations – Canterbury, Iona, Stonehenge, Bardsey Island – continue to work their magic. But newer destinations also draw us to them. It is in this spirit that the routes have been created.

ENGLAND

CHAPTER 6

The Canterbury Pilgrimage

There is a green road that runs
Through an ordinary but extraordinary garden
Where trees have been replanted
In clustered sheaths like candles

It is the Garden of the Earth

OF ALL THE pilgrimage routes in Britain, the most famous is that to Canterbury, known simply as the Pilgrims' Way. The religious capital of England is reached by traversing some of the oldest sacred landscapes in Britain – sacred long before Christ was born.

ROUTE MAPS

Each pilgrimage route in this book is illustrated in the margin with a specially commissioned "strip" map. Strip maps originated with medieval pilgrims' itineries (handbooks) and gave details of each route and any towns and villages on the way. They took the particular form that we have given them in the seventeenth and eighteenth centuries when they were developed for more general road map use and included the region surrounding the route. Each strip should be read from the bottom up.

DIRECTION BOXES

The following abbreviations are used: N = North, S = South, E = East, W = West, J = Junction, M = Motorway

This route is, of course, most remembered because of Chaucer's *Canterbury Tales* – the account of a journey by a group of pilgrims from London to Canterbury, during which they entertain each other with stories. The reason for the pilgrimage to Canterbury from the late twelfth century onward was the shrine of St Thomas à Becket, England's greatest medieval saint – a martyr to the Church and a symbol of struggle against the overweening powers of kings and the ruling class. As a former Archbishop of Canterbury who was murdered at the suggestion of the king, he was both establishment and anti-establishment. He was also a great miracle worker saint. All this and more drew people from across Britain and from much of northern Europe, so that St Thomas's shrine became the wealthiest in the land. However, long before his time pilgrims went to visit the shrines of the many archbishops who had become saints, from Augustine himself to the much-loved Dunstan.

There are two well-known routes to Canterbury. The one from Winchester to Canterbury is known as the Southern Route and is described first. The second is the Westminster to Canterbury route, called the Northern Route (see p. 89).

Southern Route: From St Swithun at Winchester to St Thomas at Canterbury

Main Route (129 miles/208 km):
WINCHESTER · FARNHAM · COMPTON ·
GUILDFORD · NEWLANDS CORNER ·
ALBURY · SHERE · CHALDON · KEMSING ·
AYLESFORD · CANTERBURY

WINCHESTER · HAMPSHIRE

One of the great ancient cities of England, Winchester started life as the Roman settlement of Venta Belgarum, built on the site of an Iron Age

fort. But others may have used this area for religious purposes long before the Romans came. Later Winchester was the traditional gathering place for medieval pilgrims setting off for Canterbury from south of London. It was a fine city with plenty of inns to provide bodily comforts and a great cathedral to offer spiritual uplift.

ST CATHERINE'S HILL

SE of Winchester between the river and the Twyford Down bypass of the M3, by exit 10

On St Catherine's Hill are an Iron Age fort and the small chapel of St Catherine, but most significantly the remains of a turf maze. It seems impossible to date, but some have suggested that it was a sacred maze in either the Roman period or, more likely, the Middle Ages. Such mazes were Christian symbols of the soul caught up and confused by the intricacies of the material world, yet always seeking to escape.

Winchester under the Romans was reputed to have had two major temples, one to Apollo and one to Concord or Peace – an unusual dedication – both supposedly on the site of the present cathedral. What is certain is that the holy well under the present cathedral was in use during Roman times, and probably the nearby St Martin's Well was too. The main well under the cathedral is called St Birinus's Well: he was the seventh-century missionary who founded the original church there, and it is claimed that he used the well for baptisms.

ST MARTIN'S WELL AND MONASTERY SITE

Near the cathedral, by the old Roman wall

There is, however, a fascinating possibility of an earlier Christian site in Winchester. Legend says that very soon after the conversion of the Roman Empire to Christianity in the fourth century AD, a monastery or headquarters of some other Christian community was built in Winchester and dedicated to St Martin. This saint founded the first monasteries in western Europe around AD 360 in southern France. Links between France and Britain, both part of the Roman Empire, were very good. It is not unreasonable to think of a similar monastery being established in such a well-settled and wealthy city as Winchester, or perhaps a Christian community had developed which later became a monastery. The dedication to St Martin might have come later, and perhaps the well bears testimony to this site. If so, this is probably the earliest monastery in Britain, pre-dating that of St Ninian at Whithorn in Dumfries and Galloway.

Winchester is thought to have been one of the places where resistance to the collapse of the Roman way of life in Britain was centered. Some have seen it as the base from which the Romano-Celtic ruler of Britain, Ambrosius Aurelianus (c.480), tried to rally a last stand against the invading Angles.

CASTLE HALL AND THE ROUND TABLE
Off High St

One of Ambrosius's commanders, mentioned in passing in a sixth-century document, was called Arthur, and the ancient link between Arthur and Winchester is demonstrated by the so-called Round Table of King Arthur to be seen in the Great Hall of the castle. Although it is an early medieval fake, someone thought it was worth doing – so the notion of a link between Arthur and Winchester was there many centuries ago.

It is said that when Winchester fell at last to the Angles and Saxons, the church/monastery of St Martin's was converted into a temple for the invaders' deities. This it remained until AD 635 and the arrival of St Birinus (see also p. 80), who fought the political and spiritual battles which established his sainthood and converted the West Saxons to Christianity.

In 648 Cynegils, King of the West Saxons, built the first church of which we have definite records on the site of the present cathedral. At that time Winchester was in the diocese of Dorchester, but soon afterward it was made a cathedral in its own right. By the eighth or early ninth century the kings of the West Saxons and then of Wessex were always crowned at Winchester.

WINCHESTER CATHEDRAL AND ST SWITHUN
In city center

The saint who made Winchester such a popular destination for pilgrims

has become a part of English folklore about the weather. His name is
Swithun or Swithin. Born probably in Winchester, and educated at the
cathedral, he became Bishop of Winchester *c*.852. Swithun was renowned
for his humility and for his generosity to the poor. Typical of this were his
instructions concerning his burial, which he commanded should take
place outside the cathedral because he felt unworthy to lie within the
sacred walls. Indeed, he wished to be buried by the door, so that all those
who entered could tread on him as a sign of his unworthiness. But when
he died in 862 the monks compromised and buried him to one side.

In 971, the then bishop decided to honor Swithun with a proper tomb
and shrine in the cathedral itself, so popular had his cult become. On July
15 his body was disinterred and carried into the cathedral, but the saint
expressed his disapproval in the form of a tremendous rainstorm. Indeed,
it is said that it rained for the next forty days. Hence the old saying:

> *If it rains on Swithun's Day,*
> *Then forty days shall it rain.*
> *If it be fine on Swithun's Day,*
> *Then forty days shall it be fine.*

The site of the shrine of St Swithun, moved yet again in the great rebuilding of 1093, is still marked and honored in the cathedral but the great
shrine itself has been destroyed. We feel that the simplicity of the remains
today actually do greater justice to this simple man – simple in his needs
and faith. Here is a place to stand and reflect upon the essentials of life, an
antidote to consumerism which sees bigger and glossier as better. This man
wanted to be dust beneath the feet of the faithful, yet the Church wanted
him to be something else. Today, stand quietly at this shrine and reflect
that in the fullness of time grandeur and pomp disappear, but the memory
of a good and humble man lives on.

Around the cathedral there are still clear signs of the importance of pilgrimage. The great fourteenth-century Pilgrims' Hall where the pilgrims
slept is open to the public.

HYDE ABBEY
Hyde Abbey Rd, just N of city center

Before leaving for Canterbury medieval pilgrims would probably have
made one last visit in Winchester, for this city was the burial place of the
greatest Christian king that England ever had. Here Alfred established
schools and hospitals, and ruled as a wise king and a tough warrior. He

built a monastery for his saintly chaplain, Grimbald, just north of the cathedral, and this is where Alfred was buried. The monastery, known as Hyde Abbey, prospered until the battle of Hastings. The then abbot, Alwyn, along with twelve of his monks, was at the side of King Harold giving spiritual support; this earned them the disfavor of William, who penalized the monastery by building a castle alongside. So in the late eleventh century the monks moved here, taking with them the remains of Alfred and many of his descendants. To this new Hyde Abbey came pilgrims to venerate Alfred's tomb. Never officially declared a saint, he was often considered one by popular acclaim, especially if it upset the Normans. For example, the little church of Monkton Deverill in Wiltshire, now a private house, was dedicated to St Alfred alongside a more conventional dedication.

The route to Farnham passes close to Alresford, with its new and old towns, which is worth a brief detour. The site was one of the original pieces of land given to the new church at Winchester while St Birinus was still there, and has long associations with the bishops of Winchester.

Winchester to Farnham (29 miles/47 km): *Follow signs to Alton out of Winchester and take A31 to Farnham. Alresford is en route, just N of A31 on B3046*

FARNHAM · SURREY

The saintly and humble St Swithun had some successors who were not of like mind. The great castle at Farnham was built by Henry de Blois, Bishop of Winchester in 1138, and until 1925 this was the residence of the bishops of Winchester. In recent years bishops have made use of their new large Bishop's House to create a Christian community – a return, perhaps, to the ways of Swithun. The importance of Winchester as an episcopal see and a political powerbase is reflected in both the magnificence of the cathedral and the solidity of this castle. Serving God and Mammon has always posed a problem for the Church.

Farnham's economic success as a medieval town was to a great extent built upon the revenue of the pilgrims passing through. The whole town was rebuilt in the twelfth century as a religious development and is truly a pilgrims' settlement.

To the south-east, on the B3001, are the ruins of Waverley Abbey. An established pilgrimage place, it achieved renewed fame after its destruction because the ruins inspired Sir Walter Scott to write his Waverley novels of medieval life.

> **Farnham to Compton (9 miles/14 km):** *Continue on A31 to Guildford. Compton is S of A31 on B3000*

COMPTON · SURREY

Stop at the village of Compton on the road to Guildford. Here is one of the strangest and oldest churches in England, famed for its two-storied sanctuary – the only one of its kind in the country. It also contains the oldest wooden screen in England, a Norman one of such hardness that it is impossible to drive a nail into it. This lovely site is undoubtedly a place that pilgrims would have visited. Pause here, where people have come to celebrate and to mourn over the centuries, to remember those who lovingly created this unique church and carved this screen so long ago.

> **Compton to Guildford (3 miles/5 km):** *Return to A31 and continue to Guildford*

GUILDFORD · SURREY

The city has long been famous for its inns, originally built to handle the pilgrim trade. The Red Lion and the White Hart are both old pilgrim inns.

SYNAGOGUE
High St

In 1994 some workmen were taking down an old wall in the cellar of a shop on High Street. They found themselves looking into a previously unknown and almost completely rubble-filled room. Once the rubble had been removed, it was found to be the ground floor of a synagogue dating from the Norman period, which makes it the oldest in England if, as seems possible, it pre-dates the one at Lincoln (see p. 123). Its restoration emphasized the fact that England has always been a multi-faith and multicultural society. At the time of writing it is not clear when access to this site will be possible.

Guildford to Albury (5 miles/8 km): *Follow A281 (signposted Horsham), then at Shalford take A248 going E. Continue to Albury*

NEWLANDS CORNER · SURREY

THE DRUID'S GROVE

Leaving Guildford, you will enter one of the most religiously dominated and shaped landscapes in England. Sites in this area, both natural and humanly constructed, go back over 2500 years. The landscape starts with two hilltop chapels just outside Guildford, St Catherine's (see p. 48) and the strange chapel of St Martha. They may both have been built on previous pagan sites, although there is scant evidence.

Just before Albury is Newlands Corner, with the remains of a druidic sacred yew grove. The trees here have been dated to around 2500 or maybe even 3000 years old. This landscape has been sacred for a very long time, as indicated by the presence of the chapels and the yew grove. It seems likely, therefore, that here at least the Pilgrims' Way is following an older pilgrims' way – one trodden perhaps for millennia before the cult of St Thomas gave it renewed significance. Here is a place to stand and be part of that landscape which has arisen from the many twists and turns of our sacred history; a place to be part of, not to observe.

ALBURY · SURREY

The church at Albury has two octagonal pillars thought to have come from a Roman temple which stood on nearby Blackheath, which still displays the remains of earthworks. Deep in the woods near a house known as Albury Park are the Sherborne Farm Pools, one of which is known as the Silent Pool and may have been a druidic sacred pool into which offerings were cast (see p. 9).

Albury to Kemsing (3 miles/5 km): *From Albury continue on A248 and go E on A25 through Dorking to Reigate. From here take A217 N to join M25. (For detour to Chaldon, leave at J7, follow signs for Redhill and then turn on to B2031 toward Caterham. Chaldon is just N of this road.) Continue E along M25 to J5, exit, take A25 E to Seal. At Seal, follow local signs to Kemsing*

SHERE · SURREY

Here, just east of Albury on the A25, there lived in the thirteenth or four-teenth century an anchoress – a female hermit who spent her life locked away in a specially constructed cell. All that remains is the squint window into the church through which the anchoress could see Mass being cele-brated at the high altar. This area seems to have been a focus for such reli-gious zeal.

CHALDON · SURREY

THE LADDER OF SALVATION

The church at Chaldon contains a magnificent Norman wall painting of the Ladder of Salvation. Here it is possible to see one of the motivating forces behind pilgrimage: many who made the long journeys did so in rec-ompense for sins committed. Without the pardon which such a pilgrimage could offer, the medieval Church taught, the soul faced the fires of Hell or the trials of Purgatory. Looking at the faces of the devils in this wall painting, it is easy to see why people would undergo an arduous pilgrimage if they felt it would save them from such horrors. It seems to us that the

"The Ladder of Salvation" in the church at Chaldon, Surrey

demons depicted are not external forces trying to catch people out, but inner forces with which each of us has to wrestle.

KEMSING · KENT

ST EDITH'S WELL

Here is another famous shrine. Just over a thousand years ago, a daughter was born here to King Edgar the Peaceful. Her name was Edith. At a very early age, possibly while still a baby, she was taken to the nunnery at

Wilton in Wiltshire. Here she lived all her short life: born in 961, she died in 984. One of her biographies describes her as "knowing not the world rather than forsaking it." She refused to become the abbess, preferring to be the humblest among the nuns, serving like Martha. The shrine beside the war memorial at Kemsing is St Edith's Well, once very popular and famous for its ability to restore sight, save crops from mildew and bring about a fruitful harvest. The first written record of a holy well here is in 926, making it one of the earliest recorded Christian wells. It was considered holy before being linked with St Edith. Pilgrims would have availed themselves of its good waters before moving on. The tradition lives on to this day in the annual church procession to the well on September 16.

Kemsing to Aylesford (14 miles/23 km): *Return to A25 and follow signs for M26 (becomes M20). Aylesford is just N of J5*

AYLESFORD · KENT

The next stop on the Canterbury pilgrims' route was Aylesford, then a major pilgrimage town. This was the site of one of Alfred the Great's major victories over the Danes in 893. Earlier, in 455, it had witnessed one of the first great defeats of the Saxons by the British, when the invaders Hengest and Horsa fought the Romano-British ruler Vortigern.

The church is interesting because of its shape. The south chancel arch and roof are out of alignment with the rest of the building, a layout which is supposed to represent the twisted head of Christ on the cross at his death.

AYLESFORD PRIORY AND ST SIMON STOCK

Today, as a modern pilgrim, you can visit a friary which still offers hospitality. Aylesford Priory was founded by a returned Crusader in 1242 as a Carmelite monastery. The second prior was St Simon Stock, another former Crusader who had undergone a conversion experience in the Holy Land and become a Carmelite. In 1254 Simon became Superior-General of the Carmelite Order and founded houses throughout Europe, in particular at university cities such as Cambridge, Oxford, Paris and Bologna. He is best remembered for his vision of the Virgin Mary, from which he devised the idea of the scapular devotion – the wearing under one's outer garments of a cloth bearing a picture of the Virgin Mary or Sacred Heart. Simon died in 1265 and was buried in Bordeaux. However, pilgrims visiting

Aylesford in the Middle Ages would have offered prayers to him at his possible place of birth, and certainly at the place where he had been prior. Today you can offer prayers at his actual shrine, for after an absence of several hundred years the Carmelites have returned and brought with them the bones of St Simon Stock. At the dissolution of the monasteries in the 1530s the priory was sold and much of it was pulled down in order to build a large house from the stones. In the 1930s a fire destroyed this house and the ruins were sold to the Carmelites, who have rebuilt the priory and made a shrine to St Simon Stock.

St Simon Stock, the second prior of Aylesford

Here one can sense what a medieval pilgrim would have found at any of the shrines along the road: hospitality and a place of prayer. The river flows alongside, and for all the world you could be back in the Middle Ages. Today the priory offers courses and conferences on the spiritual life. The intellectual tradition of St Simon Stock, established in his university town priories, is alive and well in this atmosphere. Here, though broken for nearly four centuries, the thread has been taken up again. This is a place to sit and reflect on how history is as much to do with continuing cycles as it is with the concept of progress.

NEOLITHIC STONES
Some 4 miles N of Aylesford, W of A229 going toward Rochester. Follow local signs

The most famous of these five Neolithic remains are the burial mounds known as Kit's Coty House and Little Kit's Coty House. Local legend claims that they were built to contain the bodies of Horsa and Certigorn, brother of Vortigern, killed at the famous battle of AD 455. As these were "pagan" kings it is just possible that their followers made use of old burial sites, though there is no indication that they did. But again, with the friary reopened and ancient tombs exposed to the air, one is in a charged, sacred landscape.

At Aylesford the Southern Route is joined by the Northern Route. For the final section, therefore, see pp. 96-102. It is to the urban route from London that we now turn.

Northern Route: From St Edward the Confessor at Westminster to St Thomas at Canterbury

Main Route (79 miles/128 km):
GREENWICH · DARTFORD · GRAVESEND · ROCHESTER · AYLESFORD · HARBLE-DOWN · CANTERBURY

It is also possible to follow the old pilgrim route, which leaves London via Blackheath, Kidbrooke, Bexley, Singlewell, Frindsbury and Boxley and involves detours from the more direct route described below.

LONDON

For all its antiquity and importance, London has never been in the top league of sacred places in Britain. It has, of course, the great shrine of St Edward the Confessor; the magnificence of Westminster Abbey and St Paul's Cathedral; and the glorious churches by Wren and his contemporaries. But it is not the equivalent of Canterbury or Glastonbury, Ely or Durham. London has tended to be a city to visit and leave again. Yet, as you will see in the multi-faith pilgrimage in Chapter 18, London is home to places of great significance to Christians and people of other faiths. In this section, we simply follow the Canterbury pilgrims' route. Although the official route started from Southwark, the pilgrims would undoubtedly have visited the major shrines and religious buildings of London before they departed, so we will start with these.

WESTMINSTER ABBEY
Westminster, opposite Houses of Parliament

Since the twelfth century Westminster Abbey has been the coronation church of English and then

British kings and queens. Yet when the abbey was founded, probably by Edward the Confessor c.1050 (though one legend says that an earlier king, Sebert, founded it c.959), it stood on a small natural island called Thorney in the countryside south of London itself. Here too Edward built a new royal palace – the Palace of Westminster, now, in rebuilt form, the Houses of Parliament. The name Westminster gradually replaced that of Thorney, for the new abbey was roughly west of the Old Minster – a predecessor of Wren's St Paul's Cathedral (see p. 92).

TOMB OF THE UNKNOWN WARRIOR

Set into the nave is a tomb within which is buried an unidentified soldier from the First World War. The idea of so honoring an unknown soldier to lie among memorials to the great and powerful of the land was to show how the sacrifices of such men were appreciated. The notion of an ordinary man, perhaps an unwilling conscript, perhaps an idealistic volunteer, being thus honored is very moving. The tomb is a place to reflect upon the enormous sacrifices that people have had to make down the centuries in order for their descendants to enjoy their freedom today. But it is also a terrible reminder of the destruction of war and the failure of all religions to create lasting peace. It is a place to stand and reflect upon these and many other issues affecting ordinary lives caught up in forces beyond their control.

Keith Douglas, himself killed during the Second World War, wrote movingly of compassion for the enemy in war in his poem, "Vergissmeinnicht" (Forget-me-not):

> Three weeks gone and the combatants gone
> returning over the nightmare ground
> we found the place again, and found
> the soldier sprawling in the sun. . . .
>
> Look. Here in the gunpit spoil
> the dishonoured picture of his girl
> who had put: Steffi. Vergissmeinnicht
> in a copybook gothic script. . . .
>
> But she would weep to see today
> how on his skin the swart flies move;
> the dust upon the paper eye
> and the burst stomach like a cave.
> For here the lover and killer are mingled
> who had one body and one heart.

And death who had the soldier singled
has done the lover mortal hurt.

THE SHRINE OF ST EDWARD THE CONFESSOR

Until St George was adopted in the thirteenth or fourteenth century, St Edward was the patron saint of England. Born in 1003 at Islip in Oxfordshire, he was the eldest son of King Ethelred the Unready and Emma, daughter of the Duke of the Normans. Edward became King of England in 1042 and the whole of his reign was a series of crises brought about by the struggle between the Norman party, based in northern France, and the Anglo-Saxon party, based around Earl Godwin and his son Harold. Edward died in 1066, and his vacillations about appointing a successor laid the foundations for the struggle between King Harold and Duke William which ended in the battle of Hastings in 1066. Edward was thus the last crowned Saxon king of England.

But why was he a saint? It seems that this man, torn between conflicting loyalties, found great succor in the Church. He not only built Westminster but endowed other churches and monasteries. In his own lifestyle he was monk-like in his simplicity and in his attentiveness to prayer. As such he was elevated by the Church as a model king, even if he left his poor subjects in confusion and ultimately conquered. His life was spent trying to reconcile the irreconcilable and to maintain peace in a land which even during his early life was dogged by invasion and warfare. It was for this reason that he was loved by the ordinary people; he was also popular with the monarchy and the ruling class because he gave the royal house a holy lineage. His shrine was therefore a magnificent one, covered in gold and jewels. At the Reformation the gold and jewels were stripped off and his bones exhumed and buried in an obscure part of the abbey. However, when Mary became Queen and briefly restored the Catholic faith, she had Edward put back into the rebuilt shrine. This is the shrine still visible today, and his bones have not been moved since.

We find both his shrine and the tomb of the unknown warrior very poignant. Here is the king who tried to keep the peace and who compromised and confused. Here is the commoner who paid with his life for the failure of kings and rulers to keep the peace. Playwright Alan Bennett has said that Westminster Abbey, with its place for the greatest and the most humble, with its saints and its atheists buried and respected equally, is a reflection of the best of Anglicanism and of being English – a live-and-let-live world view. It embodies a sense of the sacred which is neither exclusive nor arrogant: the good in all people is respected, regardless of what they believed.

ST PAUL'S CATHEDRAL
Ludgate Hill

The pilgrim route leads on beside the Thames from Westminster to London Bridge. Churches, monasteries and nunneries abounded here, as did the palaces of the bishops, especially on the Strand. Needless to say, the medieval pilgrims would then go a little further east to visit St Paul's in the City of London – not the magnificent Wren building of today, but its equally magnificent predecessor destroyed in the Great Fire of 1666. In 604 St Augustine consecrated Mellitus as Bishop of London, and as a result of his preaching, Ethelbert, King of the East Saxons, founded St Paul's. The saint associated with St Paul's was Erkenwald (sometimes written Earconwald), another Bishop of London. Born into the royal family, he was rich enough to found monasteries at Chertsey in Surrey and Barking in Essex. At Barking he ruled alongside his sister Ethelburga, also a saint.

The old St Paul's is also supposed to have held the burial place of St Thomas à Becket's parents, the Christian knight Gilbert and a Saracen

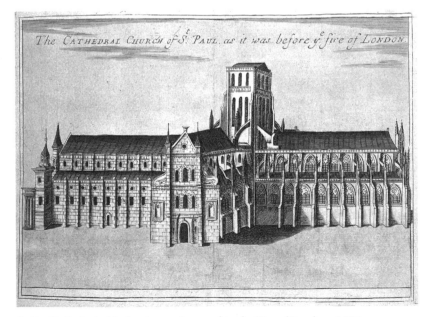

St Paul's Cathedral before it was destroyed in the Fire of London, 1666

woman called Mahaut (for more details, see p. 99). According to one medieval source, there was even a procession to their graves every year.

LONDON BRIDGE AND SOUTHWARK

Crossing London Bridge from north to south, the pilgrims would probably have stopped at the chapel in the middle, dedicated to St Thomas à Becket. What more auspicious way could there be to start their pilgrimage?

From the bridge it was on to the overnight stop at the Tabard Inn in Southwark, or, for the wealthy, a stay at the monastery church of St Mary Overy just over the bridge. This great church and priory originally faced on to London Bridge in one direction and looked out over fields in the other. Today its surroundings have been totally transformed. Its name was changed to St Saviour's at the Reformation when the priory was dissolved, and much later, in 1905, it became the cathedral church of the new diocese of Southwark. Of all the cathedrals of Britain, this must be the best example of how not to treat a sacred site. Crowded in by railway lines, surrounded by roads, filth and noise, it is hard to imagine that this is one of the oldest-known religious sites in England. For beneath the cathedral is a Roman well: when this was excavated, a broken Roman altar and three statues of gods – or possibly goddesses, in which case they are probably the Three Mothers or Matres – were found.

Next stop for the medieval pilgrims would have been the vast abbey of St Saviour at Bermondsey, now totally disappeared. Here kings and queens were often entertained on their way in or out of London. The only trace remaining is in the name Abbey Road.

Southwark to Greenwich (3 miles/5 km): *From Southwark Cathedral on S side of London Bridge head W along Tooley Street and take A2 (signposted Dover). At Deptford take A206 to Greenwich*

GREENWICH · LONDON

ST ALPHAGE

This settlement was a popular stop because of its church dedicated to another martyred Archbishop of Canterbury, St Alphage (sometimes spelled Aelfheah or Elphege), 953–1012. He was a quiet man who loved peace.

His early years as a monk were spent at Deerhurst in Gloucestershire (see p. 175), after which he retired to Somerset. Then he was asked by the Archbishop of Canterbury, St Dunstan, to become Bishop of Bath and subsequently Bishop of Winchester. He lived a very austere life but was renowned for his generosity to the poor. He was also a peacemaker who paid for it with his life.

In 1005 he became Archbishop of Canterbury at a time when the Danes were over-running the English. Canterbury was captured and Alphage was seized and imprisoned by the Danes in Greenwich. A ransom of £3000 was demanded – the equivalent of perhaps £2–3 million today. Alphage forbade anyone to try to raise such a crippling sum. This infuriated the Danes who one night, in the midst of a drunken feast, had him brought before them and beat him to death with the bones of the ox they had been eating, finishing him off with an axe. The church is thought to mark the site of this murder; here died a man who put others before himself. The medieval ballad *"Ubi sunt qui ante nos fuerunt?"* ("Where are those who lived before?") contains this pertinent verse:

> *Be wise, O Man, and gladly know*
> *A little torment here below;*
> *Shrink from your pleasures often.*
> *And when you suffer bitter pain,*
> *Consider well your heavenly gain.*

Greenwich to Dartford (10 miles/15 km): *Take A207 to Dartford. (For Pocahontas detour, take A226 to Gravesend)*

DARTFORD · KENT

This next stop was a major pilgrimage center, with a nunnery where women travelers could stay in safety, a hospital founded in the mid-fifteenth century and a leper hospital founded in the fourteenth century. Here the pilgrims could follow an old Roman road, Watling Street, which would lead them through Kent to Canterbury. Today the countryside through which they would have traveled is under threat as never before. Urban development, motorways, Channel Tunnel links and the destruction of the old orchards of the "Garden of England" have spoiled much of Kent.

GRAVESEND · KENT

POCAHONTAS

Turn aside for just a brief excursion. In St George's churchyard, Gravesend, lies a sad reminder of the results of British colonialism. Here is buried Pocahontas (1595–1617), a native American woman who befriended the early settlers in Virginia and saved the life of one of them when her tribe was about to kill him. She became a Christian, married another settler and sailed to England with her husband in 1616. In 1617 she was setting off back to Virginia but died on board ship, just off Gravesend. She was brought ashore and buried with due honor. Her tribe disappeared within a century through the incursions of the English settlers.

Today she is perhaps best known through the Disney film which turned her into a beautiful fairy-like girl in a dream world which is rudely broken into by the arrival of newcomers. The impact of the West on indigenous cultures has often been disastrous, but we do no credit to the complex issues involved by making simple good/bad dichotomies. Stand a while by her tomb and think what it must have been like to see your whole world turned upside down. Yet she tried to bridge these two worlds, just like the women saints who entered "peace marriages" between the native English and the invading Danes, Saxons and others (see p. 104).

> **Dartford to Rochester (22 miles/35 km):** *From Dartford (or from Gravesend detour) join A2, which joins M2 just before Rochester*

ROCHESTER · KENT

The next major stop for the pilgrims was Rochester. The small city is dominated by two buildings: the castle, built on a site fortified since Roman times, and the nearby cathedral, founded in 604 by St Justus, one of the early missionaries sent to England by Pope Gregory.

ROCHESTER CATHEDRAL AND THE SHRINE OF ST WILLIAM

Although Rochester was a popular stop, it was not as popular as the local monks would have liked – they resented all the money which flowed on down to Canterbury and tried to initiate a saint's cult for their own benefit. They had the shrine of St Paulinus, a missionary who came with

Augustine in 597. St Justus also had a shrine here, as did the first native-born Bishop of Rochester, St Ythamar. But these were not big-time saints and lacked the aura of St Thomas à Becket.

Then, one night in 1201, a pilgrim became a saint. He was a fisherman named William from Perth in Scotland, whose life, so the chroniclers say, was full of good deeds to the poor. He and a companion who were traveling together to the Holy Land arrived at Rochester on their way to Canterbury. The following day the companion took him to a quiet spot and murdered him, taking all his belongings. The body was supposedly found by a madwoman who, after garlanding it with honeysuckle, was apparently cured. The Hospital of St William which celebrates this healing stands today on the spot where he was murdered.

William was buried in the cathedral and soon other miracles were being recorded. As the cult grew, his body was moved to where the shrine is today, in the north-east transept. However, while the monks of Rochester may have been convinced of his sanctity, the Pope was not. In 1256 William's memory received a papal blessing but he was never officially made a saint.

> **Rochester to Aylesford (8 miles/13 km):** *Go S on A229 to Maidstone and follow local signs for Aylesford (just N of Maidstone and W of A229)*

AYLESFORD AND MAIDSTONE · KENT

From Rochester the route followed the old Roman road through Sittingbourne to Canterbury. At Faversham hospitality was offered by the great abbey, founded by King Stephen in the twelfth century and the place where he was buried; now just the gatehouse remains. From here it was straight on to Canterbury. But others might have veered off to meet the Southern Route at Aylesford, which we now rejoin.

Just after Aylesford, Maidstone has not only the magnificent church of All Saints but also the impressive remains of the Archbishop's Palace. Here archbishops shuttling between Canterbury and their London palace at Lambeth stayed the night. Much of its beauty remains to this day on the riverside.

> **Aylesford to Canterbury (33 miles/53 km):** *Return to A229, head N toward Rochester and join M2 going E to Canterbury*

HARBLEDOWN · KENT

ST NICHOLAS'S HOSPITAL

At Harbledown, south of the A2 just west of Canterbury, the city itself comes into view. Here is the Hospital of St Nicholas, founded by Archbishop Lanfranc in 1084 to care for the outcast, aged and infirm. It seems likely that this site was chosen not least for the well nearby. This is now known as the Black Prince's Well and bears above it the crest of the three feathers. The reason for this name is that when the Black Prince was dying in 1376, he asked for healing waters to be brought from here. The well obviously has a long tradition of healing.

CANTERBURY · KENT

The site of modern Canterbury was first occupied by the Cantii, a Celtic tribe that built Iron Age forts here, but the basic town shape as seen today was laid out by the Romans as Durovernum Canticorum (see p. 56 for details of Canterbury's sacred layout). This is one of only two places where it is known that a Roman church occupied a site which is still a church today (the other is Old St Pancras in London). St Martin's was the old Roman church which St Augustine reopened when he arrived in Britain in 597 to bring the gospel back to south-eastern England.

CANTERBURY CATHEDRAL

It was, of course, to the cathedral that the pilgrims came. This, one of the most magnificent medieval buildings in the world, is a world in itself. To undertake the pilgrimage round the cathedral is to do a lot more than just visit the site where Christianity returned under St Augustine, or to visit St Thomas's shrine. The whole building is a cosmological and theological statement, a model of sacred space, sacred land.

From the south porch you enter the lower part of the church. Stand and look up the aisle toward the high altar and you will begin to see the cosmic geography of this extraordinary building. The high altar is literally that, for it stands much higher than the rest of the church: to take communion you ascend the hill of Golgotha – the hill on which Christ was crucified. And beneath the high altar are chapels deep down in the ground. This exactly reproduces the situation in the church of the Holy Sepulchre in Jerusalem, where the chapel and altar of Golgotha rise from the surrounding area of the church. Beneath it is the chapel of Adam's Skull, for legend says that he was buried in a cave under Golgotha. This is clearly seen in Orthodox icons of the crucifixion, where the cross breaks through the rock and points down to a skull – that of Adam – lying in the cave beneath. In Canterbury Cathedral, this sacred geography is re-created.

Above: The inside of Canterbury Cathedral looking east toward the High Altar and Trinity Chapel

The whole cathedral is laid out as a great processional way, in order to handle the vast number of pilgrims who flocked to this, the greatest shrine in Europe after Rome. As they processed past the shrine, then down into the crypt chapels, and finally up to the high altar, the pilgrims underwent a journey both physical and metaphysical. They died with Adam and rose with Christ – powerful themes in medieval religious thought as this medieval hymn shows.

Adam lay in bondage.
Bound in fetters strong;
Four thousand winters
Thought he not too long:
And all was for an apple,
An apple that he took,
As holy men find written,
In their holy book.

Had the apple not been taken,
The apple taken been,
Never would Our Lady
Have been Heaven's Queen.
Blessed be the time
That apple taken was!
Therefore we must sing,
"Deo gracias!"

St Thomas à Becket

The story of St Thomas does not immediately indicate why he should have become the most popular of all saints. He was born the son of a wealthy London merchant, in 1118. As a young man he studied theology at Paris – his father's family were Normans – and in 1142 he joined the household of Theobald, Archbishop of Canterbury. He was a knight, a diplomat and a scholar, and few could have foreseen his end. But in 1162 he became Archbishop of Canterbury and something changed within him. He put aside courtly pleasures and became a strict ascetic. From working for King Henry II he now became the champion of the Church, standing up to the King and his nobles. This earned him few friends in high places and soon he was being accused of sequestering money and overstepping the mark. In 1164 he fled to France, fearing that Henry II would imprison him. A truce was arranged and Thomas returned to his archbishopric, but it soon broke down and Henry was threatened with excommunication.

The denouement took place on December 29, 1170. The night before, Henry had muttered a wish to be rid of "this turbulent priest" and four knights took it, rightly or wrongly, as an indication that Thomas's death would please their master. Riding all night from London, they arrived at the cathedral in time for morning Mass. Thomas was on his way to worship at the altar when the knights burst in and murdered him in cold blood.

Horror at the crime that had been committed in the most sacred place in Christian England meant that the murder achieved immediate notoriety. Henry was shocked, and four years later had to make this shock public

A WOMAN OF PERSEVERANCE

Above Thomas à Becket's tomb there is a small gilded crescent, traditionally regarded as a symbol of his mother's Islamic origins. According to a medieval story circulating as early as a hundred years after his death, Gilbert, Thomas's Crusader father, was taken captive in the Holy Land by a Saracen prince. His daughter, Mahaut, fell in love with the handsome Gilbert and offered to free him if one day he would return for her. He accepted the offer, but, after returning to England, forgot his promise. When, after several years, Mahaut realized that he was not going to come for her, she set out to find him herself. Although she knew only two words of English – his name and his home – she persevered and managed to find her lost love. They married and she became a Christian.

by walking barefoot through Canterbury, whipped by priests to venerate Thomas at the cathedral. Two years before this, the most humiliating public experience of any ruler of England, Thomas had been made a saint – just two years after his murder.

The Church certainly found it very convenient to have a stick, both literally and metaphorically, with which to beat down the overweening King and his nobles. It fitted well with the Church's increasing ascendancy over the secular authorities. This later led to many abuses, but its original purpose was a good one. The kings and barons of the Middle Ages were often little better than the mafia or drug barons today, ruling through brute force and fear. Against them the ordinary people were defenseless. The only body capable of standing up to them was the Church, whose clergy came from the same social background and could take them on as equals. This, together with the miracles credited to him, is why Thomas was so popular both during his life and afterward. He represented the curbing of the kings and barons, and the power of the Church to protect.

ST AUGUSTINE'S COLLEGE AND ST AUGUSTINE

What is interesting is that there never seems to have been much of a cult of St Augustine. He was not buried in the cathedral, nor was he ever transferred there. St Augustine is a strange figure, and one whose role in British Christianity has at times been overstated.

It used to be said that he brought Christianity to England. Yet Christianity was here long before him – he reused a Roman church, after all – and he merely brought the faith back after a gap. Furthermore, the Celtic saints such as Ninian, Columba and Cuthbert and their followers had been coming as missionaries to northern England for many years before Augustine. St Augustine was sent to southern England by Pope Gregory, who famously saw some fair-haired British slaves in Rome and asked where they came from. Being told they were Angles, he is supposed to have replied, "Not Angles, but angels." It seems he then sent a mission to bring the gospel back to Kent. To do this he chose the prior of St Andrew's monastery in Rome. This is how St Augustine and his small band were sent to England. They landed at Pegwell Bay and traveled straight to Canterbury.

Augustine was very successful and can certainly be credited with bringing Christianity to the Kentish people again. His disciples and later groups sent by the Pope spread out across England, meeting the Celtic missionaries moving south. But in 603 Augustine traveled to just north of present-day Bristol, to Aust on the Severn. Here he met the Celtic Church leaders of Wales, seeking their submission. The story goes that the Celtic leaders, fearful of the power politics that Augustine was playing, made a decision as they traveled to Aust. If, when they arrived, Augustine was seated and rose to meet them, or he was standing and remained so to greet them, they would consider being under his authority. If, however, he was seated and did not rise when they entered – in other words did not treat them as equals – then they would not work with him. Augustine re-

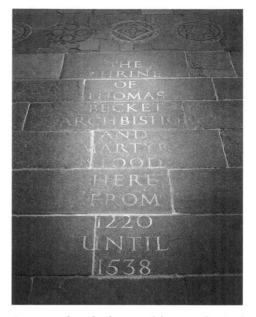

A memorial marks the spot of the great shrine of St Thomas, destroyed by Henry VIII during the Reformation

mained seated, and it was not for many many centuries that Canterbury had authority over the Welsh Church. In the light of all this it is untrue to call him the bringer of Christianity to England. This is not to decry his achievements, but to remind us that there were many churches, saints, bishops, monasteries and devout Christians in Britain long before Augustine of Rome came.

Canterbury is the burial place of many saints. St Augustine himself is buried under what is now the college, but which was previously the site of his abbey of St Peter and St Paul. Here also lie two early missionaries who put "English" Christianity into its proper international perspective. In 668 the Archbishop of Canterbury elect, Wighard, died while in Rome to receive his authority. The Pope, St Vitalian, decided to appoint in his place a man who would broaden the understanding of the newly established Roman Church and assist in establishing a Catholic hierarchy in Britain. In fact he sent two men: one was St Theodore, the other St Adrian.

Theodore was a Greek monk born c.602 in Tarsus, in what is today central Turkey. Adrian was an African – possibly a black African – who had become abbot of the great monastery of Monte Cassino. It was to him that the Pope originally offered the archbishopric, and it was the African who recommended the Greek from Turkey. The Pope agreed, so long as Adrian went as well. Adrian was in fact to live for thirty-nine years in England until his death.

Theodore laid the foundations for a just and equitable administration of the Roman Church in England and tried to heal the wounds between the Roman and Celtic Churches. It was his brilliance that set the Church on firm foundations. St Adrian became abbot of the monastery of St Peter and St Paul just outside the city walls in Canterbury. This later became St Augustine's, and today its site is occupied by St Augustine's College. This gentle but firm and utterly incorruptible African monk established the monastery as a place of high learning, teaching Greek and Latin as well as philosophy and ethics. So when you walk through Canterbury today and see and hear people from a wide range of religious and ethnic backgrounds you are part of one of England's great cosmopolitan cities – where once Greeks and Africans ran the show and did so in such a way that what we have today we owe in no small part to these two men.

Many archbishops became saints and lie in the cathedral or in St Augustine's abbey site – for example St Honorus, the last of Augustine's original companions, and his successor, St Deusdedit, the first Englishman to be Archbishop of Canterbury. St Alphage, martyred at Greenwich (see p. 93) lies in the cathedral, as do St Dunstan, who died in 988 having reformed monasticism in England, and Thomas Cranmer, who oversaw and wrote much of the great *Anglican Book of Common Prayer*. This is a holy city, though many of the sites of saints' bones are now unmarked. The great shrine of St Thomas was destroyed by Henry VIII – as much to indicate that the Church was now under his control as to plunder its gold, silver and jewels.

The Anglican Church is now a third-world Church. The vast majority of Anglicans worldwide are black and poor, and this great cathedral is their spiritual Mother Church. Every ten years Canterbury hosts the Lambeth Conference, attended by bishops of the Anglican Communion from all over the world. The city is filled with purple-robed Africans, Chinese, Americans, Indians, people from the Pacific islands, the Caribbean and elsewhere. To them, as to the nostalgic English person or the questing wanderer, Canterbury is as much a spiritual destination today as it has been for over fourteen hundred years.

CHAPTER 7

·············· ≈ ··············

*E*ly to Walsingham

Once boots trod there and carts bumped
You can feel them in your stride
And hear the soundless accents of conversation

Now it is a tractor-mown path
Flanked by waist-high wild flowers
(Where you may disturb a sleepy owl)

Leading to a landslip above a tan-brown river
That has become a precipice of fragile ground

*E*LY TO WALSINGHAM could be described as the women's or feminist pilgrim route. All along the way we encounter primarily women saints: individuals of great power, strength and authority from St Etheldreda of Ely, toughest and most popular of all the Anglo-Saxon women saints; via Mother Julian of Norwich, the greatest English Christian mystic of all time; via St Withburga and her untimely removal after death; to the Virgin Mary, whose appearance at Walsingham in 1061 to Lady Richeld gave rise to the greatest and most enduring of Marian shrines in Britain.

From St Etheldreda at Ely to Our Lady at Walsingham

Main Route (107 miles/171 km):
ELY · SOHAM · MILDENHALL · BURY ST EDMUNDS · THETFORD · ATTLEBOROUGH · WYMONDHAM · NORWICH · EAST DEREHAM · NORTH ELMHAM · WALSINGHAM

ELY · CAMBRIDGESHIRE

ELY CATHEDRAL AND ST ETHELDREDA

The great central tower of Ely Cathedral with its unique giant lantern shape rises high above the surrounding Fenlands – a magnet which has drawn pilgrims for centuries. Here lies the most famous of all England's female saints. This is a place which bears testimony to the power of women to change the world, even when the odds are against them.

Until the 1700s Ely stood on an island, surrounded by waterways and marshes with only a causeway across them to the holy place. It was to this isolated spot that a remarkable woman came in the year 673, to found not just a nunnery but also a monastery. Etheldreda was the daughter of King Anna of East Anglia and was probably born at Exning in Suffolk in 630. She was first married to Tondberht, prince of the Gyrvii, as a diplomatic move to bring peace and security; but at her insistence she remained a virgin. After her husband's death in 655, Etheldreda went to her property on the isle of Ely to contemplate. Five years on, again to strengthen bonds of peace between kingdoms, she married Egfrith, the young King of Northumberland. A devout Christian himself, he agreed that they would live as brother and sister. However, after twelve years Egfrith wished to consummate the marriage; but Etheldreda persisted and eventually her husband allowed her to take vows as a nun.

She retired to the nunnery of her aunt St Ebbe, at Coldingham in the Scottish Borders (St Ebbe is remembered in the corrupt form of her name, Abb, at St Abb's Head in Scotland, and in the St Ebbe district of Oxford). In 673 Etheldreda moved back to Ely and there founded her double monastic house. She lived a life of extreme austerity, eating only one meal a day, and died here in 679. Her body

THE DISSOLUTION OF THE MONASTERIES

By the early sixteenth century the thousands of monasteries and nunneries across Britain provided the population with basic social as well as religious services. They ran schools, hospitals and clinics, as well as providing local employment and giving shelter to travelers. But they were also tainted by the corruption of some aspects of the Church. In 1536 King Henry VIII forced the English and Welsh Church to break away from the control of the Pope. Henry made himself head of the Church and, in this role, ordered a complete survey of all the monasteries in England and Wales. Under the pretense of purging corruption, but actually driven by the desire to acquire the wealth and lands of the monasteries, Henry and his minister Thomas Cromwell began closing the smaller monasteries in 1536. The great monasteries tried to bargain for their survival, but to no avail. By 1541 all had been closed, and most were sold to local families from the newly rich merchant classes.

The closing of monasteries was often a feature of the Reformation, a movement which, taking its title from the desire to reform the Church, began in 1517 in Germany when Martin Luther published his ninety-five complaints against corruption in the Church. The English Reformation was a mixed affair arising from Henry VIII's desire to divorce his first wife, Catherine of Aragon, who had produced only a daughter, and to marry Anne Boleyn. The Pope refused permission, so Henry broke away from Rome, using the Reformation as an excuse.

was laid in a Roman sarcophagus and she was buried in her abbey with full ceremony. Soon it had become the most popular woman's shrine in the country, and continued to be so until the day of its destruction in 1541.

Etheldreda, queen, daughter of a king, niece of an abbess, sister of another and aunt of yet another, appears to have belonged to that powerful and increasingly important group of women who, in fact if not in name, were heads of the Church in their area. In more recent times many people found the memory of her role and status helpful while the Church of England dithered about ordaining women to the priesthood. Of Etheldreda's immediate family, four more became official saints: her sisters Sexburga, who succeeded her as abbess, and Withburga (whom we shall meet again at East Dereham); Werburga, granddaughter of one of Etheldreda's sisters (see Threekingham, p. 126) and her aunt St Ebbe.

What is extraordinary about Etheldreda's story is the loving respect which her husbands showed in allowing her to remain a virgin and to

fulfill her vows. Even though one of them greatly desired to consummate the marriage, he never tried using force and eventually returned to accepting her wish to remain a virgin. They must have been moved by her strength of conviction and love of God. Ely is a place to recall all those women who have fought against what society expected, even demanded; a place to recall the struggle for equality between women and men, and to recall those men who have supported them when they challenged the status quo and who have played their part in making change possible. This is a place to remember women who are still oppressed by religion, class, gender, politics, sexual slavery or anything else which demeans them. Pray here at St Etheldreda's for their lives, hopes and dreams.

Ely to Soham (6 miles/10 km): *Go SE on A142, then follow local signs to Soham*

SOHAM · CAMBRIDGESHIRE

ST FELIX

Just outside Ely, at Soham, is another holy place. Here St Felix, a Burgundian monk and first bishop of the East Angles, founded an immense abbey c.630. This was a place of great pilgrimage during Saxon times, and the remains of the cathedral and abbey of those days can still be seen. Here one can sense something of the remoteness of these early Christian sites, necessary partly for defense. Like Ely, the cathedral was destroyed by the Danes in 870 but, unlike Ely, it was never rebuilt.

Soham to Mildenhall (10 miles/15 km): *From Soham return to A142, then travel S to B1102 to Mildenhall*

MILDENHALL · SUFFOLK

We now come into territory rich in Roman associations. Mildenhall is worth visiting for its church roof, carved with biblical scenes, weird and wonderful creatures and angels. Near here in 1946 the vast fourth-century hoard of Roman silver now known as the Mildenhall Treasure was found. The objects are decorated with scenes from Greek and Roman mythology as well as Christian symbols.

HOLYWELL ROW

Just north of Mildenhall is Holywell Row, a small village once renowned for the healing powers of the holy well still visible in its churchyard.

> **Mildenhall to Bury St Edmunds (12 miles/19 km):** *Take A1101*

BURY ST EDMUNDS · SUFFOLK

Along with St Albans in Hertfordshire, Bury St Edmunds is perhaps one of the clearest place-names in England indicating a holy site. Wales is full of such place-names, but there are few in England. This is where St Edmund was buried, and pilgrims came here for centuries to revere one of the most popular martyred kings of Saxon Britain. Bury is an ancient city and was a center of Roman worship of some scale. But it is for two post-Roman events that it is famous, reflected in its motto: "Shrine of a King; Cradle of the Law."

BURY ST EDMUNDS ABBEY AND ST EDMUND

Edmund, born in 841, was king of East Anglia and a devout Christian. In 866 the Danes began to

make incursions into East Anglia, burning and looting as they went. Virtually all the great monasteries and abbeys, as well as the small parish churches of the time, were destroyed during this invasion. Many, such as Soham (see p. 106) and Icklingham, never recovered. Elsewhere it took centuries before enough people had returned to the area to produce the wealth to rebuild.

In 870 Edmund rallied his forces and tried to fight back. After a particularly ferocious battle he was captured. He refused either to swear allegiance to the Danes or to give up his faith, so they tied him to a tree and shot him with arrows. When he was almost dead, they cut off his head and, legend says, cast it into a nearby forest. They then departed, leaving his body impaled on the tree.

When Edmund's followers were able to approach, they reverently took down his body. Some of them ventured into the forest where they found the King's head resting between the paws of a wolf, which surrendered it willingly. When the head was put back on the body, it seemed to fuse with no visible sign of having been severed. Edmund's body was buried nearby in a simple little church at Hoxne. The tree where he was martyred remained alive until 1848 and its site in the fields nearby is now marked with a monument.

In 903 his body was removed from Hoxne and brought to the settlement of Beodricesworth, which changed its name to Bury St Edmunds to commemorate the event. In 925 the building of the magnificent abbey was begun, and the shrine of St Edmund attracted many pilgrims. Until Edward the Confessor took over in the late eleventh to early twelfth century, St Edmund was the patron saint of England. In an act of contrition, it was the converted Dane Canute who laid the foundations for an enlarged monastery in 1020.

Throughout the Middle Ages many kings and queens came to venerate the shrine of St Edmund, one of the most splendid in Britain. The abbey itself was second only to Glastonbury (see p. 199) in size and wealth. Many legends and stories built up around the saint, and some even influenced history. When the sons of Henry II rebelled against him in 1173, the King gathered his troops in Bury and took the sacred standard of St Edmund into battle with him. His victory was ascribed to its holy influence.

MAGNA CARTA

But Bury St Edmunds has a second claim to fame. It was at St Edmund's shrine that the barons who drew up the Magna Carta in 1215 swore to

CLASSICAL AND CHRISTIAN
ICONOGRAPHY

Roman Christians in Britain seem to have had no great difficulty in combining Christian and other religious images. The most famous Christian remains from Roman Britain, the great mosaic from Hinton St Mary in Dorset (pictured at right), illustrates this very clearly. Dating from the first half of the fourth century, it shows a beardless, plump-faced, youthful Christ with the Chi-Rho symbol behind his head at the center of the mosaic. In a smaller panel, designed for an anteroom, there is a picture of Bellerophon riding his horse Pegasus and spearing the three-headed monster Chimaera.

Roundel from the Hinton St Mary Roman mosaic in Dorset, showing Christ with the Chi-Rio symbol

ensure its adoption, hence the motto "Cradle of the Law." Here too came King John to swear upon the saint's bones that he would abide by the terms of this document, a list of sound principles of government hitherto lacking in his reign; he agreed to abolish the Norman laws and restore those of Edward the Confessor. The shrine had obviously come to stand for the glories, sacrifices and noble kingship of the vanquished Saxons. Like so many others, the shrine was destroyed in the 1530s to early 1540s and the great abbey was demolished. Little remains, but the beauty of the ruins still offers opportunity to reflect upon the saintly king who lies somewhere within these grounds. Today his shrine can be found in the cathedral, a parish church until the creation of the diocese of St Edmundsbury in 1914, in Churchgate St.

Bury St Edmunds to Thetford (12 miles/19 km): *Take A134 going N and follow signs to town center*

THETFORD · NORFOLK

Now only a small country town, Thetford was a center of political power during Anglo-Saxon times. Even in the Middle Ages it had twenty churches, eight major monasteries, twenty-four principal streets, five marketplaces, six hospitals, and numerous chapels and other religious foundations. For a brief spell Thetford was the cathedral city of East Anglia when the seat of the diocese was moved here from East Dereham (see p. 115) in the late eleventh century. Today only three churches remain and the town sits inside its old boundaries, much shrunken.

Apart from the various monastery ruins, also worth a visit is Thetford Forest Park, a wonderful survival of an ancient forest traversed by time-worn footpaths. The town is still dominated by the earthworks of the Iron Age fort, reused by both the Romans and the Normans. In this now small area it is possible to see how humanity has molded, preserved, altered and even enhanced nature for centuries.

Thetford to Attleborough (15 miles/24 km): *Take A11 going NE*

ATTLEBOROUGH · NORFOLK

This Saxon town was once the royal residence of kings of East Anglia such as Offa and St Edmund. Its main claim to fame today is that some of the Pilgrim Fathers (and presumably Mothers) came from here and sailed to America on the *Mayflower* in 1620. Norfolk was a strong Puritan area, and their resistance to persecution and willingness to risk life and limb on a long and dangerous voyage in order to create a new and better life according to their firmly held religious convictions make a powerful story even today.

Attleborough to Norwich (16 miles/26 km): *Continue on A11 through Wymondham*

WYMONDHAM · NORFOLK

CHANGES IN THE COUNTRYSIDE

The serene countryside of Norfolk is not some gentle act of grace. It has been humanly wrought – sometimes at great cost to ordinary people. Today areas of land which for many years have been accessible to everyone are increasingly being shut off as reservoirs and forests are privatized. The enclosures are happening all over again.

Wymondham is where Kett's rebellion started in 1549 – a mass objection to the enclosure of common lands by the new rich. This peasant uprising was a response to extreme times. The great monasteries had gone ten years before, and with them hospitals, schools, places of refuge, beds for the homeless and travelers, protectors of the weak, the whole world view of saints, shrines, pilgrimage and festivals which made ordinary life just a little more bearable. Although the poor had little, even that was taken away from them.

Over the last fifty years or so East Anglia has witnessed the most terrible environmental onslaught since Roman times. To make larger fields for crops, hedgerows have been removed to such an extent that some parts are threatened by desertification – especially in the light of rising temperatures and longer droughts. The eighteenth-century poet William Cowper (see p. 115) saw the divine in nature: his poem "The Poplar Fields" stands as a reminder of the beauty we lose when trees or hedges are destroyed.

> The poplars are fell'd, farewell to the shade
> And the whispering sound of the cool colonnade,
> The winds play no longer, and sing in the leaves,
> Nor Ouse on his bosom their image receives.
>
> Twelve years have elaps'd since I last took a view
> Of my favourite field and the bank where they grew
> And now in the grass behold they are laid
> And the tree is my seat that once lent me a shade.
>
> The blackbird has fled to another retreat
> Where the hazels afford him a screen from the heat,
> And the scene where his melody charm'd me before,
> Resounds with his sweet-flowing ditty no more.

My fugitive years are all hasting away,
And I must ere long lie as lowly as they,
With a turf on my breast, and a stone at my head,
Ere another such grove shall arise in its stead.

'Tis a thing to engage me, if any thing can,
To muse on the perishing pleasures of man;
Though his life be a dream, his enjoyments, I see,
Have a being less durable even than he.

The tree under which Kett launched his revolt still stands.

NORWICH · NORFOLK

The diocese moved the site of its cathedral to Norwich from Thetford in 1094 in what seems to have been a deliberate attempt to regenerate a badly damaged city. Sacked by the Danes in 1004, it was also severely damaged by the subsequent resistance it put up to William the Conqueror. Norwich goes back to Iron Age times, and nearby was a major Roman city. The first castle recorded here dates from 575 according to tradition, and the magnificent if daunting later Norman castle which, along with the cathedral, dominates the city is one of the finest examples of castle architecture in England. During the Middle Ages Norwich was second only to London in importance – Bristol and Norwich were the two greatest cities of England after the capital. There are still thirty-two medieval churches left, almost all of which are worth a visit.

ST JULIAN'S CHURCH AND MOTHER JULIAN
St Julian Alley, off Rouen Rd

Of the city's wealth of holy places, we wish to emphasize just two as having significance for Sacred Britain. The first is not the cathedral nor any of the great parish churches such as St Peter Mancroft, but the church of St Julian. In the late fourteenth century one of the most wonderful and perceptive of English mystics came to live here, taking her name from the church beside which she lived in a tiny cell.

Mother Julian of Norwich lived until some time after 1415. On May 8, 1373 she had a series of fifteen revelations or visions which lasted for five hours. The next day she had a sixteenth. These she later wrote down in her book *The Revelations of Divine Love*, which to this day is still one of the most popular of mystical texts.

MYSTICISM

The term mysticism is used to cover a considerable array of different things. It is often put up against dogmatism or scholasticism – against attempts to define God or to regulate religion. To someone such as Julian of Norwich, it meant going beyond the formal language of her faith and encountering the mystery at the heart of religion. Mysticism has frequently been a reaction to over-zealous attempts to contain God by technical terminology or to regulate religious experience to the mundane rituals. Mysticism, of which the Church has often been suspicious, takes you beyond formal language and into experience of the transcendent which passes well beyond the normal boundaries of the Church. The language of mystics is usually poetic, using images and metaphors to attempt to describe that which is beyond words – the mystery of God.

Mother Julian lived a life of considerable severity, during which she was famous for her wisdom. In recent years, with the growth of interest in Christian mysticism and especially women's spirituality, her writings have become even more popular. The core of her book concerns the issue of existence itself and the reality of evil, which she sees as essentially a failure of the human will to abide by God's loving will. Her most famous line sums up the Christian hope which shines through her work and stands as an antidote to more pessimistic visions of the world and its future: "All shall be well. All manner of things shall be well. All shall be well."

THE OLD JEWISH QUARTER
King St and adjacent streets

On the way to the cathedral you will probably go along King St, passing through an area which was inhabited by Jews until their expulsion in 1290. The Old Music House is a medieval mansion built for a wealthy Jew. Remains of Jewish cemeteries can also be found.

NORWICH CATHEDRAL AND ST ETHELBERT
Palace St

Norwich was an immensely wealthy city, as demonstrated by its superb cathedral built with money provided just by local donors and not through pilgrimage income, for no great saint lies buried here. The city also supported many monasteries – indeed, it was effectively ringed by them. But

St Ethelbert's memorial gate,
one of the entrances to
Norwich Cathedral

the cathedral is what draws the eye in Norwich, and one way in is through the gate of St Ethelbert. King of East Anglia, he died c.793 as a result of dynastic infighting in Mercia, where he had gone to marry the daughter of King Offa. His body was buried at Hereford, where a cathedral was built over his shrine and he was declared a saint and martyr because he had fought against non-Christian kings. The gate here is the only memorial to him in East Anglia.

The precincts and church of the cathedral offer one of the finest medieval sacred landscapes in England. The cathedral, placed to the east of the city center (the direction of Jerusalem), occupies a prime site, which with the Great Hospital, founded in 1249 as St Giles' Hospital and containing the lovely church of St Helen, puts this part of Norwich on a par with Wells in Somerset as an example of a sacred landscape. In the cathedral itself, note especially the roof bosses which act as a cartoon strip of Old and New Testament events.

ELIZABETH FRY AND THE QUAKER MEETING HOUSE
Upper Goat Lane

In somewhat stark contrast, visit the Quaker meeting house where Elizabeth Fry (1780–1845) worshiped. Born into the wealthy banking family of Gurney (Quakers, renowned for their honesty, became very popular bankers), she married a fellow Quaker, Joseph Fry, in 1800. In 1813 she visited Newgate prison in London where she found three hundred women, some condemned, others as yet untried, along with their children, living in terrible filth and squalor. From that day on she dedicated herself to prison reform, founding hostels for the homeless and many charitable foundations. The humanitarianism of her life bears vivid witness to her Quaker Christianity.

Norwich to East Dereham (16 miles/26 km): *Take A1074 W to A47 and continue W to B1135 (signposted East Dereham)*

EAST DEREHAM · NORFOLK

ST NICHOLAS'S CHURCH AND ST WITHBURGA

Our next stop is more humble, but speaks of a different kind of holiness. East Dereham is the site of a nunnery founded by St Withburga, youngest daughter of King Anna and sister of St Etheldreda of Ely (see p. 104) and St Sexburga. In 743 this remarkable woman died and was buried in the grounds of her abbey. The abbey church of St Nicholas now stands on the site of the Saxon church. Here Withburga lay quietly, visited by pilgrims and honored by the nuns of her order, for many years. But in 974 she was stolen: Brithnoth, abbot of Ely, wishing to have a full set of holy sisters, seized Withburga's body and took it to Ely. However, Withburga left her mark. A holy well, still flowing in the churchyard, is supposed to have arisen from her original grave, and its healing powers are valued to this day.

This is a place to recall those strong Anglo-Saxon women. There was a force in them which seems to have drained away by the time of the Normans. Never again did England produce so many remarkable women saints, renowned equally for their independence and their compassion.

WILLIAM COWPER

At East Dereham lived one of England's best-loved religious poets, William Cowper (1731–1800), whose poetry arose from deep uncertainty and pain. Cowper's combination of piety, mental instability and humanitarianism created some of the finest poetry in the hymn books. At Norwich we met Mother Julian, full of the certainty of God's love for all. In Cowper we see a man struggling with the doctrine of predestination, in which God's justice and demands for the punishment of "wicked humanity" outweigh His love. Cowper, a gentle, kind man, believed he was damned, yet through his inner turmoil he wrote so movingly that he transcended the misery of this oppressive doctrine. Best known of his hymns is "God Moves in a Mysterious Way," which describes a God manifest in all creation and contains the telling line: "Behind a frowning providence, He hides a smiling face."

East Dereham to North Elmham (5 miles/8 km): *Take B1110 going N*

NORTH ELMHAM · NORFOLK

The oldest diocesan seat in East Anglia, North Elmham was founded *c.*673. There were ten bishops here until the martyrdom of Humbert in the terrible Danish invasion of 870. The ruins of the vast Saxon cathedral are still visible, and powerful even in this dilapidated state. Oddly, the cathedral was converted into a fortified manor house by a later medieval bishop of Norwich – an unusual secular use of a great religious site.

North Elmham to Walsingham (14 miles/23 km): *Continue N on B1110, then turn L on A1067 to Fakenham, and from there take B1105*

WALSINGHAM · NORFOLK

THE SHRINE OF OUR LADY

The shrine of Our Lady at Walsingham – or Little Walsingham, to give it its proper title – must be the most special shrine in England today. Here in 1061 the lady of the manor, Lady Richeld, had a vision of the Virgin and was commanded to build a replica of the house in Nazareth where the Angel Gabriel appeared to her to announce that she would bear Christ. This the good lady did, in simple wood and mud, and in it placed a wooden statue of the Virgin. Her son, away on the First Crusade, visited the original house in Nazareth. When he returned home he magnificently endowed the shrine in order to build an English Nazareth and founded an order of Augustinian monks. The only shrine to rival it was Canterbury.

The route to Walsingham used to be marked by pilgrim shrines or way stations; the last of these was the Slipper Chapel at Houghton St Giles, a mile or so to the south, where pilgrims removed their shoes in order to walk the remainder of the way barefoot. The Slipper Chapel is today back in Roman Catholic hands, the original shrine and its cult having been destroyed at the Reformation. This chapel, opened again for worship in 1934 as part of the revival of the shrine, is fourteenth-century.

The actual site of the shrine is in dispute. Some authorities claim it stood to the north of the north aisle of the now ruined church of the priory of the shrine. Here pilgrims came throughout the Middle Ages to see the only place where Mary appeared in England. In 1897 the pilgrimage and site were revived as part of the creation of Anglican monastic movements and as an expression of the Anglo-Catholic movement in the Church of England. As at the Slipper Chapel, Roman Catholic interest was also renewed and today Walsingham is the most important pilgrim destination in England. The Greek and Russian Orthodox Churches also have shrine churches here. The former have converted the old stationmaster's house, while the Russians have a shrine by the river.

The ruins at Walsingham, Norfolk

The modern shrine, placed where some believe the shrine to have been, is not a place to inspire through its architecture. But the experience of Walsingham, as in all sacred places, is only partially dependent on the building. While some people find the High Church piety and plastic holy souvenirs somewhat hard to take, many do discover an experience of Heaven touching Earth and a place of solace. The holy wells are supposed to have arisen as a direct result of the Lady Richeld's vision and are still considered to this day to possess great holiness and healing qualities.

We end the pilgrimage here, for where could one go after Walsingham? It is fascinating that this site has revived so strongly and that where Anglican and Roman Catholic traditions have often clashed in the past there are now genuine attempts to create an ecumenical understanding of the sacred.

CHAPTER 8

ℒincoln to Crowland

And there, beyond the river, it continues
Like a vein above the sheep-grazed grass
Where a little grove of trees has grown among its stones
As it snakes towards the rising hill under its ridge

𝒲HEN WILLIAM the Conqueror had gained control of most of England, the Lincolnshire fens resisted him steadfastly. Hereward the Wake, a brilliant guerrilla warrior, harried the Normans for years. That Lincolnshire should be such a center of Anglo-Saxon resistance is hardly surprising. Here lies the most popular male Anglo-Saxon saint, St Guthlac, now almost unknown. It took the compassion, honesty and strength of St Hugh of Lincoln to show that not all Normans were bad: his defense of the Jews in his diocese and of the poor and oppressed earned him the affection of large numbers of people. Finally, England's only indigenous monastic movement, the Gilbertines, arose in this strange, flat landscape.

From St Hugh at Lincoln to St Guthlac at Crowland

Main Route (63 miles/101 km):
LINCOLN · STOW · NAVENBY · SLEAFORD · THREEKINGHAM · SEMPRINGHAM · BOURNE · MARKET DEEPING AND DEEPING · ST JAMES · PEAKIRK · CROWLAND

LINCOLN

As you come toward Lincoln, it is easy to see why it became one of the great pilgrim destinations. The hill rises suddenly from the flat plains like some ancient beast keeping guard over the land. Rising from it is its humanly constructed complement – the great church of Lincoln: cathedral, shrine and architectural wonder.

Lincoln's origin was a Celtic hill fort settlement called Lindon – the hill fort by a pool – which from c. AD 90 developed under the Romans into a *colonia*. A *colonia* was a place where retired soldiers were given land to settle on – a colony, in fact. The name Lincoln comes from the gradual conflation of Lindum (the Roman way of spelling Lindon) Colonia. Lincoln was a very fine Roman town, as recent excavations demonstrate. Indeed it is still possible to walk down streets and alongside walls running from the hilltop of Lincoln which were built by the Romans. The Newport Arch, for example, is the only Roman gateway in Britain still in use today.

It is almost certain that Christian communities existed in the city under Roman rule – if not before the legalizing of Christianity under Constantine the Great in the early fourth century, then certainly after that time. Somewhere within the city walls there must have been a church, but no trace of it has yet appeared. The first definite evidence of Christian life in the city came in AD 627. The *Anglo-Saxon Chronicle* records that the missionary bishop from Rome, St Paulinus, evangelized in Lincoln and while here consecrated Honorius as fourth Archbishop of Canterbury. It is said that he built a stone church within the city walls, but again no trace has to date been uncovered.

It was not until 1072 that Lincoln emerged as a major Christian center. The bishopric which was to make the city so famous by building its mighty cathedral had been on the move for many years, traveling from place to place including Stow (see p. 124). Eventually, because of the troubles experienced in East Anglia following the Norman Conquest of 1066, Remigius, Bishop of

Dorchester-on-Thames, was told to move his cathedral to a fortified town. Lincoln, still ringed by its Roman walls, was the only such place in the diocese.

Remigius started to build the first cathedral in 1072 and it was complete as early as 1092. Destroyed by fire in 1141, it was rebuilt by the splendidly named third bishop, Alexander the Magnificent. But in 1185 an earthquake destroyed much of Alexander's work and it fell, quite literally, to the sixth bishop to rebuild. But what this man, known to posterity as St Hugh of Lincoln, did was to bring to the diocese a love and integrity which still shine forth today.

ST HUGH

Born c.1135 at Avalon in Burgundy, Hugh took his vows as a Carthusian monk and in 1175 became procurator of the headquarters of the movement at Grand Chartreuse in France. Although he was a scholarly, gentle man he stood no nonsense from anyone – as was to become clear very soon.

In 1178 Henry II, as an act of contrition for the murder of Thomas à Becket eight years earlier (see p. 99), founded the first Carthusian monastery in Britain at Witham in Somerset. The remains of this building, usually known as Charterhouses, can still be seen in the hamlet of Witham Friary between Bruton and Frome (see p. 195). Hugh was appointed prior, and quickly began to display his organizing skills and ability to deal with the highest and lowest with equal impartiality. At the outset he refused to take up his appointment until the King had fully compensated the villagers and built them suitable new accommodation to replace that which had been taken to create space for the new buildings. Not until every last penny had been paid out did he even enter the monastery.

THE JEWS IN ENGLAND

Jews would certainly have come to England with the Romans. By the twelfth century all major cities and towns had Jewish quarters, and places such as York still have an area known as Jewry. London has Drury Lane, a corruption of Jewry Lane. The history of the Jews in England is one of slowly but inexorably increasing violence against them until their expulsion at the end of the thirteenth century. It was only under Oliver Cromwell in 1653 that the ban on Jews living in England was lifted. Recently a Jewish congregation has begun to worship again in Lincoln for the first time since 1290.

In 1186 Hugh was offered the bishopric of Lincoln, a see which had been vacant for sixteen years and was in need of not just a rebuilt cathedral but a rebuilt morale. He erected the magnificent building we see today and refounded the famous schools of Lincoln, which had fallen into decline.

Hugh is also remembered for two great acts of courage. Firstly, he defended the ordinary people against the brutal enforcement of the royal hunting and forestry laws which had been imposed upon many parts of England after the Conquest. They totally disrupted old farming patterns and brought poverty and starvation to the peasants. Hugh stood up against these laws and their enforcement by the royal foresters. In doing so he risked incurring the grave displeasure of both Henry II and later his son Richard I. But Hugh handled the situation with humor, self-deprecation and a will of iron.

It is his second act which perhaps today needs to be particularly recalled, not least because of a shrine in the cathedral to another St Hugh – of whom more in a moment. In 1187 Jerusalem, taken in 1099 during the First Crusade, was recaptured by the Muslims. In England all foreigners who were not Christian became suspect, but especially the Jews. Two years later Henry II, who had protected the Jews, died and Richard I came to the throne. Riots and attacks on Jews and their property soon became widespread. The worst one was at York, where the bulk of the Jewish population took refuge in the castle known as Clifford's Tower. Besieged for three days, the community committed mass suicide rather than face rape, mutilation and death at the hands of the mob.

Just such a tragedy could have taken place in Lincoln, then a major center of Judaism as is evident from the superb twelfth-century Jewish houses and synagogue. But when the expected violence broke out Bishop Hugh confronted the rioters and offered sanctuary to the Jews. He then traveled to

*A detail from the door
to the South Choir
aisle, Lincoln
Cathedral*

Northampton, where a similar ugly situation was brewing: again he faced down the mob and saved Jewish lives.

While these two brave stands against injustice mark the pinnacles of his life, Hugh's everyday work took him to all parts of his diocese – the largest of its time in England. He loved to be with children and animals, and, after St Cuthbert, is the nearest that England has produced to St Francis of Assisi. When Hugh died in 1200 he was buried in the Angel Choir of his great cathedral. By 1220 the Pope had declared him a saint, and within a few years the pilgrimage route to Lincoln and the devotion accorded to St Hugh were second only to the cult of St Thomas at Canterbury. The great north rose window in Lincoln Cathedral, known as the Dean's Eye, depicts Hugh's funeral in medieval stained glass.

Today his tomb is still there, a massive monument despite having been stripped of its beauty during the Reformation. Now it is a place of peace and prayer. Stop here and remember one who in his life sought to protect the weak, the poor and those caught up in the horrors of racism; one who was at home with kings but would not let their temporal power override basic human morality, and one who loved the company of children and animals. He is a saint whose influence we should seek and recall for these troubled times.

LITTLE ST HUGH

The second shrine to a saint – though not one who was ever officially recognized by the Pope – lies in the south aisle of the cathedral. It is the base of a tomb to Little St Hugh, whose story is tragic in every sense of the word. At the age of nine, in 1255, he was murdered by persons unknown and thrown down a well. When the body was found the child was buried in the cathedral, close to the tomb of the saintly Bishop Grosseteste who had died just two years earlier.

It is clear from this action that such a murder, then as today, evoked distress and horror. By burying him beside a great bishop, the townspeople were seeking his mercy and guidance for the child's soul. But some found it impossible to accept that any "ordinary" person could have committed such an act. Very rapidly, a libel grew up that Hugh had been murdered by Jews as part of some satanic ritual. In the lynch mob trials that followed, over twenty Jews were tortured and then hanged after "confessing" to having crucified the little boy. It is a tragic irony that, in the city where St Hugh defended the Jews and where Robert Grossteste taught humanity and understanding, such terrible events should have taken place. It is perhaps another reminder, similar to the rise of the Nazis in Germany, that even in the most civilized of places evil can emerge and produce true monsters.

Standing today at the site of Little St Hugh's tomb we should reflect upon the abuse and distress suffered by so many children at the hands of adults. Our age has also seen the logical outcome of racism in the terrible genocide of the Jews by the Nazis. Saints often bring to the surface issues hidden deep within our society and ourselves which need to be brought out and confronted. Visiting the two shrines of Lincoln Cathedral is to journey into both the beauty and the ugliness of humanity.

Many people find it hard to reconcile the ugliness of life with belief in a benevolent God. The Yiddish poet Jacob Glatstein attempted to hold God to account in his poem "The Dead Do Not Praise God," which begins:

> *We received the Torah at Sinai,*
> *and in Lublin we gave it back.*
> *The dead do not praise God,*
> *the Torah was given to life.*

We do well here to recall that Britain has always been sacred to people of different beliefs, traditions and customs. What defines "sacred" is not for us to dictate. We should always tread gently, for we are always walking on ground that is special to someone.

THE OLD JEWISH QUARTER
Steep Hill

Down the hill from the cathedral stands what is probably the oldest syn-agogue in Britain (but see also Guildford on p. 84). Next door to the famous Aaron's House, a twelfth-century Jewish merchant's house and reputedly the oldest inhabited house

The Old Jewish Quarter, Steep Hill, Lincoln

in England, is a smaller but contemporary building which is thought to have been the synagogue of that period. Later a larger synagogue was built, but it was probably destroyed when the Jews were expelled from England in 1290. This smaller building had probably by then become a house or shop and therefore survived. At 15 The Strait is another Jewish merchant's house from around the same time (see previous page).

Lincoln to Stow (10 miles/16 km): *Leave Lincoln on A57 and at Saxilby turn R on to B1241 to Stow*

STOW · LINCOLNSHIRE

Before following the pilgrims' route south-east to Crowland turn briefly north-west to the small village of Stow, where the church of St Mary bears the title of Dowager Minister of Lincoln. For it was here that the earliest diocese of the area was centered and the first cathedral built, on the site of the Roman town of Sidnacester.

ST ETHELDREDA'S TREE

In 660 King Egfrith of Northumberland made a dynastic marriage with Queen Etheldreda (see Ely, p. 103). Etheldreda had decided to be a nun, but when her father ignored her wishes and made her a pawn in a political alliance she swore to remain a virgin. This caused considerable argument in the royal household; the chronicler Bede records that poor King Egfrith tried to get great churchmen of the time to persuade Etheldreda to consummate their marriage, but to no avail.

On one occasion the couple quarreled and Etheldreda fled. Stopping at Stow, she drove her staff into the ground. Immediately the staff took root, flowered and became an ash tree. To commemorate this miracle her long-suffering husband had a church built upon the site, which became the cathedral church. It was destroyed by the Danes in 870 and was left as a ruin until 1040 when Leofric, Earl of Mercia, rebuilt it with the assistance of his famous wife, Lady Godiva. The building that remains today is still in essence that church, though altered and added to and now finely preserved.

What is this story about? As related earlier (see p. 64), the ash was revered by the Celts. So is this a story of the conversion of a tree? In the seventh century the inhabitants of the area around Stow and Lincoln still followed a mix of Celtic and Roman traditions; the missionary journeys of

Ship To

Bowness
Calhoun
Central Circulation
Country Hills
Crowfoot
Fish Creek
Forest Lawn
Glenmore
Interlibrary Loans
Memorial Park
Nose Hill
R:

Paulinus and others were made to a region where Christianity had died out or was barely present. In such a setting, an old Roman town with a sacred ash might well have attracted the attention of a woman like Etheldreda. It seems likely that the miraculous ash had been growing there long before her visit, but that for some reason she became associated with it and hence the church was built. This story of ash and church, staff and tree, miracle and cathedral represents a fascinating interface between different aspects of the sacred landscape.

Stow to Navenby (20 miles/32 km): *Return to Lincoln via B1241 and A57, then take A15 (signposted Sleaford) and turn off on to A607 to Navenby*

NAVENBY · LINCOLNSHIRE

The church of St Peter boasts an unusual selection of carvings and a fine Easter sepulcher. Here, on the evening of Good Friday, Christ was buried in symbolic form, only for the tomb to be found empty on Easter Day. Few of these fine stone Easter sepulchers survive. They remind the modern traveler of the dramatic reenactment of the Passion which was such a feature of medieval religious life in Britain. Each parish church, no matter how humble, could become the tomb of Jesus, part of the church of the Holy Sepulcher in Jerusalem. Through such symbols the Holy Land came to life here, and Navenby became another Jerusalem, a holy place.

Navenby to Sleaford (15 miles/24 km): *Continue S on A607 to Leadenham, then turn E on to A17 and follow signs for Sleaford*

SLEAFORD · LINCOLNSHIRE

BISHOP'S PALACE RUINS

At Sleaford, wealthy and important pilgrims would probably have stayed overnight at the superb palace of the Bishop of Lincoln just off the main street. Now virtually nothing remains, but it was once one of the great episcopal palaces of England.

Sleaford to Threekingham (10 miles/16 km): *Go S on A15, then E on A52*

THREEKINGHAM · LINCOLNSHIRE

ST WERBURGA

From Sleaford the pilgrims might have gone south via Threekingham to the site of St Werburga's seventh-century nunnery and the place where she died. Her body was taken from here to be buried at her other nunnery at Hanbury in Staffordshire. From there in later years she was taken for safe-keeping during the Danish raids to Chester, where her cult became one of the greatest in Britain (see p. 215). The name Threekingham is supposed to derive from the death of three kings in battle against the Danes here in 870. Their tombs can be seen in the church.

SEMPRINGHAM · LINCOLNSHIRE

10 miles N of Bourne, off B1177

ST GILBERT

At Sempringham there are the faint remains of the only native English religious order. St Gilbert, its energetic, charismatic founder, had a troubled old age. When he was eighty he was arrested on the charge of

THE GILBERTINE ORDER

St Gilbert was born c.1085 and lived to be over a hundred, dying in 1189; he was made a saint in 1202. In 1131, as vicar of the little church at Sempringham, he organized a group of women in his parish into a religious community under the Benedictine rule, then the most common monastic rule in Europe. The order grew and an organization of lay brothers and sisters was founded here as well. In 1148 Gilbert established an order of monks to be priests for the nuns, following the Augustinian rule. Soon the Gilbertine order was building houses in many places, distinctive for the fact that the nunneries and monasteries stood side by side – a tradition of the Celtic churches but not favored by Rome! The Gilbertines ran leper hospitals and orphanages and were highly regarded.

helping St Thomas à Becket oppose King Henry II. Then in his nineties various charges were brought against him by lay brothers who revolted against his rule. The case was tried in Rome and St Gilbert won.

Today at Sempringham only St Gilbert's church remains: the former monastery, nunnery and village have all gone. Only an outline of a moat can be seen north of the church. But centuries ago pilgrims worshiped at the tomb of St Gilbert and were welcomed by the members of his order.

It is sad to reflect upon the problems which plagued Gilbert as an old man. Charismatic figures are not easy to live with – yet it is their very charisma that is responsible for their achievements. Religious leadership is capable of abuse as well as glory. Who knows what tensions were felt here so long ago? What matters is that for some four hundred years the Gilbertines offered hospitality and healing to those who needed them. Our age is full of people claiming to speak for God. Stop here a while and reflect on the dangers and joys of strong religious figures.

Threekingham to Bourne (11 miles/18 km): *Return to A15 via A52 and continue S*

BOURNE · LINCOLNSHIRE

ROBERT MANNYNG

At Bourne an Augustinian monastery, founded in 1138, awaited the pilgrims. Its remains can be seen in the church. Here c.1260 was born the monk Robert Mannyng, also known as Robert de Brunne (the old spelling of Bourne), who became famous for his development of English as a literary language.

Bourne to Peakirk (10 miles/16 km): *Go S on A15 via Market Deeping, then at Glinton turn L on B1443 to Peakirk*

MARKET DEEPING AND DEEPING ST JAMES · LINCOLNSHIRE

At Market Deeping the pilgrims could have stayed in the priory, the remains of which, probably the refectory or dormitory, can be seen in the

Old Rectory. But many would probably have pushed on to the Benedictine monastery at Deeping St James, just south-east; the great abbey church is now the parish church.

PEAKIRK · CAMBRIDGESHIRE

ST PEGA

Peakirk is the site of the simple hermitage, then in a remote and barren part of the country, built by St Pega, the sister of St Guthlac (see below). Here in 714 she settled in a cell, and after dying in Rome in 719 her relics were venerated. The hermitage, east of the church, was founded in Saxon times as a monastery and twice destroyed by the Danes. The present ruined building dates from c.1280, though a fragment of Anglo-Saxon carving, perhaps from the original monastery, survives. The church of St Pega – hence the village name Peakirk, meaning Pega's church – is the only one dedicated to this saint. The church is a Norman gem with contemporary wall paintings.

Peakirk is now famous for the Waterfowl Gardens founded by Sir Peter Scott and making use of the old Roman canal. It is fitting that wildlife should be protected here, for both Pega and her brother Guthlac at nearby Crowland are famous for their love of animals and birds. Indeed, it seems that both places became sanctuaries. A story is told of Guthlac that he would not harm even the crows and magpies who stole his food; he said people ought to set an example of patience even to wild creatures. At Peakirk we come very close to the simplicity and wonder of the Anglo-Saxon saints. Here it is possible to reflect upon a life of withdrawal and contemplation, surrounded by the world of nature of which you see yourself as a part – not apart.

Peakirk to Crowland (7 miles/11 km): *Continue E along B1443, then take A1073 N to Crowland*

CROWLAND · LINCOLNSHIRE

ST GUTHLAC

When Guthlac came to Crowland it was a desolate spot – the very reason that he chose it. He was born c.673 into the Mercian tribe of Guthlacingas and became a soldier – legend says a very debauched one – at the age of fifteen. But after nine years of fighting his blood lust waned and his soul longed for peace. He entered the great monastery at Repton in Derbyshire but, finding this existence too easy, then took what the Celtic and Anglo-Saxon Churches called green martyrdom and sought a life of solitude.

THE THREE MARTYRDOMS

There were three forms of martyrdom in the old Church of Britain. Red martyrdom involved being put to death for being a Christian. White martyrdom was to leave all you knew and loved and to set out to preach the gospel in unknown parts of the world where it had not been heard before. Green martyrdom meant going alone to a place of great wildness and barrenness, there to lead a solitary life of prayer, fasting and meditation.

The monastic tradition in Christianity springs from Egypt in the first few centuries after the death of Christ. Here, disgust with the worldly ways of the Church in the great cities led men such as St Anthony to seek God in solitude and austerity. He went off into the desert, and soon hundreds of men and women followed his example. Eventually communities emerged there which formed the beginnings of monasticism.

Celtic and Anglo-Saxon Christianity were deeply affected by the examples set by these fervent ascetics. Egyptian and Coptic monks were regular visitors to Ireland and Wales and brought with them the traditions of the Desert Fathers and Mothers, as they were known. Many monks seeking to find wild places called their sites "deserts" in memory of Egypt: to this day there are places in Wales and elsewhere which include some variation of the word in their names.

It was in the fenland desolation of Crowland that Guthlac found his green martyrdom, in a place famous even then for its wildlife and wildfowl. Welsh legend says that perhaps a century and a half earlier St David had come here and founded a church – but of that nothing is known. Guthlac's quest is perhaps well caught in this Wish of Manchan of Liath, a tenth-century hermit:

I wish, ancient and eternal King, to live in a hidden hut in the wilderness. A narrow blue stream beside it, and a clear pool for washing away my sins by the grace of the Holy Spirit. A beautiful wood all round, where birds of every kind of voice grow up and find shelter. Facing southward to catch the sun, with fertile soil around it suitable for every plant.

Life here was hard. The local peasants often attacked Guthlac, stealing his few possessions. But he was also subject to what he believed were attacks by the devil, which he found far more difficult to contend with. He gathered around him here a small band of followers, Cissa, Bettelin, Egbert and Tatwin, and it was they and his sister who buried him here by his simple cell when he died in 714. Soon people from far and wide were visiting this, one of the earliest pilgrim sites in England. Wiglaf, King of Mercia came, as did Ceolnoth, Archbishop of Canterbury, who was cured of ague after his visit. Guthlac's influence spread. An entire hundred (an old county division) of Leicestershire was named Guthlaxton, and there are at least nine ancient churches named after him.

On August 24, 716 Guthlac's great friend Aethelbald, King of Mercia, laid the foundation stone of Crowland Abbey, a Benedictine monastery dedicated to St Mary, St Bartholomew and St Guthlac. Here his feast day of April 11 is still celebrated. The monastery was destroyed by the Danes in 870, rebuilt by King Edred in 948, destroyed by fire in 1091, rebuilt in 1112, burned again c.1150 and rebuilt in even grander style. It was pulled down at the Reformation, and the remaining ruins were almost totally destroyed when they were used as a garrison during the Civil War in the seventeenth century. The great west front gives a hint of what this place must have been like, while the church preserves the north aisle of the original nave – which again gives some idea of the scale of this place. Stand and look at the tympanum above the west front doorway, with its carving of the life of Guthlac. Here is a man of God reaching out to us over thirteen centuries – a green martyr whose message of living simply and in peace with all God's creation has great relevance for us today.

ST WALTHEOF

Another saint buried here is St Waltheof or Waldef, who died in 1076. His story is very different from that of Guthlac. Waltheof was a Saxon count, son of Siward, Earl of Northumberland and himself Count of Huntingdon and Northampton. He fought beside King Harold at the battle of Hastings in 1066, and again at York when it was besieged by the Normans, but was pardoned by William the Conqueror, restored to his lands and even married William's niece Judith. Obviously William felt it important to gain him as an ally. But in 1075 Waltheof was one of a number of Saxon earls who rebelled against the Normans. When it became clear that the rebellion would fail, Waltheof confessed everything to the Archbishop of Canterbury, Lanfranc, who suggested that he throw himself on William's mercy. But William was not disposed to show mercy. Waltheof was imprisoned for a year and then beheaded, after which his body was brought to Crowland and buried in the chapter house.

Crowland was clearly already a center of Anglo-Saxon opposition to the Normans and soon an extraordinary cult grew up around Waltheof, who was popularly declared a saint. To the Normans, he was a traitor; to the Anglo-Saxons, a martyr. In 1092 his body was moved into the church and was found to be in a perfect state of preservation – a traditional sign of a saint. Soon miraculous cures took place and, even more popular, a Norman monk who cursed him dropped dead!

There is no other saint quite like Waltheof in England. His story and cult are a reminder of the resistance to the Normans, whose invasion of England caused tremendous suffering and thousands of deaths among the ordinary people, quite apart from the men killed in battle. William's policies displaced thousands of people from their homes and destroyed towns and villages alike. At this distance in time it is easy to forget how unpopular the Normans were. Hereward the Wake, a more famous resistance fighter against the Normans, is also buried here. At Crowland we are reminded of the desire for freedom and the right to rule themselves which so many people have fought for all around the world – often against the British as an occupying colonial power. Here is a reminder that we too were once occupied and our native culture prohibited and crushed.

Stand here a while and think of all the freedom fighters, so often labeled terrorists or traitors, who in later life, having secured their people's freedom, were hailed as heroes. Guthlac despised violence and left the world of war, whereas Waltheof used war as a means of resistance: two very different men – two very contemporary men.

·························· ✍ ··························

CHAPTER 9

Lichfield to Mam Tor

And as you walk on its soft springy turf now
You can be a part of all that your heart feels,
And know that its threading blood-line is real

Human, as you are, from your sky into your feet.

FROM THE violence of emperors to the strange brooding silence of the Mother Mountain, Mam Tor, this pilgrimage route more than any other intertwines pre-Christian and Christian sites. It takes the pilgrim from the apocalyptic vision of the Quaker George Fox, via the sad stillness of St Bertram, to the unknown ones of the stone circles, traversing a sacred landscape of great antiquity.

From St Chad at Lichfield to Mam Tor, the Mother Mountain in Derbyshire

Main Route (71 miles/114 km):
LICHFIELD · BURTON UPON TRENT · REPTON · ILAM · BUXTON · MAM TOR

LICHFIELD · STAFFORDSHIRE

The three mighty spires of Lichfield, known as the Three Ladies of the Vale, make the cathedral of St Chad highly visible to all who travel past the city. But long before this cathedral or its two predecessors stood here Christians gave their lives for their faith, if an ancient tradition is to be believed. The name "Lichfield" is said to mean "The Field of the Dead." During the last and worst period of persecution under the Roman Empire, up to a thousand Christians may have perished here. In 303 the Emperor Diocletian launched a savage campaign against Christianity, which by this time was probably, in terms of numbers, the main religion of the Empire. Persecutions of staggering brutality and scale are recorded from Syria, Africa, Germany and France. The site of the original Lichfield lay just outside the Roman fort and settlement of Letocetum. The Romans rarely killed people within the city boundaries and never buried them within the walls. So if a massacre of local Christians did take place, it is possible that this was where they died.

HOLY WELLS

Lichfield is also rich in holy wells. Just outside the city, in the village of Stowe, is St Chad's Well, a Roman well which appears to have been taken over as a Christian well at an early stage. It is even possible that there was a Celtic monastery here before the arrival of St Chad – it might explain why he chose this area as his diocesan center. Another ancient holy well can be seen at St Mary's church, while under the chapel of St Peter in the cathedral there is evidence of yet another.

ST CHAD

Lichfield therefore seems to have had powerful religious significance long before St Chad arrived here c.670. Chad is one of those interesting transitional figures in English Christianity. Born in Northumberland some time in the very early seventh century and known then by his Celtic name of Ceadda, he studied Celtic Christianity under the great St Aidan at Lindisfarne (see p. 270). He then followed his brother, St Cedd, as abbot of the increasingly influential monastery, founded by Cedd, at Lastingham in Yorkshire.

The Council of Whitby in 664 set about destroying the Celtic Church from which Chad had emerged, and at first he seems to have got caught up in the ensuing struggles. In particular he was made Archbishop of York, c.668, in opposition to the appointment of that great protagonist of Roman Christianity, St Wilfrid (see p. 143). But St Theodore, the Greek Archbishop of Canterbury, removed Chad in order to restore a degree of harmony; he was deeply impressed when Chad took this demotion in good spirit and went quietly for the sake of the Church.

Theodore now made Chad Bishop of Mercia, then still a relatively undeveloped mission field. Chad founded his cathedral at Lichfield but died only three years later; however, he had laid the foundations for the development of the Church in Mercia. He was buried in his church and it became a center for pilgrimage, though never on the grand scale. Today the remains of his shrine are to be seen in the Lady Chapel. Pilgrimage has resumed in recent decades, and Chad's memory is once again treasured.

GEORGE FOX

But not everyone cherished Lichfield. It was once the scene of a most startling vision and denunciation, fit for the cities of Sodom or Gomorrah. George Fox (1624–90) was a most remarkable man, a shoemaker's apprentice who at the age of nineteen had a call from God which set him off on a journey which ended only with his death. Bible in hand he wandered the country, preaching, protesting and organizing what was to become the Society of Friends – better known by their nickname derived from their enthusiastic shudders when caught up in prayer or prophecy: the Quakers. England was in turmoil when Fox took to the roads. Civil war was upon the land; strange and dramatic sects were appearing; visions and Messianic pretensions were almost a daily occurrence. And through all this strode the man in leather breeches who took on all comers and yet who, despite his rudeness, drew people to him.

His link with Lichfield is a dramatic one. One day in 1650 as he approached the city he experienced a terrible vision, seeing a channel of blood running through the streets. He entered the city shouting, "Woe unto the bloody city of Lichfield!" Still shouting, he saw the marketplace as a pool of blood. The locals looked on in curiosity while some friends helped him away. This outburst seems to have been one of the turning points in Fox's life: he stopped ranting and became a great teacher. From destruction he turned to construction, creating the Society of Friends. Sydney Carter expresses Fox's beliefs beautifully in his hymn "George Fox":

*There's a light that is shining in the heart
    of a man,
It's the light that was shining when the
    world began,
There's a light that is shining in the Turk
    and the Jew,
And a light that is shining, friend, in me
    and in you.*

The story of George Fox and Lichfield is an important one for today. All religions combine hope and doom. There is a tension between what they see as humanity's folly and humanity's glory. Through faith, many teach ways of developing that which is best within each person for the good of the wider community. But some pervert this into doctrines of vengeance and doom for all who do not follow their particular teachings.

Religions are called to play a prophetic role. To see the world as a whole and to recognize its vulnerability and its beauty means that many religions today are in the forefront of environmental action, looking for new economic models which do not destroy or oppress and seeking new ways of living in community. This is what religions do best – fusing vision and practice. But some exploit vulnerable people and incite fears for the future. Religion stirs up the most powerful of emotions. It can produce great saints and teachers, or it can produce great monsters. The story of Lichfield and Fox is a lesson in religious skepticism and in looking for the balance within religion, not just the extremes.

Lichfield to Burton upon Trent (12 miles/19 km): *Take A38*

BURTON UPON TRENT · STAFFORDSHIRE

ST MODWENA

Burton upon Trent is a sacred place for many beer drinkers, and indeed this aspect of the town has a religious connection! There was already a substantial settlement here when the exiled Irish saint Modwena arrived. She is supposed to have been granted refuge by King Ethelwulf as a reward for a miraculous cure performed on his son Alfred, later to become the Great, which places her at around 830. A shrine grew up around her church in an area still known as St Modwena's Garden, but she never became a major cult. Nearby a monastery was founded in 1004 by the Benedictines, who were the first to exploit the excellent local spring water for brewing. After the destruction of the monastery in the 1530s brewing was taken over by a number of small companies, and now the town is dominated by Bass Charrington. It is sad how God is sometimes seen as a repressive, strictly ascetic being. The story of Burton upon Trent's beer, and these fine lines from an Irish prayer, paint a very different picture: "I should like to have a great ale-feast for the King of Kings; I should like the Heavenly Host to be drinking it for all eternity."

> **Burton upon Trent to Repton (8 miles/13 km):** *Continue N on A38, then turn E on to A5132 (signposted Willington) and follow local signs*

REPTON · DERBYSHIRE

Outside Burton and slightly off the direct route lies the very important site of Repton. It was the capital of the kingdom of Mercia and there was a nunnery here before 660 – one of the earliest in England. Lying under the ruins of the later monastery are kings of Mercia in what amounts to a royal funeral church. The nunnery and much of Repton were destroyed by the Danes in 874, and it was not until 1172 that a monastic order returned to the site. However, the medieval church contains a magnificent Saxon crypt, if not from the nunnery itself then perhaps from a royal church in the town.

The Saxon crypt at St Wystan's Church, Repton, Derbyshire

Repton to Ilam (22 miles/35 km): *Return to Willington and go back to A38 via A5132. Travel N on A38 to Derby and take A52 (signposted Ashbourne). At Ashbourne take A515 toward Buxton, and after about 1 mile turn L. Follow local signs to Thorpe, Dovedale and Ilam*

ILAM · DERBYSHIRE

ST BERTRAM

Ilam is the site of a famous hermit's cave, well and church. It was here, in the eighth century or possibly earlier, that St Bertram or Bertelin took refuge in a cave just above the place where the water flows out near the present church. It is said that he became a hermit after his Irish-born wife and child were killed by wolves in the area. Heartbroken, he took to a life of renunciation. This is a lovely area with woods full of flowers and scenery of great beauty; it is easy to see why a hermit might come here. It would have been a remote area when he arrived, but soon a community formed, drawn by his wisdom. Some time between 900 and 1000 a rough cross was carved and placed in the churchyard: its

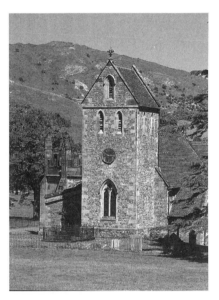

Holy Cross Church, Ilam, Derbyshire, near where St Bertram took refuge in a cave in the eighth century.

design shows the fusion of Viking art with Christianity and it is a very important artifact for this reason alone. Another cross, or the base of one, was found during renovations and also stands in the churchyard. It is believed to have been carved in 1050 to celebrate a victory by the local Saxons over the invading Danes.

This was obviously a place of great holiness and sanctity, where people came to celebrate their conversion or their victories. It is hard to imagine now the dangers that a saint such as Bertram might have faced. But this was no rural retreat, beautiful though it was. It was a hard place, the "desert" of Celtic green martyrdom (see p. 129) where souls were hard won from their violent past.

From Ilam you can explore one of the largest concentrations of stone circles, standing stones and other Neolithic sites in England. Visit Arbor Low, described here (see p. 22 for directions), and some of the sites already discussed in Chapter 2: Minning Low, a stunning collection of Bronze Age burial mounds, some of which are now open and exposed (see p. 4), Nine Stone Close (see p. 30) and the Nine Ladies (see p. 25). All these sites are in the vicinity of Youlgreave, which lies west of the A515 from Ashbourne to Buxton.

ARBOR LOW

This famous circle began as a collapsed Neolithic burial mound with a cove in the center. It was subsequently given a henge which later had a burial mound built on it, while the stone circle seems to have come last – perhaps c.1500 BC. The shape of the ditch, meant to keep the inhabitants in rather than keep intruders out, is quite clear. Traces of a ceremonial avenue of earthen ramparts can be seen curving away toward the burial mound on nearby Gib Hill. Aubrey Burl describes Arbor Low's religious significance in *A Guide to Stone Circles of Britain, Ireland and Brittany*:

> That the circle-henge was the sub-tribal focus of a well-populated countryside, usurping the roles of earlier family shrines, seems indisputable. It lies at the heart of a landscape of eight Early Neolithic chambered tombs including Five Wells, Burshfield and Harborough Rocks. In turn it became the center of dozens of Bronze Age cairns. It is one of the wonders of megalithic Britain.

Here we are in sacred landscape par excellence. This was a major cult center, a cathedral of the unknown religion of Neolithic and Bronze Age Britain. The Peak District offers limitless beautiful vistas, sites of great antiquity and churches of striking loveliness. Here Christian and pre-Christian co-exist in magnificent harmony.

BUXTON · DERBYSHIRE

The whole of the Peak District is a sacred landscape of quite extraordinary potency. One element is the well-dressing revived in recent years, which was discussed in detail in Chapter 3. The holy wells of the Peak District are a major factor in the sacredness of the area, and the most special of them is the pre-Roman one at Buxton (see p. 38).

LUD'S CHURCH

A small detour worth taking before continuing north to Mam Tor is to Lud's Church near Allgreave in Cheshire, a few miles out of Buxton on the A54 going south-west toward Congleton. This cave was the site of illegal church meetings by the earliest reformers. Here in the fifteenth century followers of John Wycliffe, who wanted to make the Bible available to the ordinary people in their own language rather than Latin which they could not understand, and who saw no need for priests, met at great risk of death. The name Lud comes from their leader, Walter de Ludbank. This place is a reminder that in the past freedom of worship and assembly was often hard won.

The cave is also reputed to be the site of the Green Chapel of the medieval poem *Sir Gawain and the Green Knight*. It is therefore the place where this noble knight of the Round Table vanquished the terrible Green Knight.

GODDESS WORSHIP

There is widespread evidence, both archaeological and mythological, of the worship of goddesses in pre-Celtic religion (see below). This ranges from goddesses associated with different aspects of nature – for example Danu and great rivers, Anu and holy wells – to the debate about a primeval worship of the goddess as creator. Some scholars argue that pre-Bronze Age cultures of the Middle East and Europe were matriarchal and worshiped the Mother. This was gradually replaced by patriarchy as the Bronze Age gave rise to a male, military caste. Others argue that pre-Bronze Age culture was neither matriarchal nor patriarchal. It was equal. Worship was addressed to a dominant god and goddess and the priests were both male and female.

MAM TOR · DERBYSHIRE

To end this pilgrimage, travel north from Buxton to visit the famous Mam Tor. It is also known as the shivering mountain because of the landslides

Mam Tor from Winnats Pass, Derbyshire

which occur there. The name Mam Tor, along with the pre-Roman well at Buxton dedicated to a female deity and the Nine Ladies at Birchover, all point to a considerable goddess cult in this area (see preceding page). At present all we have are the names. Perhaps archaeologists of the future will be able to unearth more substantial evidence to explain why this whole area had such great religious significance to pre-Roman, pre-Celtic peoples, and why a goddess or goddesses seem to be so revered here.

CHAPTER 10

Ripon to Jarrow

Start here (or anywhere you are): seeing
That to call this journey pilgrimage
Means an echoing in your heart
That changes it

Meaning who you are, too
Suddenly in your innermost unnamed self
That has always called itself you –
Being who you were always meant to be

THIS PILGRIMAGE takes us deep into Anglo-Saxon Christianity and the struggles between Celtic Christianity and Catholic, Roman Christianity. From cities now as peaceful as a lamb, but which were once scenes of terrible warfare, to an ancient monastery built in the wilderness and now lost in the debris of post-industrial Britain, this route looks into the uncomfortable face of violence and destruction and seeks the divine spark within.

From St Wilfrid at Ripon to the Venerable Bede at Jarrow

Main Route (98 miles/159 km):
RIPON · SOCKBURN · BISHOP AUCKLAND · DURHAM ·
MONKWEARMOUTH · JARROW · TYNEMOUTH · YORK AND
THE GREAT ABBEYS

RIPON · NORTH YORKSHIRE

Ripon, today a quiet, historic town, looks as if nothing much has happened

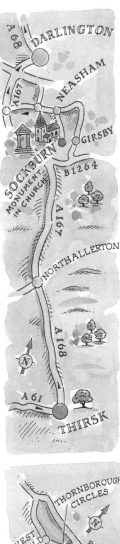

there over the centuries. But until the early 1300s it was one of the most regularly destroyed cities in England, often at the hands of Scottish raiders.

RIPON CATHEDRAL AND ST CUTHBERT

Around 650, the local king invited monks from the famous monastery at Melrose in the Borders, founded by St Aidan, to come and establish a monastery. The founder abbot was St Eata, a pupil of St Aidan. Possibly using the site of a holy well, now known as St Wilfrid's Well, the monks founded their monastery. Here the great St Cuthbert was guest master (see p. 270). In Bede's *Life of Cuthbert*, he tells how one morning Cuthbert went to the guest quarters and found a young man sitting inside. It was midwinter and snow lay thick on the ground. Cuthbert greeted the visitor kindly and took care of him. After terce – morning prayers – Cuthbert brought him food and drink and then left to go about his duties. When he returned he found that the youth had disappeared. But, although fresh snow lay all around, there were no footprints. Furthermore, the room now smelled of some sweet fragrance. Cuthbert looked around and found three fresh, fine white loaves of bread. "Now I know that it was an angel, come not to be fed, but to feed," he is reported to have said. Here, in Ripon, an angel did appear to Cuthbert.

But it was not just angels who had their eyes on this place. Bede goes on tell us how Eata, Cuthbert and their followers were ejected from Ripon. The problem arose because, like St Aidan and all the leaders of the Celtic Church, they followed a non-Roman calendar and way of life. Their monasticism and Christianity were rural and nature-based, and they followed a simple lifestyle that was community-based rather than hierarchical and included both men and women. They were therefore out

of step with the conformity that Rome was enforc-
ing across Europe as the Papacy tried to fashion the
remains of the Roman Empire into Christendom.
In particular, attention focused on the date of
Easter – each year the Celtic and Orthodox calen-
dars produced a different date from the Roman calendar. But while Easter became the cause célèbre,
the real issue was the conflict between the freedom
and community of Celtic Christianity and the hierarchical structures of Rome and its bishops.

Eata and Cuthbert refused to change their ways
and so were turned out of their monastery – some
accounts say with violence. The man who brought
Ripon into the fold of Rome, as he was to do to the
English Church as a whole, was St Wilfrid. Today
the cathedral built on the site of the monastery
where Cuthbert entertained an angel is dedicated
to St Peter and St Wilfrid.

ST WILFRID

Born in Northumberland in 634, Wilfrid was educated in the Celtic Christian tradition at
Lindisfarne (see Chapter 17) and then went abroad
to Lyons and Rome to complete his education. His
time in Rome turned him against his upbringing
and tradition, and he returned to England a fervent
supporter of Rome and its ecclesiastical policies. In
660 he persuaded the Northumbrian king who had
founded the monastery at Ripon to dispossess the
Celtic monks and let him take over. At the famous
Synod of Whitby in 664, Wilfrid argued the case for
the submission to Rome of the English and, by
implication, the whole British Church against the
Celtic case as presented by St Colman. Rome won
the day, and from that date onward, in some places
swiftly and even brutally, in other places more slowly, the old, gentler Celtic Christianity was extinguished. At least officially: for at a lay level Celtic
spirituality, with its love of nature, its communal

outlook and its vision of the Trinity as three lovers, continues to this day in some areas of Britain. Perhaps one of the most unexpected religious movements of the late twentieth century is the revival of Celtic Christianity.

Wilfrid, the main protagonist of the pro-Rome lobby, was rewarded with the archbishopric of York, displacing the Celtic supporter St Chad (see p. 133) in 669. But in 678 Wilfrid and his patron St Theodore of Canterbury fell out over ecclesiastical matters, and Wilfrid took his case to Rome for a legal decision. On the way he spent a year evangelizing in the still unconverted region of Frisia in the present-day Netherlands, where he is still revered. He won his case but it cost him dearly. On his return, his former royal supporter Egfrith had him imprisoned.

Wilfrid was eventually exiled to Sussex, and from Selsey Abbey, where he founded the diocese of Chichester, he became a great missionary among the still unconverted South Saxons. In 686 he was allowed back north, but by 691 was in trouble again and returned to Rome to plead his case. Once more he won, but had to agree to a compromise: he ceased to be Archbishop of York and became Bishop of Hexham, founding the magnificent church there – the finest north of the Alps in his time – and working from his monastery at Ripon. There, the crypt which he built – or which was built shortly after his death – can still be seen. Along with that at Hexham, Ripon's Saxon crypt is the best in England.

Wilfrid died at Ripon in 709 or 710 and was buried there; his shrine is beneath the east window of the church. The crypt, housing some of his belongings, also became a shrine to him – as it is to this day. Indeed, he is still commemorated with an annual procession to his church on the first Saturday in August, led by a man dressed as St Wilfrid riding a white horse.

What is one to make of a saint like Wilfrid? All those whom he opposed are described, even by those sympathetic to Rome, as models of gentleness, holiness, simplicity of lifestyle and compassion for the poor and weak. Saints such as Eata, Cuthbert, Colman, Chad and Theodore of Canterbury (see p. 101) were all loved for their warmth, humility and love of nature. But Wilfrid is very different. He is remembered for his opposition to such men, for his litigious nature and his force of personality. To be frank, he is not very likable. Yet when he stops being a great church politician, when he is evangelizing in Sussex or Frisia, he becomes a different person.

Here is a man who turns against his own form of faith and against his earliest teachers. He is the epitome of the zealous convert – and the zealous convert is almost always deeply intolerant. Something happened to Wilfrid which turned him against his past, and he attacked it with all his energy. He stands as an example of the almost superhuman energies that a convert brings to his or her new faith, but he also demonstrates the concomitant dangers of arrogance and intolerance. Today, this phenomenon can be seen in many sections of society. Converts to religions or specific teachers, converts to political parties, converts to forms of personal development or psychoanalysis, converts to types of diet or ethical stances – their enthusiasm is without doubt but they often lack tolerance of those less convinced or of opposing views. Ripon, site of a visit by an angel and now a shrine to the man who expelled the angel's friend, is a reminder to beware of the zealot and to celebrate those who are compassionate and open-minded.

THORNBOROUGH CIRCLES
N of Ripon on B6267

Take the A6108 from Ripon and turn off at West Tanfield for a short detour to a fascinating Neolithic ritual site. Thornborough Circles contain not just standing stones, but two other features which are usually thought to indicate special ritual use. First, underlying the circle is a cursus of long parallel banks with outside ditches. These banks are not there for defensive purposes because they do not enclose the area, but they might have been used for processions, like some of the processional ways at other Neolithic sites. They are clearly ritual in some way, though archaeologists cannot yet explain why. There are only a few such sites in Britain, and Thornborough is one of the best known.

The other ritual feature is the arrangement of three rings of ditches and banks around the site. Again, this is unusual and its meaning is unclear, other than that it marks out what is clearly a sacred space.

> **Ripon to Sockburn (11 miles/18 km):** *Take A61 NE from Ripon, then turn N on A167 through Northallerton toward Darlington. At High Entercommon take B1264 going E and follow local signs on L to Girsby, Neasham and Sockburn*

SOCKBURN . DURHAM

THE SOCKBURN WORM

This legendary venomous serpent or dragon is said to have lived in the River Tees, which virtually surrounds Sockburn. The creature's evil influence

MODERN DRAGONS, MODERN KNIGHTS

The idea of a poisoned river being a symbol of evil at work has considerable resonance today. The Tees is now a heavily polluted river – not as bad as earlier in the twentieth century, but that is due mainly to the decline of heavy industry along its banks. In modern India, the legend of Krishna battling with a giant evil serpent in the sacred River Jumna has been used as a way of helping Hindus to see that fighting pollution (the Jumna flows through Delhi and is filthy) is akin to joining the god in his battle against evil. Perhaps this ancient story at Sockburn contains a warning that should be heeded. Who are the brave knights who ride to the rescue today? Greenpeace? Friends of the Earth? The World Wide Fund for Nature? And are we able to help in some way? Old myths and legends have a way of returning to challenge us just when we think we have outgrown them.

poisoned the water and brought death to many people in the area. In the church is a monument to the brave knight who slew it, cunningly forging spikes on to his armor so that when the Worm wrapped itself around him it was ripped to pieces. The site of the battle is marked by a standing stone nearby.

Sockburn to Bishop Auckland (18 miles/29 km): *Return to Neasham, turn L to Hurworth-on-Tees and at Croft-on-Tees take A167 N. Pick up A68 out of Darlington, then turn R on to A688 at West Auckland*

BISHOP AUCKLAND · DURHAM

Once a great oak forest – perhaps a local druidic center – Bishop Auckland has been for many centuries the home of the bishops of Durham. The church of St Andrew at South Church, south of the town, has a very rare eighth-century cross relic which almost certainly once would have held a piece of the True Cross. The reason for believing this is its shape and the dedication of nearby St Helen's, Auckland. If there was a piece of the True Cross in a town, a church in the vicinity would be called St Helen's in memory of the mother of Constantine the Great, who, it is claimed, found the True Cross in Jerusalem c.320 (see also p. 49). The church also possesses a holy water stoup made from a reused Roman altar – one of the very few such reuses of an older altar within a church. Surrounded as it now is by the remains of the heavy industrial age and new industrial estates, this little medieval church is a poignant sight that speaks of a gentler past.

> **Bishop Auckland to Durham (11 miles/18 km):** *Take A688, then A167*

DURHAM

What an example of sacred space and landscape is offered by the city of Durham. The setting of the cathedral, towering above the surrounding area on its clifftop above the river, is one of the most dramatic imaginable.

THE CITY AND ST CUTHBERT'S BODY

When the monks bearing St Cuthbert's body came here in 995, something very strange happened. They had exhumed Cuthbert's body from his

beloved monastery on Lindisfarne in 875 to save it from being destroyed by the Vikings. From then until 995 the body had been on the move, though it did rest for over a hundred years at Chester-le-Street. As the monks passed through the area where Durham now stands, at that time virtually uninhabited, they rested. When the time came for the wagon to move on, it would not. No manner of force could make it shift and this, along with other miracles, was taken as a sign that the saint wished to remain here. Accepting the sign, the monks built a simple edifice known as the White Church. To this day Cuthbert's body still lies in the cathedral and his relics can be seen in the monks' dormitory.

St Cuthbert, head in hand – Durham Cathedral

The presence of the saint's body caused Durham to develop, for Cuthbert and Etheldreda (see p. 104) were the two most popular saints in England before the birth of the cult of St Thomas of Canterbury. Soon Durham was thriving – but a great shock was in the offing.

DURHAM CASTLE

The clifftop of Durham is dominated as much by its castle as by its cathedral – and this is exactly what William the Conqueror wanted. It was here at Durham that the Anglo-Saxon nobles gathered to resist him, although they fled at his approach. William at first treated the inhabitants well. But then in 1069 came an occupying force of seven hundred soldiers led by Robert, Earl of Northumberland, who meted out such brutality to Durham and its citizens that one night the city rose up and slaughtered all but one man who managed to escape. It was this act which brought William up from the south to lay waste most of the north-east. The great Norman castle was subsequently built to ensure the future obedience of the city, and to this day it competes with the cathedral on the hilltop.

DURHAM CATHEDRAL

THE SANCTUARY KNOCKER

Before you even enter the cathedral, there is a sacred sign which tells you that this is a special and holy space. On the great north door is a Norman knocker with a lion's head grasping the ring (see right). This is the famous sanctuary knocker. Anyone fleeing from the law, but who could reach and grasp hold of this knocker, was automatically entitled to forty days' sanctuary within the great cathedral. In a world in which summary justice was often practiced, this opportunity to defend yourself was essential. Between 1464 and 1524, 331 people sought and were given sanctuary; the majority of them were charged with murder.

The Sanctuary Knocker, Durham Cathedral. Anyone fleeing from the law who could reach the knocker was entitled to forty days, sanctuary in the cathedral

Stand here and call to mind all those people who today seek sanctuary from violence, warfare and famine. Nor is it just humans who need sanctuary. Bring to mind all those creatures, hunted by humanity, who long for sanctuary in which to rear their young. There is a story told of the Prophet Muhammad. One day he saw some of his followers throwing stones at baby birds in a nest and laughing at the mother bird's distress. Muhammad was angry and spoke to his followers, saying how dare they cause a mother distress – did she not have feelings like them? Remember here all mothers, of whatever species, who long for sanctuary for their young.

THE INTERIOR

Inside the cathedral, the overwhelming sensation is the sheer massiveness of the building with its vast yet astonishingly elegant Norman pillars. The shrine of St Cuthbert, or what remains of it, is in the Chapel of the Nine Altars. The cathedral is quite clear of other monuments for the simple reason that tradition forbade the burial of anyone else near to Cuthbert. Only very exceptional people were allowed to be buried there, such as Ralph, Lord Neville, the English commander of the force which defeated the Scots at the battle of Neville's Cross in 1346.

At the other end of the cathedral, in the Galilee Chapel, lies one who loved Cuthbert dearly. The Venerable Bede, monk at Jarrow (see p. 151), died in 735 having produced the first history of England together with many other histories and lives of the saints. It is, however, for his *History of the English Church and People* that Bede is most remembered. Bede's record of Cuthbert's life has helped preserve his memory to this day.

Walk along the walls at the top of the bluff, look out over the view and see why the body of St Cuthbert was happy to stay here. Or walk down by the curving river to sense the almost perfect contribution that humanity has made to what nature has created. This is indeed holy ground upon

THE CONCEPT OF SANCTUARY

To seek sanctuary meant to place yourself under the protection of the Church, and no one was allowed to violate it. Officially, the ancient right of sanctuary was abolished throughout England in 1623. Yet to this day people who feel that the law is being used unfairly against them take refuge in churches. Most recently those involved have been immigrants to Britain who are about to be deported. In Manchester one inner city church offered sanctuary for almost eighteen months to a Sri Lankan, while in the south-west Methodists gave sanctuary to a Chinese man. Even today, the authorities are reluctant to break into a church to apprehend someone. Nor is it an accident that we call places where endangered species can live and breed in safety "sanctuaries" – the notion of a place where compassion and protection are afforded even to those who may have done wrong is a very important one.

which you walk, and a recent poem by Prue FitzGerald captures something of this experience:

> We have forgotten the names
> We ignore the places
> And the face of God
> Lies unrecognised
> In the fallow fields
> Of our desecration
>
> Become the flower
> Of the rock's memory
> Be heard as the groan
> Of the high mountains of the world
> And in the curve
> Of the straight line
> Behold your God.

Durham to Monkwearmouth (15 miles/24 km): *Take A690 to Sunderland, then A1018 toward South Shields and turn on to A183 to Monkwearmouth*

MONKWEARMOUTH · SUNDERLAND

Situated on the north of the River Wear, Monkwearmouth was a monastic establishment; Bishop Wearmouth to the south, founded by the bishops of Durham and Sunderland, was "sundered" from the monastic lands back in the Middle Ages. Monkwearmouth has two ancient foundations. The earliest is its parish church of St Peter, believed to have been founded in 634 and with interesting Saxon remains. The name "monk" comes from the monastery founded c.674 by Biscopius, a Saxon noble of the court of King Oswy of Northumberland. The monastery was sacked in the Danish raids of 870, and by 1080 most of the monks had moved away from here to St Cuthbert's monastery at Durham. Monkwearmouth's claim to fame is that the Venerable Bede started his monastic life here.

Here for centuries monks and clergy praised God and wondered at the natural beauty of this place by the sea with its fine river flowing through. But when the industrial revolution began, others came and saw the natural features in a different light. The riversides and orchards became vast shipyards and the waters of the river carried not fish but the trading ships of the Empire. Today, virtually all the shipbuilding has gone. But the churches survive, and around these ancient sites and along the exhausted river banks people are trying to bring nature back into this town. The old industrial sites are being greened with considerable success, and fish are returning to the river. Here is perhaps a place to stop and reflect that things can change, that what has been destroyed or forced out can return.

Monkwearmouth to Jarrow (10 miles/16 km): *Take A1018 toward South Shields, then L on to A1300 and R on to A19*

JARROW · SOUTH TYNESIDE

JARROW MONASTERY
Jarrow Rd

The monastery of St Paul, one of the most famous Anglo-Saxon monasteries in England, was built on the site of a Roman temple. During rebuilding in the late eighteenth century, fragments of a Roman altar and inscribed tablets were found in the walls. The dedication stone inscribed in Latin and set into the surviving monastic church of St Paul tells us that the original building was erected in 681. This church contains many Saxon and Norman features, including the only Saxon window with contemporary glass in Britain (pictured on next page). The ruins of the monastery have been well excavated and the museum provides a wonderful insight into life in such a monastery and the significance of its most famous member, Bede.

THE VENERABLE BEDE

Bede, never made a saint and only officially recognized as a Doctor of the Church by the Pope in 1899, was declared Venerable – that is, worthy of honor – by a Church Council at Aachen in 836. For many centuries he was venerated not only for his learning and scholarship but also for his healing powers. He was born in 673, probably near Sunderland, and was sent at an early age to study at the new monastery at Monkwearmouth. When he was seven he moved to the new monastery at Jarrow, where he remained until his death in 735. In his own words, "[I] devoted my energies to the study of the scriptures, observing monastic discipline and singing the daily services in church; study, teaching and writing have always been my delight."

Bede wrote not only in Latin but also in early English – Anglo-Saxon. As such he is father not just to English history but also to English itself. Nor was he just a provincial monk writing in obscurity: his translations, histories and scholarship brought him fame across Europe. When Bede died, St Boniface, at work in Germany, wrote that "the candle of the church, lit by the Holy Spirit, was extinguished." He died as he had lived, seated on the floor of his cell, surrounded by his community, having just completed his translation of St John's Gospel.

Bede was buried in a special porch built on the north side of the

The Saxon window at Jarrow Monastery, South Tyneside

monastery church, but later was moved to the high altar area where his shrine became the scene of miraculous healings. Today his chair, of uncertain date, is there still and miraculous powers are ascribed to it, almost all focused around women, including love, magic, fertility and the easing of pregnancy. But his body is now in Durham (see p. 149), for in the eleventh century monks from there came and took his bones away to add to the sanctity of their cathedral.

THE JARROW CRUSADE

By the nineteenth century the new Jarrow was a center of shipbuilding and mining. The ravages of industry are still clear in the landscape, and the human cost too has been high. It was the outpouring of the pain of unemployment by the men and women of Jarrow in the mid-1930s which etched the name of the town on the collective consciousness of the nation. In 1934 Palmer's shipyard closed down with the loss of many jobs. The Depression was at its height and the prospect of alternative employment was nil. Poverty and debt stared the shipbuilders in the face. Hundreds of them set off to march the length of England, being housed and fed by trades union groups, churches, colleges and many others as they went. As they drew nearer to London the press picked up on their story, and for a brief period their plight rose to the top of the social and political agenda.

The government made polite noises, but nothing was done. Only the demands of the Second World War created further work for them. The postwar Welfare State aimed to cushion the effects of unemployment and other social problems, but sadly much of its structure has been dismantled in recent years. If Britain is to become a Sacred Land, then part of that sacredness must be to care for the poor, the weak, the vulnerable, the defenseless and the broken.

Any sacredness which fails to address the human condition is nothing more than romanticism. Care for the environment means first and foremost care for humanity within the setting of the rest of creation. Jarrow, oscillating between its scholarly, retiring monk Bede and its gaunt-faced marchers, perfectly embodies this idea.

Jarrow to Tynemouth (8 miles/13 km): *Take A19 N to River Tyne, then turn R on to A193*

TYNEMOUTH · NORTHUMBERLAND

TYNEMOUTH PRIORY
In castle grounds at junction of Tynemouth Rd and Front St

To get to Tynemouth we pass through Wallsend where Hadrian's great wall, built in the early second century to keep out the marauding Picts, ends. Some of its remains can still be seen here. A simple wooden chapel was built as early as 625 by King Edwin of Northumberland; it was rebuilt by Oswald in stone in the eighth century and then, after destruction by the Danes, rebuilt again by Tostig, Earl of Northumberland, in 1074. The monastery seems to have been founded in 651 and went through various vicissi-

A section of Hadrian's Wall, built in the second century to keep out the plundering Picts

tudes, especially after being sacked three times by the Danes. Uniquely, it lies within the walls of the castle, and the monks ruled the castle! As a result they were frequently attacked by invaders.

ST OSWYN

The church contains the site of the shrines of St Oswyn and St Henry of Coquet Island. Oswyn, rightful king of Deria in Northumberland from 644 to 651, was opposed by his ambitious cousin Oswy. When the two leaders each raised an army Oswyn realized that his own forces were inadequate to win the day and, rather than have lives lost to no avail, bravely disbanded his own men. After seeking safety with his trusted soldier-servant Tondhere he was betrayed, and the two men were brutally murdered at Gilling in Yorkshire. The crime deeply shocked England, and years later Oswy built a monastery at Gilling to expiate his sins. Not a trace of it remains today. The body of Oswyn was brought to Tynemouth monastery and buried there as befits a martyr. It might seem odd that Oswyn was declared a martyr saint. But as one twelfth-century chronicler put it, he died "if not for the faith of Christ, at least for the justice of Christ." It would be hard to find a finer epitaph for any king or powerful leader.

ST HENRY OF COQUET ISLAND

The second saint of Tynemouth does not really belong here at all. Coquet Island lies just off Amble in Northumberland. Here in the late eleventh century came a Danish Christian called Henry, seeking escape from a proposed arranged marriage and a sanctuary in which to become a hermit. Tynemouth gave permission for him to use Coquet Island and there he stayed despite requests from his family that he should return home. He was famous for his wisdom, his ability to know what troubled people before they opened their mouths, and his gift of prophecy. One famous story tells how he quite spontaneously rebuked a visiting pilgrim for having forbidden his wife sex during Lent! Henry died on the island in 1127 and his body was brought to Tynemouth, to become the second saint buried within the monastery walls.

In the built-up, run-down yet enterprising North-east, it is sometimes difficult to imagine the life of these ancient saints and the sacredness that flowed from them. Yet it would be to exactly such an area that those saints would return today. The Celtic saints often came from royal or noble families. Yet their lives were mostly spent in the service of God, the Church as a community, and the poor and defenseless. They went to areas of poverty, to places notorious for their lawlessness or bleakness. That they often made them places of great beauty and holiness is even more remarkable. It is right and proper to end this pilgrimage, which has brought us in touch with so many of the Celtic saints, at a place where today their presence is still to be felt and where they themselves would have come willingly. Every place is sacred if you have the eyes to see it, the heart to know it and the willingness to hear the sound of the angels over the din of the world around.

YORK AND THE GREAT ABBEYS

While not officially part of the described pilgrim route Ripon to Jarrow, we highly recommend a visit of York and the great ruined abbeys of North Yorkshire, surely some of the most powerful sacred sites in all of England. Our suggested route runs west-east, but of course you can plan your visit in a number of ways.

> **Ripon to Fountains Abbey:** *Fountains Abbey is a mere 5 miles/8 km SW of Ripon. Just follow the signs on B6265*

FOUNTAINS ABBEY . NORTH YORKSHIRE

There can be little doubt that Fountains Abbey is one of the most famous ruins in England, a great reminder of medieval monastic life. Today we see the ruins in their river valley and they are the epitome of the Romantic view of nature and humanity. But this was not always the case, for most of what we see today is the eighteenth and nineteenth remodeling, carried out by successive owners of first Fountains Hall, and then Studley Royal. In fact the monks first came here because it was bleak, wild, a landscape probably broken by overfarming by the Romans and then by neglect. They came to build a beautiful place but also a functional place.

The history of the abbey begins in October 1132, when 13 monks from the Benedictine Abbey of St Mary, York, came to Ripon with Richard, the prior of that abbey as their leader, in protest against lax ways that had become normal in York. They came here because life would be harder. Archbishop Thurston, whose palace was at Ripon, received them sympathetically and gave them the land in the Skell Valley on which the great abbey now stands.

After two years of poverty and privation the monks sent Richard to France, to ask St Bernard of Clairvaux to accept them into the Cistercian order. Then a miracle happened. While he was away the Dean and two Canons of York, all wealthy men, decided to throw in their lot with the Fountains community. An architect was sent by St Bernard, and the actual building of the abbey was begun in 1134. The greater part of it was complete by 1147. There were the usual setbacks, such as the incendiary fire which broke out the same year and destroyed many of the wooden buildings and damaged the abbey church, but the repairs began immediately.

Richard, the first Abbot of Fountains, died on April 30, 1139. He lies at Rome, where his body was taken by Alberic, Bishop of Ostia.

This was a mighty place. The austerity of the founders soon gave way to wealth and power and this is reflected in the buildings which survive. The cellarium, the monastery storehouse and cellar, is an astonishing Gothic building more than 300 feet long, 40 feet longer than Ripon Cathedral.

After the dissolution by King Henry VIII in 1539 the abbey and its lands passed into the hands of the Gresham Family. It was Sir Stephen Proctor who built Fountains Hall and, according to the figures on the left-hand pillar of the entrance gate, it was completed in 1611. It was built from stones from the lay brothers' infirmary, of which only the front now remains.

Fountains Abbey to York: *Follow signs to Markington and Ripley. In Ripley take B6165 E to Knaresborough, then follow the A59 into York*

YORK . NORTH YORKSHIRE

For almost 2000 years the City of York has been the great sanctuary and stronghold in the north of England. Bounded by its ancient walls and dominated by its towering Minster, it sits in the midst of the vast Plain of York. Through the center of the city flows the River Ouse. York has retained so much of its medieval structure that walking into its center is like entering a living museum.

York was first founded by the Romans in AD 71 and called Eboracum. On one side of the river was the legionary fortress, base for the legions which controlled the north of the Roman Province of Britain. As such it was one of the greatest powerhouses of the Roman Empire. On the other side of the river was the civilian settlement that served the fortress and the industry which was the Roman Army.

At one level, York is perhaps the most important sacred site in Northern Europe. For it was here in York in AD 306 that Constantine was proclaimed Caesar. He became sole emperor, having defeated all other contenders and in particular having won his major battle with the aid of a vision of the Cross. As a result, Constantine became the first Roman Emperor to be a Christian and made Christianity an official and recognized religion of the Empire. From his reign onward, Christianity entered the mainstream of social, religious and political life in Europe, and his reign inaugurated the Christian Roman (Byzantium) Empire based at Constantinople. Here in York, the Christianization of the Roman Empire began. Some see this as the greatest event after the Crucifixion — certainly Constantine did! Others see it as the end of pure Christianity and the beginning of politically compromised Christianity.

The Roman name of York is remembered down to this day, as the present Archbishop of York signs himself David Ebor+ as have all his predecessors.

YORK MINSTER

Today part of the site of the fortress is occupied by York Minster. It is the largest Gothic church north of the Alps. York Minster is 543 feet (163 m) long and 249 feet (76 m) wide and houses the largest collection of medieval stained glass in Britain. The present church is the fourth to stand on the site, built between 1220 and 1472. Interestingly, York was never a monastic foundation, for it was built as a mission center and as a cathedral to rival Canterbury.

All churches to which the name "Minster" is attached were mission centers in the early days of the evangelization of Anglo-Saxon England. The word comes from the Latin *monastrium* which could describe not only a monastery but also any church looked after by a group of clergy living together.

For many centuries the Archbishops of York disputed with those of Canterbury for supremacy in the English Church, and there were times when the king and the Archbishop of Canterbury refused to recognize the Pope's nomination to York, preferring their own nomination.

There is so much of interest to see in the Minster that it is difficult to know where to start. If you want to know more about the early history, then make your way to the crypt and the treasury. We know that the earliest church on the site was a wooden structure (a chapel) built by King Edwin of Northumbria in AD 627. The following year he started on the first Minster. This was finished by Oswald in AD 635.

Wander here where archbishops have fought to defend the faith against invaders and against the claims of the South. Where kings have met in council and where century by century the people of Yorkshire have come in their individual way to give thanks, pray for help and to celebrate the faith and the Northern and in particular the Yorkshire Archbishopric.

OTHER SITES IN YORK

A very sacred place in York is Clifford's Tower. This Norman fortification was the scene in 1182 of the worst massacre of Jews that ever took place in England. Over a hundred Jews, mostly families, took refuge there, initially protected by the Crown and Church. However, after three days of riots, both Crown and Church withdrew their help. Realizing that death faced them, they all agreed to die by their own hand — or rather, by the hand of a chosen few. When the mob broke in every Jew was dead. To this day, this awful place is visited by people praying for the souls of those who died there. It is an example of how terrible deeds can also make a sacred place. Enter here and recall all those hounded to death for being different.

York is also famous for its Quaker families, in particular the Rowntree and Terry families, immortalized in the names of sweets and chocolate. They have, in the spirit of the Quakers, been major benefactors to the city through schools, the university and many other philanthropic organizations.

York to Rievaulx Abbey: *Take B1363 N out of York and follow it until Oswaldkirk, where it joins B1257. Continue N on B1257 through Helmsley, and you will see the ruins of Rievaulx on the banks of the river*

RIEVAULX ABBEY . NORTH YORKSHIRE

On your way to Rievaulx Abbey you come through James Herriot country, the famous veterinarian author whose stories of life in this part of the world in the last half of the 20th century remind us of the timelessness as well as the change which is so typical of this part of the world. Thirsk is the real name for Darrowby which is the name he gives to the town where he had his veterinarian practice.

Founded in 1131, the abbey, which was intended as a Cistercian mission center, was soon in a position to send out colonies to Melrose and Warden in 1136, Dundrennan in 1142 and Ravesby in 1143. Its prosperity is also shown by the fact that the construction of its church, the first large Cistercian church in Britain, must have begun not long after the abbey's foundation, and that by the last quarter of the 12th century practically the whole of the monastic buildings had been completed. Under the 3rd abbot Ailred (1147-1167), afterward canonized, there are said to have been at Rievaulx 140 monks and 500 lay brothers "so that the church swarmed with them like a hive with bees." Ailred was much loved as a scholar and man of God.

Because of the river you will notice that the abbey church doesn't run east-west, but north-south. This is unique, for Christian geomancy calls for churches to face the rising sun in celebration of the Son of God who rose from the dead. It must have required very special permission for the design to be turned around.

At the dissolution in 1538 there were 22 monks and the income of the house was £351. One of the best places to get an overall view of Rievaulx is from the terrace of the same name that was built in the eighteenth century halfway up the hill behind the abbey, a beautiful stretch of lawn flanked by two classical temples.

Rievaulx Abbey to Whitby: *Drive back to Helmsley and take A170 E to Pickering. In Pickering turn N onto A169, a scenic road through the North York Moors National Park which brings you straight to Whitby*

WHITBY . NORTH YORKSHIRE

Whichever way you approach the town you can't miss the ruins of the abbey, rising like broken teeth on the hilltop above the town. The abbey was first founded in AD 657 by King Oswy of Northumbria in fulfillment of a vow before his great victory over the heathen Penda, King of Mercia, at Winwaed in 655. Oswy promised, in the event of victory, to found twelve monasteries, six in Deira, and six in Bernica, and further to devote his daughter Elfled to the religious life. At this time St Hilda was Abbess of Hartlepool (a monastery founded in 640) and Elfled was placed in her care. In 657, two years after the victory, Hilda set up the Abbey of Whitby as one of the six votive monasteries in the province of Deira, moved there herself and took Elfled with her. It was in the style of the Celtic Church, a double monastery with both nuns and monks living in separate parts of the site but ruled by one abbess, Hilda. She appears also to have had the power to appoint clergy and even bishops.

Whitby figures largely in Bede's *History*. It rapidly achieved a high reputation for both piety and for ecclesiastical training, and also became the burial place of King Oswy, his Queen Eanfled, their daughter Elfled and other members of his royal house.

But without doubt the two main events that stand out are the Synod of Whitby and the career of Caedmon.

THE SYNOD OF WHITBY AND CAEDMON

The Synod took place in 664 and was summoned by King Oswy to decide the difference between the Roman and Celtic elements of the English Church as to the time of Easter and other matters. Bishop St Colman of Lindisfarne was the spokesman for the Celtic Church. One of his party was a young man from Melrose called Cuthbert (see pages 142, 270), England's first patron saint (as such he was replaced by Edward the Confessor, who in turn was replaced by Thomas à Becket, and he in turn was replaced by St George). For the Roman party the spokesman was St Wilfrid (see pages 143-145).

Bede's description of the debate is moving for although he was of the Roman Party, his sympathy is clearly with the Celtic Party, not least because Colman comes across as much more humane than Wilfrid.

Despite the saintliness of Colman, the king decided that if the Pope was the successor of St Peter and St Peter held the Keys to Heaven, then the Pope was more likely to be useful than all the Celtic saints. Thus it was that the Celtic Church, once the most radical and astonishing Church in Europe, began its long retreat first from England, then from Scotland and finally from Wales and Ireland. Many mourn the decision to abandon what was to all intents and purposes the indigenous Christianity of Britain. In its place came the power and might, skills and intellectual rigor of Rome. Out went a gentler version of Christianity in many ways and one which found itself at ease with nature and with the world of the senses as is beautifully illustrated by the story of Caedmon.

Caedmon, the most celebrated of the vernacular poets of Northumbria, was a peasant living on the lands of the abbey in the days of the Abbess Hilda. He was very shy and kept to himself. At night he slept in the barn with the horses. Here one night he had a vision of One who called him to sing of the beginning of all created things, and inspired by his vision he began to do so. St Hilda heard of his sudden discovery of the gift of song and she persuaded Caedmon to enter the religious life. Here in the abbey "he sang the creation of the world, the origin of man and all the history of Genesis," the "story of the Exodus, the incarnation and passion of our Lord, the preaching of the apostles, the last judgment, the pains of hell and the delights of heaven." No one had ever heard anything like it, and sadly, we can only get the slightest hint of his power of song and creative composition through a tiny fragment that remains of one such song. But it is not too hard to stand on the hilltop, the wind blowing through the ruins, and to imagine that one can catch far off in the distance a note or two of his singing.

CHAPTER 11

Cartmel to Aspatria

And as you go, read the signs
What is gathering around you?
Everything is secretly written on air
To feed, sustain and awaken you:

The journey is itself, and it is your eyes
And something vaster than us is speaking
Through the intricate text of Its Being
Beat by beat and breath for breath –

WE CHOSE THIS route because of its links with early Christian saints, Anglian and Viking sites and Cistercian abbeys. The journey takes you to ruined Lakeland abbeys and small, remote churches, many of which reflect a time when Christianity was struggling to survive among the Romano-Celtic peoples, when the Anglo-Saxon invaders spread into the northern kingdoms and the Vikings invaded the area like "stinging hornets," as the *Anglo-Saxon Chronicle* so graphically put it. The route is interspersed with stone circles, barrows and Dark Age remains. There are links with Ireland – some claim St Patrick was born in Cumbria – and ties to St Cuthbert, whose diocese at Lindisfarne stretched right across to northern Cumbria. Further to the south, at Ulverston, is the first Friends' meeting house, and nearby is Furness Abbey, by the time of the dissolution of the monasteries under Henry VIII the second largest and wealthiest abbey in the kingdom.

This was one of the greatest of Celtic areas, hence the many sites associated with leading Celtic saints such as Ninian, Cuthbert and Kentigern. In the northern parts of this region the English were foreigners until the twelfth century, and here Cumbrian shepherds still count using a version of Welsh numbers.

From the monks at Cartmel to St Kentigern at Aspatria

Main Route (125 miles/200 km):
CARTMEL · THE LEVEN SANDS AND ULVERSTON · GREAT
AND LITTLE URSWICK · DALTON-IN-FURNESS · GOSFORTH ·
ST BEES · KESWICK · DEARHAM · CROSSCANONBY · ASPATRIA

CARTMEL · CUMBRIA

CARTMEL PRIORY

We start where saints have trod and where strange miracles determined why the church stands where it does today. The land on which the priory stands was given to St Cuthbert by King Egfrith of Northumberland in 686 in order to spread the Christian message, though he built no church here. Cartmel was founded in 1188 and, according to tradition, the saint appeared in a vision to the priory's architect telling him to build between two springs flowing in the opposite direction. The architect laid the foundation stones on an appropriate site, but the next morning they had been flung to a lower field where two springs were found. This is where the church stands today.

Cartmel was never as wealthy as the nearby abbey at Furness. After the dissolution very little of Cartmel was left standing. Its church was, however, spared since it was used as a local parish church, and parishes were excluded from the dissolution laws. The church is still used, while the original gatehouse of the priory stands in the center of Cartmel village.

Cartmel to Ulverston (15 miles/24 km): *Follow local signs to B5278 and head to Haverthwaite, then take A590 around estuary to Ulverston*

THE LEVEN SANDS AND ULVERSTON
CUMBRIA

It is now possible to drive or take the train around the estuary to Ulverston, but the old and more perilous way from Lancashire was across the Leven Sands. For centuries this was the route used by monks and pilgrims, and before the monks organized paid guides many lives were lost when people were cut off by the tide. Chapel Island is on the Leven Sands; it is said that the monks of Conishead Priory built a chapel here which was also used as a resting place by the monks of Furness on the way to their fisheries. The only remains were turned into a folly in the early nineteenth century by the then owners of Ulverston Priory. The tides here are still dangerous, and no crossing should be attempted without a sand pilot.

CONISHEAD PRIORY

Not far from the shore of the Leven Sands, south of Ulverston, the present nineteenth-century building stands on the remains of a twelfth-century priory and hospital which was run by Augustinian canons. The priory is now home to a Buddhist community, and visits can be arranged at weekends (see p. 289).

SWARTHMOOR HALL

In Ulverston you can encounter the earliest traces of the Quakers: the simplicity and peace that characterize the movement are reflected in the setting of sixteenth-century Swarthmoor Hall. Although the original owner, Judge Fell, was not a Quaker he and his wife gave the founder of the movement, George Fox, refuge here when he was persecuted for his teachings. After Judge Fell died, George Fox married his widow who was a convert to Quakerism. Nearby in Meeting House Lane is the first Friends' meeting house, which was established in 1691.

Beyond the end of this journey is another seventeenth-century meeting house in Carlisle, situated opposite the town jail – a familiar place to the large numbers of Quakers who were imprisoned for refusing to pay tithes or swear oaths. They were eventually granted freedom to practice their faith under the Toleration Act of 1689.

Here is a good place to sit quietly, in the spirit of the Quakers. They believe, as George Fox put it, in the light of God in everyone. Perhaps here you can look within and find that light for yourself.

SKELMORE HEADS

Just over 2 miles south are the hill fort earthworks of Skelmore Heads. Although the fort is Iron Age, the site is thought to have been used earlier by Neolithic settlers. To the south-east is the Iron Age and Bronze Age site at Birkrigg Common, where the remains of a double stone circle can be found. Known as the Druids' Temple, the outer ring is about 87 feet in diameter and contained within it is the smaller circle, approximately 27 feet across. Excavations have revealed that the two circles stand on a cobbled platform – an unusual feature. The center of the inner ring contains burial mounds. As you continue down to Great Urswick you will travel through an area farmed by Anglo-Saxon and Norse people; the present field boundaries cover an open field created c.400, possibly by the Roman Iron Age settlers of Skelmore Heads.

> **Ulverston to Great Urswick (6 miles/10 km):** *Continue on A590 about 3 miles, then turn L following local signs for Great Urswick*

GREAT AND LITTLE URSWICK · CUMBRIA

CHURCH OF ST MARY AND ST MICHAEL

Between the villages of Great and Little Urswick lies the church of St Mary and St Michael. Ian Brodie, in his book *Cistercian Way*, points out that the villages were built in the same period by Anglian farmers who chose a church site which would be convenient for both. Although the church has been rebuilt there are still fragments of a ninth-century Anglo-Saxon cross bearing the runic inscription: "This cross Tunwini erected in

memory of Thorhtred, a monument to his Lord. Pray for the soul." There is also a cross shaft which is a reminder of the Viking settlement.

Here, in an area which reveals traces of occupation for at least two thousand years, it is possible to reflect on more than ten centuries of Christian tradition. There are links left in the porch from the chain that the vicar pulled across to prevent his cow from sleeping there, particularly since parishioners traditionally slept here for two nights after a funeral to prevent the grave being robbed. There are also scratch marks in the porch where arrows were sharpened before target practice held after church services. Near the church, marked by limestone boulders, are the remains of a Neolithic or Early Bronze Age burial chamber.

Great Urswick to Dalton-in-Furness (7 miles/11 km): *Follow local signs*

DALTON-IN-FURNESS · CUMBRIA

FURNESS ABBEY

The next stop on the journey is the town of Dalton and the ruins of Furness Abbey (see below) just south of it. The monks moved here in 1127 from Preston in Lancashire, in search of a more remote and contemplative setting; the name "Furness" is said to mean "obscure." Access to the site itself was difficult, across the Leven Sands, and the land upon which they built was so marshy that huge oak trunks had to be placed in the soft ground first to provide solidity. The abbey still stands on the ancient wood foundations.

Dalton flourished when the monks began holding fairs here in the thirteenth century to trade charcoal, iron, wool and agricultural produce, all from the abbey's

The once wealthy Furness Abbey in Cumbria which was sacked during the Reformation

extensive landholdings, but fell into decline when the monks were forced to leave and the abbey stripped at the dissolution. At that time Furness was a very wealthy foundation, but it incurred the wrath of the state in 1536 when some of its monks took part in the Pilgrimage of Grace, the northern rebellion against the closure of the monasteries. The dissolution of the smaller monasteries began soon afterward, but Furness was picked out for its role in the protest and despite its size was sacked the following year. The abbey was given to the statesman Thomas Cromwell, who transferred it to the Cavendish family.

While it was in their ownership the nineteenth-century poet William Wordsworth visited several times. There is a Latin quotation found in all Cistercian houses which he translated in the third of his ecclesiastical sonnets:

> Here Man more purely lives, less oft does fall,
> More promptly rises, walks with stricter heed,
> More safely rests, dies happier, is freed
> Earlier from cleansing fires, and gains withal
> A brighter crown

In other poems he bemoaned the abbey's sad state of repair and criticized the railway builders whose intrusive presence spoiled its tranquillity. A visit to Furness gives you a chance to reflect on modern-day parallels: the search for a place that allows space for reflection and serenity, and the potential incompatibility of the interests of religion and state.

Dalton-in-Furness to Gosforth (38 miles/61 km): *Follow local signs to A595; follow it to junction with B5344 and turn R to Gosforth*

GOSFORTH · CUMBRIA

THE GOSFORTH CROSS

The Viking link continues: here in the churchyard of St Mary's is the famous Gosforth Cross, which recalls the time when the Vikings settled in Britain and the future of Christianity was in danger. In the words of an Anglo-Saxon chronicler they "robbed, tore and slaughtered, not only beasts of burden, sheep and oxen, but even priests and deacons, and companies of monks and nuns."

The Vikings slowly accepted Christianity and were tamed by it, and in the Gosforth Cross you can see how the Church gave Norse myths a Christian interpretation which could accommodate the traditions of these newcomers. The carvings on the Gosforth Cross depict both the crucifixion of Christ and the Viking hero Vidor slaying the wolf which had killed his father, Odin – a sign of the triumph of good over evil.

Gosforth to St Bees (9 miles/14 km): *Return to A595 and continue N (signposted Workington), then take B5345 to St Bees*

The Gosforth Cross, Cumbria

ST BEES · CUMBRIA

On your way to St Bees you will pass through Calder Bridge where there was once a Cistercian abbey, built in 1134 in honor of the Virgin Mary. There are few remains but it is set in a beautiful wooded vale that befits the contemplative tradition of the order.

ST BEGA AND THE CHURCH OF ST BEES

Seven miles north of Calder Bridge, the headland, village and church at St Bees are associated with the legendary St Bega. There is evidence of a church on this site at the time of the Viking raids in this area c.900, and a large church was built here for Benedictine monks in 1120.

According to an account of Bega's life written in the thirteenth century, she was the pious daughter of an Irish king who gave her a bracelet or arm-ring bearing the sign of the cross. He wanted to arrange a marriage between Bega and a Norwegian prince, but she refused. One night, after her father and suitor had drunk too much and were sleeping deeply, Bega prayed for an escape. A heavenly voice told her to travel to England, where she would find that the locks in doors would open at the touch of her bracelet. On the shore she found a ship waiting for her: she sailed across the Irish Sea in it and arrived at Copeland, now St Bees. Here she built a cell in a wooded area and lived a monastic life. After several years pirates began to raid the Cumbrian shores; Bega fled eastward but left her bracelet, having "forgotten it by the will of God."

The arm-ring tradition could have developed from the Viking pagan tradition of swearing oaths on a ring. Bega's bracelet was used for oath-taking at St Bees in the twelfth and thirteenth centuries – another sign of the Vikings having been reconciled with the Christian Church in this area. The Chronicle of St Mary's Abbey in York contains entries between 1298 and 1316 which cast a light on the popularity of the cult of St Bega at this time: "In 1310 God worked many miracles by the prayers and merits of St Bega – giving speech to the dumb, sanity to the demented, purging to the dropsical, with many seeing and hearing."

> **St Bees to Keswick (24 miles/38 km):** *Take B5345 to Whitehaven, then A595 toward Cockermouth, then A66 to Bassenthwaite Lake and Keswick*

KESWICK · CUMBRIA

To the Celts in Cumbria as elsewhere, the world was full of miracles. To them, all events spoke of divine powers at work. The mundane or the strange glowed with light from beyond this world. Here, in this wild countryside, stand a while and imagine the world filled with the glory of God, diffused with love. Enter for yourself the magical world of the Celts and the early Christians.

CHURCH OF ST BEGA

As you travel alongside the beautiful lake at Bassenthwaite, approximately 4 miles before Keswick is a turning for Bassenthwaite old church which is dedicated to St Bega. To reach the church you have to walk down a track or follow the lake-shore footpaths. The Norman church is believed to have replaced a seventh-century building, and there are suggestions that the church stands on a former place of worship for druids. In 1835, when Tennyson was a guest at nearby Mirehouse, he was writing *Morte d'Arthur*, and it is thought that this church may have been the setting for the opening lines:

> *. . . to a chapel nigh the field,*
> *A broken chancel with a broken cross,*
> *That stood on a dark straight of barren land*

CHURCH OF ST KENTIGERN

At Crosthwaite, on the outskirts of Keswick, according to legend St Kentigern set up a cross in 550; there has been a church on this site ever since. The present building dates from 1523 and is unique in England in that it still has a full set of twelve consecration crosses. They are sixteenth-century and were placed at the points at which the bishop blessed the new building. St Kentigern's at Crosthwaite is the first of three churches on this journey that are dedicated to this early Cumbrian saint, who is also known by his Celtic name of Mungo.

CASTLERIGG STONE CIRCLE

1½ miles E of town center

This famous site on the outskirts of Keswick is believed to be one of the earliest stone circles tentatively dated to c.3200 BC. This is a spectacular setting, clearly designed to impress and awe. The ring is made of meta-morphasized slate and thirty-eight stones remain from the original forty-two. Unusually its tallest stone indicates the November or Samain (Celtic New Year) sunrise. Stone axes have been found in and around the circle; it is thought that they may have been exchanged here at festivals (see also p. 25).

DERWENTWATER

THE ISLAND OF ST HERBERT

Just south of Keswick lies Derwentwater or Herbert Holm, to give it its Norse name. The island in the middle of the lake, which is now National Trust property, was the isolated home of the anchorite monk St Herbert. When St Cuthbert came on a visit Herbert left the island to receive instruction and pray with him. Cuthbert asked Herbert to speak his mind because they would never meet again in this life. Kneeling and weeping, Herbert begged him to ask the Holy Trinity for him to die at the same time as Cuthbert so that "I may not be left bereft of you after death, but that He may receive me with you into the joy of the eternal kingdom." Cuthbert told him to "rise and rejoice," for his request had been granted. Both men died on March 20, 687. Although Herbert's hermitage was located "in the islands of a western lake," according to the anonymous author of the life of St Cuthbert, not long afterward Bede named the lake, in his writings, as Derwentwater.

Keswick to Dearham (19 miles/30 km): *Return on A66 to Cockermouth, then take A594 toward Maryport. After 5 miles follow local signs to Dearham*

DEARHAM · CUMBRIA

CHURCH OF ST MUNGO

This church has a history of Christian worship going back 850 years. Its peaceful setting and that of the church at Crosscanonby (see below) offer a chance to reflect not just on the long history of Christianity here but also on the variety of human settlement that gives the area both diversity and continuity. Although this remote part of the west coast has had its share of invaders and skirmishes, it retains a calm and natural beauty. The church tower was built as a defense against the Scots, while the windows and doorways show its Norman origins. An ancient Viking cross from c.850 stands inside the church and there are also Dark Age carvings. Here, ordinary life has gone on for centuries, given special shape and meaning by the ancient church and faith at its heart. No great cathedral this. Just a place made sacred by prayer.

Dearham to Crosscanonby (2 miles/3 km): *Take local roads to A596 and follow signs for Crosby, then follow sign for Crosscanonby*

CROSSCANONBY · CUMBRIA

CHURCH OF ST JOHN

The church was founded in the eighth or ninth century and has ancient connections with the priory and cathedral at Carlisle. In the porch is a section of a carved sandstone Viking cross, while the churchyard contains a Viking hog back gravestone. It was once the parish church of nearby Maryport, and in the eighteenth century one of its parishioners brought in a Roman arch from the fort at Maryport – it still stands as the chancel arch.

Here again the radically different worlds of the Vikings and Celts meet, brought together and purged of their violence by Christianity. In the beauty of the Viking cross we can see how these fierce people came to live in peace with their neighbors. But for such a cross to exist, many Christians gave their lives – victims of the cruelty of the Vikings.

Crosscanonby to Aspatria (5 miles/8 km): *Return to Crosby and take A596 NE*

ASPATRIA · CUMBRIA

CHURCH OF ST KENTIGERN

At Aspatria stands a Saxon church of St Kentigern, one of the earliest dedications to this saint (the other tenth-century dedication is at Bromfield, some 3 miles north of here). In the churchyard stand pieces of carved Anglo-Danish crosses, reminders once again of this area's Viking past. This is one of nine churches in northern Cumbria dedicated to this early Christian missionary, who died in 612, demonstrating his popularity. Part of his mission as Bishop of Glasgow was to spread the Christian message through this area in the post-Roman period, and places were still named after him in the eleventh century.

This is the last stop. Not in some grand monastery ruin, or powerful cathedral, but in a humble, ancient church. For it is in places such as this that the timelessness of ordinary, humble faith can be found. Here prayers have been said for centuries, loved ones mourned, new birth celebrated. Here the greatness and the sadness of everyday life have slipped deep into the very fabric of the church. Magnificent cathedrals or great stone circles inspire, but to catch the true spirit of faith walk humbly to this humble place.

The journey ends at Aspatria with a memory of the early roots of Christianity. This chapter has followed a route through a rural corner of northern England which was witness to the struggles and successes of Christianity from Roman times through the Dark and Middle Ages and on to the present day. The area saw sweeping raids, times when the Vikings "spread on all sides like fearful wolves," as the *Anglo-Saxon Chronicle* says, and survived skirmishes both religious and political; but it also saw peaceful times when the Christian message thrived in remote villages and powerful monasteries.

CHAPTER 12

❧

*W*orcester to Dorchester-on-Thames

And as the journey grows
Weaving you in with your companions,
Why these people? This motley bunch,
Seemingly random, but assured . . . as boundaries soften

Bringing up all you need to see and feel, until
We are all One Body – straggling or smiling
We are messengers for each other, like a medicine
We are stories to be told and heard: a cargo of treasure.

*T*HE PILGRIM to Worcester knew that he or she was coming to a city long revered for its shrines and church. From here, following the footprints of kings and peasants down the ages, we find out of the way churches and visit the place where the Virgin Mary first appeared in England. The route takes us to a monastery so powerful that it once ruled the land, and to a little village with a lost cathedral. On the way we visit a saint who shares her shrine with a doubter. This journey takes us into many hidden and unusual corners of life.

From St Oswald and St Wulfstan at Worcester to St Birinus at Dorchester

Route (115 miles/184 km):
WORCESTER · EVESHAM · TEWKESBURY · DEERHURST ·
WINCHCOMBE · BURFORD · BINSEY · OXFORD · ABINGDON ·
DORCHESTER-ON-THAMES

WORCESTER

Our starting point is beside the Severn, an ancient sacred river revered by the Celtic tribes of the region. Worcester was a Celtic settlement long before the Romans made it one of their towns. In the early seventh century the first post-Roman Christian church was built here, and by 679 Worcester was the seat of the diocese. The city's two saints were both bishops here, and reflected the different needs of the church in relation to itself and the wider community. Both are buried in the cathedral.

ST OSWALD

Born c.925, Oswald was a Danish settler whose family moved to England and whose uncle was St Odo, Archbishop of Canterbury. In 962 Oswald was made Bishop of Worcester and, in collaboration with St Dunstan and St Ethelwold, set about reforming monasticism in England. He founded many monasteries, the most notable being at Westbury-on-Trym near Bristol, Pershore and Evesham (see next page). In 972 he was made Archbishop of York, but also, uniquely, remained Bishop of Worcester. It was in Worcester that he died in 992. His biographies tell of a gentle man, renowned for his kindness and for the love which people felt for him. Certainly his city and cathedral remember him with gladness, as the shrine to him has testified.

ST WULFSTAN

Born at Long Itchington in Warwickshire in 1009, Wulfstan spent twenty-five years as a monk at Worcester before, much against his will, being elected bishop in 1062. Once in office, however, he set about putting his diocese in order. He was not a learned man, but he was a good man. In particular he was appalled by the slave trade between Bristol and Ireland: raiders seized the inhabitants of the shores of the Bristol Channel and South Wales and sold them into slavery with the Vikings in Ireland. Wulfstan, within whose diocese the newly emerging city of Bristol lay, put all his spiritual, emotional and physical energies into stopping the trade. He succeeded, and from his time until the sixteenth century Bristol was saved from the horrors and disgrace of being a slaving city.

Here was a man who, seven hundred or more years before the anti-slavery movement, eight hundred years before the American Civil War and the freeing of the southern slaves, banned slavery within his territory as an

un-Christian activity. Here is a place to remember all those today who are still slaves in fact if not in name; those who have no freedom over their lives or movement.

Worcester to Evesham (15 miles/25 km):
Follow A44

EVESHAM · WORCESTERSHIRE

Both the development and name of this town are due to a vision of the Virgin Mary. There was a settlement here from ancient times, but its sacred history begins at the end of the seventh century. Around 695 a swineherd called Evves, who kept pigs for the Bishop of Worcester, had a vision of the Virgin and two other heavenly women beside the river. The Virgin indicated that she wished to have a church built here. By 702 an abbey was rising and the place had started to be called Evves ham ("Evves' home or village"). The great monastery was finished in 714 and dedicated, not surprisingly, to the Virgin Mary. The popularity of this, the earliest English Marian shrine – Walsingham (see p. 116) dates from 1060 – brought great prosperity.

In 1265 this serene place became the scene of a terrible battle between Simon de Montfort, who had forced an early form of Parliament upon King Henry III, and the King's son, Prince Edward. Montfort was at the time holding the King captive. The fighting between the older order and the early signs of a new order was particularly fierce and shocked the chroniclers of the time: over four thousand men died that day and were buried at the abbey.

Evesham to Tewkesbury (15 miles/24 km):
Take A435 S, then A438, crossing over M5

TEWKESBURY ·
GLOUCESTERSHIRE

The former abbey church at Tewkesbury is now one of the great treasures among English parish churches. But here again we encounter violence and the violation of the right of sanctuary. One of the most decisive battles of the Wars of the Roses, England's fifteenth-century civil war, took place at Tewkesbury in 1471. The Yorkists were triumphant and many of the leaders of the Lancastrian forces took refuge in the abbey, but were dragged outside by their enemies and brutally murdered.

Tewkesbury to Deerhurst (7 miles/11 km): *Go S on A38, then turn R on to B4213 and follow signs to Deerhurst*

DEERHURST ·
GLOUCESTERSHIRE

ST MARY'S CHURCH

This little settlement concealed beside the River Severn just below Tewkesbury contains one of the most perfect examples of Saxon church building and of Saxon Christianity in England. There are two churches in fields by the river, a place which was once the royal capital or at least the ecclesiastical capital of the long vanquished Saxon kingdom of Hwicce. St Mary's, begun *c.*790, was the church of the great monastery here which was founded *c.*715. Probably the finest Saxon church in England, it displays the interaction between Celtic and Saxon craftsmen and theologies in all its decoration, from the magnificent Saxon font to the Saxon angel.

But this now obscure part of the world also

The Saxon church of St Mary's, Deerhurst

seems to have been in touch with streams of Christian life far beyond these shores. It is well known that Irish Celtic Christianity had close links with the Coptic Church of Egypt: a number of Coptic monks are recorded as having been buried in Ireland. Cornwall too seems to have had connections with Egypt, and much Celtic Christian art is echoed in that of the Copts. What seems likely from the architecture of Deerhurst is that Ethiopian monks were visitors here, for the high window in the central wall of the church, looking out to the north, is almost unique in design. There is only one other window like it, also dating from the eighth century – and that is in the cathedral at Addis Ababa in Ethiopia. Such links might seem far-fetched, but when we consider that the British Church had Greek, Italian and African archbishops, bishops and archdeacons, they begin to seem less unlikely.

It was in this church or nearby that Canute and Edmund Ironside met in 1015 to conclude the treaty which formally divided England between the Danes and the Saxons. Away from the church, now part of a farmhouse, stands the Saxon chapel of Offa. We know its date exactly, for a dedication stone bearing the date April 12, 1056 is still here. Used as a barn for many years, the chapel has now been sensitively restored.

Time has passed this place by. Yet here kings once made and broke each other and kingdoms rose and fell. The works of humanity are indeed puny in comparison to the works of God. When the works of humanity are in such glorious harmony with the material environment and with the love of God, as one senses at Deerhurst, then humans participate in the divine.

Deerhurst to Winchcombe (21 miles/34 km): *Return to A38, go S, then take A4019 to Cheltenham and B4632 out of Cheltenham (signposted Winchcombe)*

WINCHCOMBE · GLOUCESTERSHIRE

BELAS KNAP BURIAL CHAMBER
Turn off B4632 just before Winchcombe, following local signs

This tomb of c.2000 BC is wonderfully preserved and gives a powerful sense of the corporate burial place of Neolithic people. Crouching in one of the side chambers you are back in the ancient past, while to stand in front of the tomb in the curved horns of the entrance wall is to understand something of the dances and rituals which it is believed took place before these great tombs.

Belas Knap Burial Chamber, Gloucestershire dates from c.2000 BC

A great monastery was founded in Winchcombe in 798 by King Kenulf and refounded c.960 by St Oswald of Worcester. By the fifteenth century it was reputed to be equal to a university, so great was the level of scholarship. Alas, all was swept away in the dissolution of the monasteries, as was the nunnery founded in 787 by King Offa. Winchcombe was for some time a royal city of the Mercian kings and the site of a royal palace c.780. It is from the royal family of Mercia that Winchcombe derives its own saint, who lies buried somewhere in the ruins of the abbey.

ST KENELM

Kenelm, to whom, along with the Virgin Mary, the monastery was dedicated, was the son of King Kenulf. The story of Kenelm is much confused by later legends. The core of the story is that Kenelm died before his father, possibly in battle against the Welsh, c.812 and was buried at Winchcombe. When the monastery was revived by St Oswald in the late tenth century Kenelm was revered as a martyr, and his cult became very popular throughout the south-west. A number of churches were dedicated to him.

How and why did a young prince killed in battle become a saint and martyr? One cynical answer would be to say that a saint is always good for income and restarting a monastery is an expensive task. However, a legend grew up in the eleventh century which goes some way to explaining the cult. The legend says that Kenelm became king at the tender age of seven and ruled for just a few months. He died at the treacherous hands of his own tutor at the instigation of his jealous sister, Queen Quendreda. The chapel of St Kenelm at Clent near Halesowen in Dudley is supposed to mark the site of his murder. The body was apparently hidden and only dis-covered by a miracle. While the Pope was saying mass at St Peter's in Rome, a dove dropped a message in Anglo-Saxon on the high altar. Anglo-Saxon pilgrims present were able to translate it and the hiding place was uncovered. The body was borne in ceremony to Winchcombe where the Queen, trying to cast the evil eye on the proceedings, recited a psalm backward – whereupon her own eyes dropped out!

This story seems a little incredible, not least because Queen Quendreda was a saintly woman who was abbess of Minster in Kent. Winchcombe still has a chapel to St Kenelm and his holy well, plus a pilgrims' house and a lovely fifteenth-century wool church – a proud expression of the wealth that wool from Cotswold sheep brought to this town. In 1815, near the site of the old monastery's high altar, two stone coffins containing the bones of a child and a man were found – supposedly those of Kenelm and his father. The bones have since been lost, but the coffins are still kept in Winchcombe church.

Winchcombe to Burford (24 miles/42 km): *Take B4632 N, turn R on to B4077 and at Stow-on-the-Wold turn S on to A424 to Burford. Directions for the Hailes and Temple Guiting detours are given below*

HAILES ABBEY
3 miles N of Winchcombe off B4632

Enfolded in the curve of a little valley lie the remains of one of the great pilgrimage centers of Britain, one mentioned by Chaucer. Hailes Abbey had in its possession a vial of Christ's blood, which miraculously became liquid at certain times. At the Reformation the reformers took great delight in exposing this relic as a fraud, claiming that the blood in the vial was pig's blood which was renewed daily!

Nevertheless this Cistercian monastery was immensely popular during the later Middle Ages. It was founded in 1246 in fulfillment of a vow made by Richard, Earl of Cornwall, after nearly drowning at sea in a storm. The irony of Hailes is that the Cistercian order favored an austere lifestyle and was very much opposed to relics and the kind of conspicuous wealth that they created. But when the son of their founder brought the vial home from his travels, they could hardly refuse it. Pilgrims' money funded the building of a stunning splay of seven chapels radiating out from the high altar, with the shrine holding the vial at its center. At the dissolution of the monasteries in

Hailes parish church, Gloucestershire. A medieval "hare hunting" painting can still be seen on the right-hand wall of the church

the 1530s Hailes was earmarked for obliteration as a reaction against the "superstitious" cult of the Holy Blood. Today very little remains and, while there is a good museum, the site of the shrine is unimaginatively laid out.

But beside the gate leading to the ruins is a little church (see above) which was already a hundred years old when the abbey was built. It has outlasted the abbey by nearly five hundred years so far and looks set to be here for many centuries to come. Inside is one of the most perfect pre-Victorian interiors of any church in England. The old floor and old pews are still there, and in the window niches are the most lovely thirteenth-century frescoes. In the simplicity of this little parish church one sees the essence of holiness and sacredness. It still serves the needs of local people as it has done for centuries. Gone are the grandeur and power, authority and wealth of Hailes. But here, week by week, God is worshiped, milestones in people's lives are celebrated, sadnesses are addressed and prayers offered.

What is honored here in this church is the perennial search for meaning at the most humble level.

TEMPLE GUITING

From Hailes, follow local signs via Farmcote to Temple Guiting. Afterward go N and join B4077 E to Stow-on-the-Wold, then S on A424 to Burford

Here the Knights Templar (a military religious order founded by Crusaders c.1118) had their church, but what is most striking has nothing to do with the Templars. On the outside walls of the chancel, high up where the roof meets the walls, are some remarkable early carvings. Despite the presence of a lovely carved cross, most of the heads seem to have nothing to do with Christianity. Here is one of the places, like Kilpeck in Herefordshire, where Christian and pre-Christian iconography meet. The question is whether the one had adopted and resanctified the other, or whether the old religion was expressing its enduring capabilities and to some extent cocking its finger at the newer religion. We prefer to think that, as at most places where new religions superseded old ones, the old found a place within the new. One only has to look at the major Christian festivals, one of which, Easter, is still named after the pre-Christian Celtic goddess, Eostre, whose festival fell in spring, to see this in action (see p. 70).

BURFORD · OXFORDSHIRE

This beautiful small town has seen some interesting events during its history. In 685 a synod of the Church was held here to denounce certain Celtic practices such as the date of Easter. The fighting between King Ethelbald of Mercia and King Cuthred of the West Saxons at Battle-Edge just outside Burford in 752 led to the defeat of Ethelbald and the capture of his sacred banner with its emblem of a golden dragon. This dramatic event used to be reenacted in a mock battle on the streets of Burford between a vast dragon and a giant.

THE LEVELLERS

It is the church which is of interest here – not primarily for its architecture, but for what happened here during the Civil War. In May 1649, certain sections of the Parliamentarian army, members of the radical Christian sect known as Levellers, mutinied at Burford and made the church their head-

SEVENTEENTH-CENTURY SOCIALISTS

The Levellers believed that all people should share the same social standing and that property should be held in common. They were particularly opposed to the enclosure of common land which had brought terrible poverty to the ordinary people of England. Theirs was a form of Christian Communism and their aims were the destruction of all status and power so that everyone would have enough to live on.

quarters. After three days Cromwell surrounded the church and attacked the occupying force. The mutiny soon crumbled and its three leaders were taken into the churchyard and shot. Cromwell then addressed the mutineers from the pulpit and brought them back into the army.

Throughout English history there have been periodic attempts by Christians to protest against the power and wealth of the rich and to call for radical social action for the poor. Time and time again they were crushed, but the vision of a more equitable Britain continued and found its clearest expression in the postwar Welfare State. Burford is one place where the revolt against power was crushed, though the ideas lived on. In the words of Robert Crowley, written in 1551:

> But such Scriptures you could not brook
> As bade you give ought to the poor;
> You writed them out of the book,
> But you were sure to have in store,
> Plenty of Scriptures, ever more
> To prove that you might aye be bold,
> With your own to do what you would.

Today, the abuse of power by the powerful and the demeaning of the poor continue. The Protest aspect of "Protestantism" has contributed in considerable degree to the vision of a just society. The tradition of the importance of the individual and the need for rebels is especially strong in the non-conformist churches. Their very title is a clear statement of the centrality of doing what you believe to be right – not just what society expects.

Burford to Oxford (19 miles/30 km): *Take A40 through Eynsham*

BINSEY · OXFORDSHIRE

At the tiny village of Binsey, on the Thames just north of Oxford, are a lovely church and a holy well dedicated to St Frideswide. This is the first trace of the patron saint of Oxford, who had a considerable cult in the early Middle Ages. Binsey is a good place to get a sense of the sacred geography of the Saxon period, for its layout – combining sacred well and church in a sacred landscape which draws upon pre-Christian and Christian motifs – has probably not changed much since the eighth century and Frideswide's visit. Binsey can also be reached via the Thames path from Godstow. Use an Ordnance Survey map to find this lovely place by the Thames.

OXFORD

So into Oxford, stopping first at the ruins of the formerly vast monastery of Osney in Mill Lane, off Botley Rd, beside the railway line. This Augustinian abbey, founded in 1129, was by the mid-twelfth century the wealthy owner of some 120 properties and thus had great wealth. In fact it was so wealthy that in the thirteenth century it set up a banking system for the citizens of Oxford. Today virtually all the site is buried beneath railway lines, except for a small fifteenth-century outbuilding which is now part of Osney Mill.

Oxford and its colleges, many of which began as monasteries, are a prime example of sacred geography in action and of how easily this can be despoiled by careless building on its edges. Right at the heart of the city are the college and cathedral of Christ Church, which are intimately connected with the extraordinary story of St Frideswide.

CHRIST CHURCH AND ST FRIDESWIDE

St Frideswide was an eighth-century princess from the kingdom of Wessex who had vowed to become a nun or at the least remain a virgin. However, a young prince had other ideas and courted her with the intention of marriage. To avoid his attentions she fled into the woods at Binsey – hence her well there – but he pursued her. She then fled to Oxford and, when he followed her, he was struck blind. Through her prayers she gave him back his sight, whereupon he vowed to leave her alone. Here on the banks of the Thames, or Isis as it is known locally, she founded a double monastery, for both men and women, and ruled over it as abbess. When she died she was buried to the south of her original church.

Her cult grew slowly, but in 1002 the monastery was destroyed by the Vikings. King Aethelred ordered its rebuilding, which was carried out in such a way as to bring the tomb of Frideswide into its center. This is the earliest account of her shrine being significant. In the twelfth century, rumors abounded that her bones had been stolen by the monks of Abingdon (see p. 185). Her tomb was opened, and the bones within confirmed their holiness by extinguishing the candles of the excavators.

The shrine of St Frideswide, Christ Church Cathedral, Oxford. The wimpled face of St Frideswide can be seen peeping out of foliage

A thirteenth-century manuscript includes descriptions of miracles at her shrine. All involve emissions of light, some emanating from the top of the church tower. Once a golden column rose from her grave and went up through the top of the tower. Frideswide seems to have been particularly popular with women.

By 1434 she had become the patron saint of the university, which paid formal respect twice a year at her shrine until it was destroyed in 1538. However, her monastery had already disappeared. In 1524, Cardinal Wolsey obtained papal permission to close it and move the monks to other houses so that he could found his own college at Oxford. So it was that Christ Church came into existence, with a saint's shrine at its center. In 1546 the old monastic church became the cathedral of the newly created diocese of Oxford. Under Queen Mary during the 1550s the shrine of St Frideswide was restored as part of the reintroduction of Catholic practices. But the reaction was very great and in 1558, as soon as Mary was dead, the tomb was opened and Frideswide's bones and dust taken out.

CATHERINE DAMMARTIN

At this point in the Frideswide story, something very strange happened. Her bones were mixed with those of another dead woman, Catherine Dammartin. An ex-nun, she had married a former monk called Peter Martyr Vermigli, who was a follower of the radical Swiss Protestant reformer Zwingli. Catherine's husband had become Regius Professor of Divinity at the university in 1548, which is where she died. It was the idea of James Calfhill, a Calvinist, to mingle the remains of an apostate nun and wife of a radical Protestant critic of all things Catholic with the bones of a saint. Together they were put back into the tomb below where Frideswide's shrine stood and there they lie to this day, commingled in the ground. What a curious tale! And what an interesting insight into different views of what is sacred and holy.

MARTYRS' MEMORIAL, ST GILES

Opposite Ashmolean Museum

The other key holy site in Oxford commemorates the martyrdom in the city of Ridley, Latimer and Cranmer, three of the greatest scholars and reformers of the English Church, who died at the stake in the fires of the Catholic reaction to the Reformation. A bronze cross is set into the road on Broad Street, where the execution took place.

Never a great scholar, Latimer was loved for his forthrightness and his ability to speak to the hearts of ordinary people. It is his words which ring down the centuries, for as the flames leaped up to devour Ridley and himself he turned to his fellow victim and said: "Be of good comfort, Master Ridley, and play the man. We shall this day light such a candle by God's grace in England as I trust shall never be put out." He was referring, of course, to the Protestant Reformation and the release to the ordinary people of the Bible, the prayer book and much else within the Church which had formerly been kept as the preserve of the clergy. It was also the movement which extinguished the cults of the saints.

Cranmer's death was delayed for a few months because he signed seven declarations of heresy, recanted on all scores and asked for forgiveness. But

RIDLEY, LATIMER AND CRANMER— PROTESTANT MARTYRS

In October 1555 Ridley and Latimer went to the stake for their beliefs. Ridley had been Bishop of Rochester and London and one of the leading intellectuals in the Reformation of the English Church. Latimer rose from humble origins to become Bishop of Worcester, and preached two sermons which in effect launched the Reformation of the Church in 1536. Cranmer was burned here in March 1556. As Archbishop of Canterbury he had been responsible for sending Catholics and extreme Protestants to the stake, but he also laid the liturgical foundations and episcopal structures of the Church of England, which has remained one of the great glories of Sacred England.

at the last, when brought publicly to recant at the university church in Oxford, he refused and was sentenced to death. As the flames crackled around him he thrust into the fire his right hand, the one that had signed the recantations, saying, "This hath offended! Oh this unworthy hand!"

This is a place to stand and reflect upon the cruelty that can be practiced in the name of religion. Down the ages, in every faith, there have been those who felt that their version of the truth was better than that of others. This idea can drive people to view those who stand against them as unworthy of life. That in Christianity this should be done in the name of the God of Love is, perhaps, the greatest blasphemy of all.

In recent years Catholics and Protestants have healed many wounds, yet Britain is still home to violence based at least in part on the forces which led to this monument being raised. Northern Ireland is a reminder of the dangers of sectarian violence and of the teachings of those who believe that their truth allows them to view those who oppose them as inhuman and not worthy of life. Pray here for those who have died, are dying and will die through religious intolerance all round the world.

Oxford to Abingdon (8 miles/13 km): *Follow signs for S, leaving by A4144, then take A34 (signposted to Newbury) and turn on to A4183 for Abingdon*

ABINGDON · OXFORDSHIRE

When the great abbey here was founded in 675 it gave the town its name. King Offa of Mercia visited the monastery and so liked the place that he built a palace here where he and two of his successors often stayed. The town and monastery were sacked during the terrible incursions of the Danes in 870, and the monastery was not restored until 948. From then until it was dissolved in 1538 the abbey grew to be immensely rich and was deeply hated by many of the townspeople. Riots broke out on a number of occasions, the most serious of which was in 1327. The records show that £10,000 worth of damage was done (something like £10 million in present-day values).

To pilgrims, the abbey was famous for two reasons. It had a piece of the True Cross and it was the birthplace and early home of St Edmund, Archbishop of Canterbury.

ST EDMUND

Born *c*.1170, Edmund showed great scholarly aptitude from an early age and was awarded a place to study at Oxford, from where he walked every day to Abingdon, his spiritual home. After going to Paris to study further he returned to Oxford as a teacher and monk. He was caught up in the scholasticism of the universities – the attempt to combine revelation with rational and philosophical study, thus treating the Bible as both a source of revelation and a product of history.

Edmund became known for his intellectual skills and for his generosity to the poor, often reducing himself to near poverty in so doing. In 1233 he was elected Archbishop of Canterbury but was not really comfortable as an administrator – he was by nature a scholar and writer. But in what turned out to be a very difficult seven years as archbishop he worked hard, averted war in the Welsh Marches and assisted in reforming the government. Edmund died in France on his way to Rome in 1240. So great was his fame as a saintly man that by 1246 he was canonized and thus began the cult of St Edmund, which in England focused upon Abingdon and helped increase the wealth of the abbey even further.

Abingdon to Dorchester-on-Thames (6 miles/10 km): *Take A415 E from Abingdon, then go S on A4074*

DORCHESTER-ON-THAMES · OXFORDSHIRE

This quiet little village with its enormous church was once the seat of a mighty bishopric and center of power for the kingdom of Wessex. But it has been removed from the affairs of state for a considerable time – even in 1140 a chronicler was reporting that the place was small and thinly inhabited.

ST BIRINUS

The Romans had a town here, and it struggled on into Saxon times as a place of uninterrupted habitation. It is just possible that a Roman church once stood on the site of the present building, for it was here in 634 that St Birinus founded his cathedral church and community in the still unconverted lands of the West Saxons. The following year he baptized Cynegils, King of Wessex, as a Christian, which laid the foundations for the conversion of this region.

ST BIRINUS'S PILGRIMAGE

The one day pilgrimage in memory of St Birinus starts on Churn Knob, just south of Blewbury, off the A417. The route follows footpaths all the way, skirting Blewbury to the east and going cross-country to South Moreton. From South Moreton take footpaths north to Brightwell-cum-Sotwell and then head north-west to Wittenham Clumps, the Iron Age fortified hill between Little Wittenham and Dorchester. The pilgrimage ends by crossing the Thames and walking into Dorchester.

Birinus was probably a Lombard who had been appointed by the Pope and dispatched from Rome to convert those areas still untouched by the Roman mission begun by St Augustine in 597. In 650 Birinus died and was buried in his cathedral. In the 660s war with Mercia threatened the area and his body and the see were moved to Winchester. Dorchester only returned to cathedral status in the 870s after the Danes had extinguished the cathedrals and churches of eastern England. In 1070 the last Bishop of Dorchester removed the bishopric to Lincoln (see p. 119) and Dorchester began its rapid decline into obscurity.

Then in 1224 the tomb of St Birinus was opened, a shrine was built and pilgrims began to come. This led to new funds which facilitated the building of much of the church that we see today. The south choir aisle was where Birinus finally came to rest in 1320. His shrine was destroyed and the monastery dissolved in 1536.

The church is a wonderful building, with a real feel of the medieval period because it has been so unaffected by Victorian restoration. It is also the renewed center for pilgrimage to the shrine of St Birinus. We are most grateful to the vicar of Dorchester, the Rev Canon John Y. Crowe, for sending us the following details. "The 12-mile route from Churn Knob (Blewbury), where tradition has it that St Birinus preached to the pagan King Cynegils of Wessex in 635, follows a route specially opened up for the day of our annual pilgrimage. The modern Ecumenical Pilgrimage, started twenty years ago, takes place each year at the beginning of July."

Canon Crowe also sent a copy of an article which appeared in the weekly Catholic journal *The Tablet*. It seems to sum up the essence of pilgrimage and in particular asks us to reflect on the landscape – sacred and profane – around this lovely pilgrim church where, as at the time of the saint himself, all Christians are united in prayer and pilgrimage.

Birinus brought the light of faith to great tracts of England, south and west of Dorchester, which Augustine had not reached. . . . And it was to renew that honor that so many surprisingly gathered on Churn Knob, first to picnic, then to walk the eleven miles to Dorchester abbey. They were of all ages, conditions and shapes. Tiny children aged six or seven. Scores of teenagers. Robust fathers and mothers. Elderly men and women counting a diminishing supply of years. . . . There was the Blewbury village band. There was the knoll, marked with a cross, where Birinus and Cynegils had met some 1400 years ago. . . .

I thought how every Christian should go on pilgrimage at least once a year to relearn the evergreen truths of that primary metaphor. He travels light. He has no settled roof, assured rest or nourishment, except at his destination. He meets strangers. He must stay alongside people he does not greatly care for, and say farewell to others he quickly warms to. He is asked to share with those in need, to support those weaker than himself. . . .

I thought too of power. Below Churn Knob, on the valley floor, stands Didcot power station. It carries light and energy to roughly the area Birinus carried the light and power of the Christian faith. It smacks, like all power stations, of up-to-the-minute twentieth-century modernity. It seems more important to our daily life than any old Roman missionary of centuries ago. But, in 1400 years from now, will it even be a scar on the grass? Will it be remembered with honor and affection? Will it be a place of pilgrimage? Power is relative. And there is no power quite like that of a man who once came from the "lofty and conspicuous citadel of Rome" to a strange country and a barbarous people, and so transformed them and their way of life that 1400 years later their descendants, survivors in a century of slow-searing, mind-shattering shock and discoveries, still hold his memory in veneration and gather at his shrine.

CHAPTER 13

Stonehenge to Glastonbury

What are these ruined shells? Shrine or castle
Where the sun warms or the wind blows –

What does it mean for us to remember
Injustice and power, beside true loving?

These stones speak for themselves: but we must read them
To see what our history could be again

As it hangs in the balance of our wakefulness
To stand up and be counted, to renew and mend.

FOR MANY people Sacred Britain means places like Stonehenge and Glastonbury. Pilgrims have come to Stonehenge for over five thousand years and will continue to come long after what we understand Britain to be has faded into antiquity. At Glastonbury, the legends take us back to Christ himself and to that timeless wonder, the Holy Grail. On the route in between we encounter gentle saints, powerful kings and aggressive barons, in some of the most tranquil countryside that England has to offer.

From the Stone Circle at Stonehenge to the Holy Grail at Avalon

Main Route (77 miles/123 km):
STONEHENGE · SALISBURY · WILTON · SHAFTESBURY · FROME ·
DOULTING · SHEPTON MALLET · WELLS · GLASTONBURY

STONEHENGE · WILTSHIRE

This is the best-known of all Britain's sacred sites, yet in many ways what

is known about it bears little relationship to the archaeological facts. For centuries Stonehenge has acted as a kind of symbolic magnet, drawing to it all kinds of people and their theories. Today it is the prime example of how not to treat a sacred site, and even though there are plans to reshape the visitors' area and approaches, damage has been done which far exceeds what the passing of time has inflicted upon this place.

In Chapter 2 we looked in some detail at Stonehenge, so all that is needed here is a recapitulation of the key points. This is the largest surviving stone circle in Britain and the grandest. It should be viewed in the same way that a great cathedral is viewed, for what we see now is the result of many periods of building spread over nearly two thousand years.

The earliest section of Stonehenge consisted of a large earth rampart, the henge, and a wooden structure. (Just a few miles away are the remains of Woodhenge, of similar date but never converted into stone.) The early part of Stonehenge was constructed c.3200 BC. Its orientation was toward the south, to the direction in which the midwinter full moon rose. The posts are linked to the varying directions of the moon over two cycles of 18.61 years. Essentially this was a lunar religious center, probably associated with death.

The second stage dates from c.2200 BC when two incomplete circles of Welsh bluestone were put into the places previously marked by the wooden posts. At the same time an earthen rampart or avenue was built. More importantly, the henge was reorientated to face the direction of the midsummer sunrise, marking a switch from lunar to solar culture by the newcomers who had taken over from the earlier Neolithic peoples.

Around 2000 BC, these incomplete circles were uprooted and the whole site redesigned in a monumental act of coordinated building. The result was the familiar shape of Stonehenge today, with two uprights crossed by a lintel stone. The bluestones were discarded. Quite what inspired this rebuilding is anyone's guess: it may have been raised to celebrate an individual's power, but we shall probably never know.

The final stage was completed c.1600 BC. The bluestones were placed rather haphazardly around the circle and carved with daggers, axes and other shapes, indicating that their Bronze Age craftsmen had links with Bronze Age culture in Brittany and Greece. In or around 1100 BC a start was made on building an extension of the avenue to the River Avon, but it was never completed and Stonehenge was then abandoned.

By the time the druids came, c.500 BC, Stonehenge was already a deserted, tumbledown ruin, shunned by the incoming Celts who preferred the woods and forests for their worship. Today it stands as a major testimony to the passion and energy that religion and the dead can unleash. It also stands cut off, badly served by its facilities and roared past by traffic – a sad monument to official insensitivity.

Stonehenge is a monument to the failure of religion. Whatever or whoever was worshiped here for two thousand years failed. Changes swept through the lives of the people and destroyed their faith in the old deities and rituals. Faith is only as strong as its believers. Stand here and reflect on how faith changes. No amount of nostalgia replaces living faith. Today all religions face immense changes. Where do you find yourself in the midst of such dramatic times?

Stonehenge to Salisbury (10 miles/16 km): *Take A303 E to Amesbury, then turn S on to A345*

SALISBURY · WILTSHIRE

This is the church and the city that moved. Originally Salisbury – Sarum as it was called – stood on the hill above the town now called Old Sarum. Here a cathedral was founded in 1078, inside the grounds of a castle erected at the same time. The diocese thus created took over from various Saxon dioceses and seems to be part of the Normanization of England after the Conquest – hence the cathedral being in the pocket of the castle.

By the start of the thirteenth century relations with the military authorities had deteriorated so badly that the then bishop, Jocelin, decided to move away. He chose a magnificent site on the water meadows of the Avon and there in 1220 laid out not just his splendid cathedral but the town as well. The cathedral was finished by 1265, though the tower and

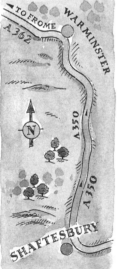

spire were added later. At the top of the spire was placed a reliquary with a fragment of the clothing of the Virgin Mary. What remains is still there.

The whole design of Salisbury – cathedral, close and city – is an act of Christian geomancy, designed to honor peace and Christian values (see Chapter 4). To this day the surroundings of the cathedral offer unparalleled examples of human building in harmony with nature. It is very much to be hoped that a proposed bypass which would cut across the water meadows south of the cathedral is never built, for in so doing the geomantic balance of the area would be disturbed and more than just a fine view lost.

ST OSMUND

Osmund, Bishop of Salisbury after the Conquest and its main architect when at Old Sarum, is honored here in two shrines. He came over with

THE PATIENCE OF A SAINT

After Osmund died in 1099 miracles were ascribed to his tomb and it became a place of pilgrimage. However, the journey to full canonization took centuries. The process began in 1228. Nothing had happened by 1387, so pressure was brought to bear on the Pope. Again nothing happened, so Salisbury tried again in 1406. There was still no result. In 1412 Robert Hallam, then Bishop of Salisbury, set up a budget for what was probably the first official PR program in England: he allocated a tenth of the income of the canons to promote Osmund's canonization. Kings Henry V and VI were involved and commissions came from Rome and studied the case. Finally, in 1456, Osmund was canonized. But it had cost the cathedral £731 13s - equivalent to several million today.

William the Conqueror, yet was surprisingly loyal and attentive to the Anglo-Saxon saints and bishops. He was involved with the Domesday Book, which was formally presented to William at Old Sarum in 1086. Liturgically he is credited with writing the Sarum Rite, a modification of the standard Roman rites to English use which was immensely popular in the Middle Ages. It was used by the Reformers in the mid-sixteenth century as the basis for what became the *Book of Common Prayer*.

Salisbury to Wilton (3 miles/5 km): *Take A36 W (signposted Warminster), then turn on to A30 (signposted Wilton)*

WILTON · WILTSHIRE

ST EDITH

Here was one of the greatest nunneries in England. This is an old Christian site, for in 800 Wulstan, Earl of Wiltshire, restored the old parish church of St Mary and founded a college for priests, beginning the links between Wilton and education. In 830 King Egbert upgraded the oratory to a priory and appointed his sister Alburga as first prioress. In 890 Alfred the Great made the priory a nunnery. King Edgar added greatly to the wealth of the place to honor his daughter Edith, who had died young here and became patron saint of the nunnery (see also p. 86). Soon stories of miraculous healings and visions associated with her tomb began to circulate. Her shrine became one of the best-known in England and she was often invoked in times of crisis. The shrine was destroyed in the 1530s and the abbey itself has gone. Wilton House occupies its site, and presumably St Edith still lies hereabouts.

Wilton to Shaftesbury (18 miles/29 km): *Return to A30 and head SW. At junction with A350 follow signs for Shaftesbury*

SHAFTESBURY · DORSET

This was a major pilgrimage center, especially in pre-Conquest times, and could be so again. Shaftesbury almost certainly owes its current existence to Alfred the Great, who founded a walled town here c.880. It seems likely, however, that some sort of settlement existed here earlier – such a naturally advantageous hilltop site asks to be inhabited. There is also some evidence that the parish church was here *c*.670. Two centuries later Alfred founded a nunnery dedicated to St Mary and whose first abbess was his own daughter, Elgiva or Aethelgeofu.

Shaftesbury is an exceptional place. The old church (there used to be ten here), the abbey and the general sense of being a little above the rest of the world make this a special landscape. It is a sacred landscape of streets and ruins, of hill and valley. One can see immediately see why Alfred built here. Standing in the ruins of the abbey, one can appreciate why the nuns came here. Today it still has a special feeling.

KING EDWARD, SAINT AND MARTYR

Being a royal foundation, the nunnery was often given lands by later kings and became immensely wealthy. It was said that if the Abbot of Glastonbury were to marry the Abbess of Shaftesbury, they would own more of England than the King! Further wealth accrued as a result of the burial of King Edward, saint and martyr, in the nunnery church *c*.980. Edward was born in 962, son of Edgar, and in 975 became King of England on the death of his father. Three years later he fell victim to his scheming half-brother Ethelred, who lured him to Corfe Castle in Dorset and had him murdered. Edward's stepmother Elfrida, who was involved in the plot, founded the nunnery at Amesbury in expiation of her sins.

Edward did not die for his religion, nor is there any tradition of him being holy. So why did he acquire the status of saint and martyr? It seems to have been the power of the story itself. Here was a harmless young person, slain for no good reason – an innocent done to death. The echoes of the story of Christ would have turned this horror story into something more profound.

Today there are similar movements within Christianity which can help us to understand why this boy's death struck a chord. One only has to think of the significance of Anne Frank, the young Jewish girl who kept a diary of her time in hiding in Amsterdam under the Nazi occupation and who eventually died in a concentration camp. Or the cult that has grown up around John F. Kennedy, struck down in his prime – apparently no saint in his private life, but a powerful figure to many nonetheless. Deaths such as these speak of forces which, unless confronted, threaten to make life meaningless and allow chaos to triumph. This is what we believe lies at the root of St Edward, king and martyr.

At the time of the dissolution in the 1530s, Shaftesbury suffered the fate of other monasteries and nunneries and was closed. The abbey church was soon in ruins and a private house rose from the remains of the nunnery buildings. But before these events someone took Edward's bones from their reliquary and hid them in a lead box which was then buried in a wall. There they lay until in 1931 they were rediscovered. By now the land was private, so the relics became the property of the family living there.

The Two Shrines

Due to family disagreements, there are now two shrines to St Edward. One is in the care of the Russian Orthodox community of St Edward's Brotherhood, St Cyprian Ave, Brookwood, Surrey, where the bones are to be found. Orthodox Christians venerate any saint who died before 1054, the date of the formal excommunication of the Eastern (Orthodox) Church by Rome, and have a special devotion to saintly kings. But at the ruins of Shaftesbury Abbey there is a new shrine in a new high altar, ready for the return of the bones. It would be good to see them back here, in the royal church, even though their shrine would be washed by rain and blown by wind. When Edward was buried here a thousand years ago, there was only one Church in England. Today, after the Reformation and the Schism between East and West in 1054, there are many denominations. This site at Shaftesbury Abbey has been prepared ecumenically. An ecumenical shrine to a martyred king could perhaps help bring the Churches together, which would be a miracle worthy of St Edward.

WITHAM FRIARY AND ST HUGH

This friary is all that remains of the great monastery founded by Henry II in 1178 and whose first abbot was St Hugh, later Bishop of Lincoln (see p. 120). The abbey had been built on land taken forcibly from the peasants, so Hugh insisted that the King compensate them all before he would take up residence. It was here that Hugh liked to retreat from his negotiations with the King and court in an attempt to establish justice for the poor. Here too he kept his pet swans, which are among his symbols today. In this quiet corner, think of his honesty, modesty and sense of justice for all.

> **Shaftesbury to Frome (21 miles/34 km):** *Take A350 N toward Warminster, then turn on to A362 (signposted Frome). Alternately, you can visit* **Stourhead** *on your way to Frome, one of the supreme examples of English landscape gardening. At the A350 A303 Crossroads take A303 W and B3092 to Stourhead. You can then continue on B3092 to Frome.*

FROME · SOMERSET

ST ALDHELM

Here in 705 a monastery was founded by Aldhelm, and later a nunnery was added. They were sacked by the Danes but the remains can still be seen. Aldhelm, the first great English scholar, was born c.640 probably near here. He studied at Malmesbury Abbey and then with St Theodore and St Adrian at Canterbury (see p. 101). He became Abbot of Malmesbury c.675 and in 705 was made Bishop of Sherborne. He was a great evangelist and founder of churches, of which Frome was one of the greatest. It is said that when he preached in the open, he would clown and juggle to attract a crowd first. He died at Doulting (see below) and was buried at Malmesbury.

Frome to Doulting (10 miles/16 km): *Leave by B3090, then take A361 W (signposted Shepton Mallet)*

DOULTING · SOMERSET

Nothing remains of the Saxon church built by the monks of Glastonbury in memory of St Aldhelm, to whom it was dedicated. However, the churchyard does contain the remains of a very fine carved standing cross. It was around such crosses that traveling monks and preachers would gather a crowd for open air preaching. Standing in Aldhelm's old parish, this is a good place to recall that one of the images of Christ, celebrated for example in the musical *Godspell*, is that of the clown – the one who goes through life laughing and joking and making people feel that the world is a bit brighter, but who at the same time can plunge into deepest tragedy and touch human pain in a way that few others can. Aldhelm seems to have been a clown of God, and we could do with a few more of those!

Doulting to Shepton Mallet (2½ miles/4 km): *Continue on A361*

SHEPTON MALLET · SOMERSET

This quiet market town has a wonderful church over which the architectural historian Nikolaus Pevsner enthuses in *The Buildings of England: North Somerset and Bristol*: "And then the roof, the most glorious of all the wagon roofs of England, solid and trustworthy, the back of a strong and nimble animal and yet extremely richly wrought. There are 350 panels and over 300 bosses, every one of them of a design not repeated in any other."

The solidity of the roof reflects the solidity of the surrounding farmland. Yet here, in 1685, many took up primitive arms and marched to join the Duke of Monmouth in his rebellion against James II. The beautiful countryside of this region has been created only at great price. Many of the peasant farmers who rose up felt their lands and traditional ways to be under threat – as indeed they were, by enclosure and by the growth in power of the great landed families. It is well to remember the human costs that lie behind all that is humanly wrought, and the great injustices which often lie behind the most charming facades.

JUDGE JEFFREYS AND THE BLOODY ASSIZES

The rebellion of 1685 against James II never stood a chance. The poorly armed West Country peasants were brutally crushed by the King's army, and then by the infamous Judge Jeffreys who masterminded the so-called Bloody Assizes. In Shepton Mallet alone, thirteen people were hanged. Altogether some two hundred were put to death and eight hundred sentenced to be transported to the colonies, while a huge number were punished by imprisonment or whipping. The uprising cast a long shadow over much of the south-west from Lyme Regis in Dorset, where the Duke of Monmouth landed, to Somerset, where his army was broken at the battle of Sedgemoor.

Shepton Mallet to Wells (10¹/₂ miles/17 km): *Continue on A361, then take A371*

WELLS · SOMERSET

WELLS CATHEDRAL

We have to confess that this is our favorite cathedral in the world. As children we would walk here from our housing estate on the edge of

Bristol, as if drawn by a magnet of history, beauty, power and magnificence. Here is an almost unchanged sacred landscape of cathedral, monastery buildings, bishop's palace, city and countryside, woven together into perfection. If you want to see what the medieval mind and hand could produce in partnership with the beauties of nature, go to Wells.

As the name indicates, the place owes its existence to holy wells which still bubble up behind the cathedral. But what exactly is the relationship between the wells and the church? In his book *The Living Stream* James Rattue says:

> Here the minster seems to have been set up over a Roman mausoleum, with several springs distributed around the site, though there does not appear to have been a great deal of settlement hereabouts. It is quite obvious that the wells were the focal point of the minster settlement; the first recorded place-name is Fontanelium in 725, and in 766 we hear of "the minster which is situated next to the great spring which is called Wiela."

The first church was built here in 705 by King Ina of the West Saxons. In 909 it was raised to the status of a cathedral and handsomely endowed. From the site of the church a settlement began to spread out; from an early date there was a parish church of St Cuthbert – itself a Celtic dedication – at the far end of the town, almost balancing the cathedral at the other end.

BISHOP JOCELIN

During his long incumbency (1206–42) Bishop Jocelin Troteman de Wells built the cathedral as we now see it. But he did more than this: he was a classic Christian builder and endowed the city with many other edifices, as did so many medieval bishops. They were creating communities and entire Christian societies, which is why you find around almost all the old cathedrals and mighty parish churches in Britain, schools, hospitals, almshouses, shelter for travelers and workplaces for the unemployed.

At Wells Jocelin built a grammar school, a choir school, a hospital and houses for his clergy; most of this work is still standing. He also established regular almsgiving for the poor and elderly. A rather touching comment has been made about his long life and great vision: "God, to square his great undertakings, gave him a long life to his large heart."

Wells to Glastonbury (7 miles/11 km): *Take A39*

GLASTONBURY · SOMERSET

The final port of call on this pilgrimage is Glastonbury, surely the best-known if most misunderstood of all English sacred sites. Here is a center not just of revived pilgrimage, nor just of ancient Christian myths which claim that Christ came here as a child, nor is it even just a place where the Holy Grail and King Arthur are supposed to lie. For many people Glastonbury has become a place where anything could have happened or could still happen – a place so charged with spiritual and mystical forces as to be a religious powerhouse. Again, as with Wells, this is a sacred land-scape largely constructed by human hands. Here natural features such as the Tor, the hill behind the ruins of the great abbey, bear traces of an ancient maze pathway and, if some authorities are to be believed, the twelve signs of the zodiac are etched into the very fabric of the country-side.

Glastonbury is the original Avalon – it was by this name that the area was known because of its abundance of apples. In ancient Welsh it was also called Ynyswytryn, which means grassy island, and in Saxon this became Glastney. Like so much of lowland Somerset, Glastonbury was to all intents and purposes an island until England tilted in the ninth century and Somerset rose a few inches above sea level. Even then, the Levels were marshy and often flooded, and only eighteenth- and nineteenth-century drainage created the scenery that we see now.

THE RIDERS' WAY

Joan Collins, a sailor and rider from Wells, has uncovered what may well be the route taken by pilgrims from Wales and Ireland to Glastonbury. Looking at tidal currents, she found that Barnstaple in North Devon, a major port until the eighteenth century, is where the tides would bring ships from those parts. From here she followed middle contour lines, neither going to the top of hills and ridges where the wind cuts across, nor descending into the valleys which in centuries past were the haunts of wolves and robbers. Riding at a comfortable pace of around 20 miles a day, she found that each logical stop was marked by a stand-ing cross and a holy well. Her route took her to Branton, North Molton, Barlynch, Cothelstone, Wembdon, Chilton Polden and Shapwick before, having received special permission, she rode into Glastonbury Abbey as pilgrims did for over a thousand years.

JOSEPH OF ARIMATHEA

Legend says that when Christ was a child his uncle, a wealthy trader called Joseph of Arimathea, brought him here. While Joseph was bartering for goods, Christ built a simple wattle church and prayed. A more commonly recorded legend says that, after the Crucifixion and Resurrection, Joseph came here to bring the gospel to the Britons. Having traveled great distances, he and his weary band of followers rested on a small hillock outside the town, which to this day is known as Weary All Hill. He then stuck his staff into the ground, where it blossomed and grew.

Joseph then built a wattle church – the first church in Britain – on the site now occupied by the abbey ruins, and founded the first Christian community in Britain. He is also supposed to have brought with him the Holy Grail, the cup used by Christ at the Last Supper and in which Joseph caught some of Christ's blood shed on Calvary. This later became the central focus of the legends of King Arthur's knights and a symbol of the pursuit of the impossible – a reminder that what we seek often lies within as well as without.

What are we to make of all this? As British mythology it is without equal and has fed the imagination of writers and poets through the ages, from the tales of the Knights of the Round Table to Blake's "Jerusalem" and on to the mystic travelers of today. Certainly something outstanding has been here for a very long time. In the most ancient charters and references to Glastonbury it is styled: "The fountain and origin of all religion

THE GLASTONBURY THORN

Joseph of Arimathea's staff became the famous Glastonbury Thorn, which flowers at Christmas; a sprig is still sent every year to decorate the table of the monarch on Christmas Day. The Puritans tried to destroy the thorn because they regarded it as superstitious, but local clergy made cuttings and hid them. From these the thorn has continued to this day.

Weary All Hill, Somerset

in the realm of Britain." Great saints of early Christianity such as St David/Dewi of Wales came here to seek inspiration in the fifth and sixth centuries. The earliest Roman missionaries, such as St Paulinus in the seventh century, sent money to protect the "old church" with a roof of lead – very rare at that time – and boards to clad it externally. What exactly was being protected? What was King Gwrgan of Damnonia referring to when he made a grant of land in 601 to the "old church" at Glastonbury?

Whatever was here was special and treasured since at least the fifth century, and probably much earlier. This is a place of great mystery and magic and it is doubtful if we shall ever be sure what we are dealing with here – myth, legend or truth.

GLASTONBURY ABBEY

There has been an abbey here since at least the fifth century, as attested by St David, and it grew to be the most powerful and wealthy one in England. It also stood out against the closures of the monasteries, for in 1539 the last abbot refused to go quietly and stood up to the commissioners sent by Henry VIII. This was interpreted as treason and he and two fellow monks were hanged, drawn and quartered, after which his head was placed over the abbey entrance. What was it about this place which called forth such brutality in those sent to suppress it?

King Arthur

One reason why this great abbey, home to so many saints over the centuries, was so powerful was that King Arthur was buried here. At least this is what the monks claimed when, in the reign of Henry II, they unearthed a tomb and found a crude lead cross on which was carved in Latin the inscription: "Here lies the famous King Arthur, buried in the Isle of Avalon." The body found below was reburied in the abbey and became a famous shrine. Near him lay the shrine of the greatest of the abbots of Glastonbury and quite probably a local lad – St Dunstan.

St Dunstan

Dunstan was born in or near Glastonbury c.909, a distant relation of Alfred the Great. Educated here, he was marked out as a high flier destined for a powerful role at court. But after a mysterious illness he turned his back on the secular world and became a monk. Around 943 he was appointed abbot at Glastonbury, where he brought in a strict Benedictine

St Dunstan was a great educator and was in part responsible for a renaissance in English religious life

rule and lived a life of great asceticism; he also greatly raised the educational standards of the monastery. Between 946 and 955 Dunstan, in collaboration with St Ethelwold and St Oswald of Worcester (see p. 173), undertook a complete overhaul of English monastic life. Invasion, destruction and laxity had brought the monastic houses into disrepute, but with the active support of King Edmund I and King Edred these three men created a renaissance in English religious life.

Dunstan is one of the great reformers and political thinkers of Saxon England. But he was also a great educator and composer of liturgy who enjoyed illuminating manuscripts, playing musical instruments and working in metal. He had the drive of a man with spiritual vision – and that vision was for the betterment of all people. He founded or refounded monasteries at Malmesbury, Bath, Westminster, Exeter, Peterborough and Ely. He composed music, wrote prayers and taught the vital importance of education. He was very greatly loved and his faith was one which moved people. It was said that, when he sang in church, "he seemed to be talking with the Lord face to face."

He died greatly mourned and his body was brought to Glastonbury for burial. Soon a significant cult grew up around his tomb and it became a center of devotion, not least to those who shared his vision of a reformed Church at the service of the people.

SACRED GLASTONBURY BEYOND THE ABBEY

When the last abbot was hanged in 1539, pilgrimage ceased. The abbey was destroyed and its library scattered. But the abbey and the legends associated with it have survived and today Glastonbury Abbey is once again a pilgrim destination as diverse and interesting as anything that people might have seen in the Middle Ages. For Glastonbury Abbey is only one site among many in an area redolent with sacredness.

Weary All Hill has already been mentioned. The sharply inclined hill called the Tor is topped by St Michael's Tower. Michael, as explained in Chapter 4, protects sacred sites by standing to their north. He is also often associated with earlier religious sites, and it is clear that the Tor was used for some form of ceremonial rites long before Christianity came to the area. Traces of what appear to be a ceremonial way up and around the Tor can still be seen. There can be little doubt that such an unusual physical feature would have attracted attention – not least because, in a marshy area, it was dry.

At the base of the Tor is the Chalice Well. This is where, according to one tradition, the Holy Grail was hidden by Joseph of Arimathea and eventually found by the Knights of the Round Table. Even after the destruction of the monastery this well remained popular. In 1750 a local man dreamed of being cured by the well water, came and drank, and was cured. By the following year ten thousand people had come to the well for healing, and a special subterranean chamber had been cut to accommodate them.

Two other wells exist here, both of great age. St Edmund's Well, northwest of the Tor, may commemorate King Edmund II, known as Edmund

Chalice Well Gardens, Glastonbury, Somerset – once home to the Holy Grail?

Ironside, who is supposed to be buried at Glastonbury. It is also called Elder Well and, with the nearby Ashwell spring, indicates that the focus of worship here before the arrival of Christianity may have been a sacred grove. This would also explain the cult of the Glastonbury Thorn – it could be a survival of the older tree cult.

Today Glastonbury remains its enigmatic self. Here you can find the highest concentration of religious nonsense and spiritual tat in Britain. But you can also find people who are working to make sense of an insensitive world, who find here a place of great spiritual power and who have helped us rediscover the sacredness of this landscape – sacredness which is actually a quintessential fusion between the old Celtic and earliest Christian traditions.

Glastonbury is a place to reflect on our need to feel special, to feel especially touched by God in our lives and in our landscape. You will have your own places of magic and power – your own Glastonburys. Perhaps it is time to revisit them and to find again why you and certain places are special.

CHAPTER 14

St Michael's Mount to Tintagel

Soul that breaks the mould
That sees what a far-flung landscape is
And blends to it

That gets out and walks
The whole way to feel -
To witness the unforgettable

Heron-bird of life and death,
And the light on the longed-for island raying down

THE DRAMA of St Michael's Mount, guardian deity and archangel of Cornwall, leads on to the shattered remains of one of the country's most sacred and haunting castles. This journey through the ancient sites and saints of Cornwall rivals the Welsh and Scottish routes for its encounter with the unexpected and the mysterious.

From St Michael on his Rock to King Arthur at Tintagel

Main Route (94 miles/150 km):
ST MICHAEL'S MOUNT · MARAZION · ST IVES · ST AGNES ·
PERRANPORTH · PADSTOW · ST ENDELLION · TINTAGEL

ST MICHAEL'S MOUNT · CORNWALL

This is one of the wonders of Britain: the church and castle perched upon their dramatic rocky outcrop seem to come from some fairy tale or children's

picture book. The dedication of this rock to St Michael is a classic example of the Christianizing of an older site. St Michael and St Catherine (see pp. 48-49) are the customary dedications for churches on hills – from this aerie, he was believed to keep watch over the land and to protect against invaders. The local legend behind the dedication is that in 495 some hermit monks or local fishermen saw a vision of St Michael standing on a ledge of rock on the island.

There is no evidence of any ritual or religious use of the island before the arrival of Christianity. Many claim that it was the island Ixtis or Ictis, spoken of by the first-century BC Greek geographer and historian Diodorus Siculus. He describes how the Phoenicians from the Eastern Mediterranean traded with the Cornish from an island reached only by an isthmus, dry at low tide; this exactly describes St Michael's link to the old town of Marazion. It seems that the Cornish tin miners brought their ore to be purchased by the Phoenicians from perhaps as long ago as 1000 BC.

The earliest record of any religious body here is in 1044, when Edward the Confessor gave the Benedictines both St Michael's Mount and Mont St-Michel in Brittany. Because of its exposed situation, the church and monastery appear to have been fortified from the earliest days. But the wars with France in the fourteenth and fifteenth centuries, combined with the Black Death in the midfourteenth century, left the Mount badly understaffed and the monastery struggling to cope. The king took over responsibility for the fortifications and in 1410 tried to suppress the monastery on the grounds of it being run from France. It limped on until 1425, when it finally closed. From then on, the Mount was primarily a secular castle, though pilgrims still came. The Henry VI Society still makes pilgrimages to the Mount as it is considered sacred to the memory of that king, who was murdered here in 1471. He founded Eton and King's College, Cambridge, and is considered a saint by some.

MARAZION · CORNWALL

This town, on the mainland opposite St Michael's Mount, has a strange name and an even stranger explanation for it. It is said to commemorate the Jewish traders who came here to hold fairs at which they bought tin, and Marazion is supposed to mean Bitter Zion, as a reminder to them of the Sweet Zion – Jerusalem – which they had left behind.

The town was badly sacked by the French in the reigns of Henry VIII and Edward VI and never really recovered. The end of the pilgrimages in the mid-sixteenth century also added its death knell to the town. Interestingly, Marazion church is dedicated to St Catherine, the other great saint of mountains, hills and high places.

Marazion to St Ives (11 miles/18 km): *From A394, take A30 N and then A3074*

ST IVES · CORNWALL

The route north to Tintagel passes many villages named after unfamiliar saints – places such as St Erth, St Day, St Columb and St Eval. These saints are extremely local and seem to be hermits or priests who were sanctified in popular legend. At St Ives we meet a saint whose legend is known but who leaves us none the wiser. This beautiful place, home to so many artists in recent years, is named after St Ia or Hya and when just a tin and fishing town was known as Porth-Ia. She is supposed to have been the daughter of an Irish chieftain who sailed here on a leaf in the fifth century or a little later. Probably she was an Irish saint who visited Cornwall, for the links between the Cornish and Breton peoples, the Welsh and Irish were very strong from before the Roman invasion right through to the Middle Ages. Ia died here, and is buried where her church is today.

To stand where one who was deemed special has stood before is, or should be, a reminder of the importance of ordinary things. Fame and fortune we know do not last. But a presence of gentleness can and does live on in these churches and villages dedicated to forgotten saints. You will have met unsung saints in your own life. Stand or kneel here and give

thanks for people whose love, care or concern for you has helped you at times of crisis; or for those who have encouraged you to be who you are. Give thanks for these saints.

St Ives to St Agnes (28 miles/45 km):
Return on A3074 to B3301 to Redruth. Pick up A30 and then B3277 into St Agnes

ST AGNES · CORNWALL

Take the coastal road as far as you can, avoiding the built-up areas of Camborne and Redruth and enjoying some of the most spectacular coastal scenery in Britain. St Agnes is famous for its holy well in Chapelcomb, where the remains of an ancient chapel are also to be found. The well is linked with many stories concerning healings and apparitions – spirits who bring healing or foretell the future.

St Agnes to Perranporth (4 miles/6 km):
Follow signs on B3285 to Perranporth

PERRANPORTH · CORNWALL

Perran is a version of Piran, a saint whose influence in this area accounts for the many place-names based on his name. A saint of the fifth to seventh century, St Piran later became mixed up with St Ciaran, a missionary who arrived in Ireland before St Patrick. Until 1764, if not later, the tin miners of the area observed St Piran's Day, March 5, as a holiday, for he was their patron saint. The remains of his ancient church, overtaken by the sand; his holy well on the edge of Penhale Point; and St Perran's Round, an ancient amphitheater on the downs, all bear witness to the sacred landscape which Piran entered and then added to in his own way.

As with so many sites in Cornwall, we really know nothing of the saint at the heart of the local area. All we know is that they were loved or feared or respected – or possibly all three. Who were they and what drove them? We cannot say, but we respect their memory and forget it at our peril, for by such women and men is the world created and then turned upside down. The *Tao Te Ching*, the Chinese classic text of the fourth century BC, describes the way in which the sage or wise one affects the world around him:

> *Heaven and Earth are enduring.*
>
> *The universe can live for ever,*
> *because it does not live for itself.*
>
> *And so both last – outliving themselves.*
>
> *The sage guides his people*
> *by putting himself last*
>
> *Desiring nothing for himself,*
> *he knows how to channel desires.*
>
> *And is it not because he wants nothing*
> *that he is able to achieve everything?*

Perranporth to Padstow (18 miles/29 km): *Take B3285, then turn L on to A3075 to Newquay. Leave on A3058, then take B3276 coast road to Padstow*

PADSTOW · CORNWALL

This is a sacred place, and here it is possible to be in touch not just with ancient Christianity but with a still-practiced ritual which pre-dates Christianity and perhaps even the Celts. The town is recorded in ancient Cornish texts as Lodenek or Heglemith and thus has a history from before the arrival of Christianity: the relevance of this will become apparent later.

The earliest Christian church here is supposed to have been built by St Patrick in 432 and called Laffenack. In or around 513 St Petroc came here from South Wales and founded a monastery which was, for much of his life, his missionary base. He is often associated with animals, especially the

AN ANCIENT RITUAL IN PADSTOW

Today it is the Padstow Hobby Horse festival on May Day which draws most visitors here; it seems to be a rare survival of pre-Christian or pre-Celtic ritual dance. The Hobby Horse, or 'Oss as it is known locally, dances through the streets – a strange mixture of horse and pantomime. No one knows where it comes from or what it is sup-

posed to be. Is it connected with fertility? Or does it hark back to the horse cult of early Britain and other early societies such as that of India? Whatever the truth, the tradition that this is the oldest dance festival in Europe ensures popularity and continuity.

stag, for he sheltered wild animals in all his monasteries and especially on the wild moors where he went to pray. The name Padstow is a corruption of Patrickstow or Petrocstown, signifying the importance that the monastery and church had here.

Because of the link with St Petroc – his body was originally buried here after he died in his hermitage on Bodmin Moor – thousands of Irish and Welsh pilgrims came here on their way to Spain or the Holy Land. It was thought that his relics, which after various adventures ended up at Bodmin parish church, were destroyed at the Reformation. But in the nineteenth century a beautiful ivory reliquary worked by Sicilian-Islamic artists was found hidden over the porch; it contained Petroc's head.

Perhaps Padstow is a good place to stop and reflect on how diverse the traditions which shape our faith – or lack of faith – are. Christianity in Britain is a mixture of pre-Christian and Christian ideas and practices. The same is true for all religions. Today new movements are sweeping the religious world. Some are dangerous, but some can help us to come to a deeper sense of what it means to struggle with faith or the lack of it.

Padstow to St Endellion (15 miles/24 km): *Leave on A389, turn L on A39 through Wadebridge, then L on to B3314 to St Endellion*

ST ENDELLION · CORNWALL

To reach here you pass close to a succession of saintly villages – St Issey, St Minver, and St Breock with its delightful church and marvelous site: one can imagine what drew the saint here in the first place. On the St Breock Downs above there is a fine cromlech – a form of stone circle; it is well worth the effort of climbing to see it and then to enjoy the view.

St Endellion is named after St Edelienta, a sixth-century princess from Wales who, forswearing marriage, came and lived here as a simple hermit. She lived on nothing but milk from her cows, but was attacked and killed by a local landowner. Foreseeing her death, she had given instructions that her body should be placed upon a bier and drawn by her cows. When the cows stopped, her followers would know that this was where she wanted to be buried. The church marks the spot to this day.

This story bears close similarities to the horse traditions of ancient societies: the sacred horse was allowed to roam free, but wherever it went the people had to follow and settle, even if this meant fighting others to obtain the land on to which the horse had wandered. Perhaps this is what Padstow celebrates with its 'Oss, and St Edelienta turned it to a more docile creature, the cow, in the light of the gentle gospel.

Gandhi loved the cow, which is sacred in India, and saw in its sacredness a message for the whole world about how we live and how we treat our fellow creatures. He said: "Cow protection to me is one of the most wonderful phenomena in all human evolution, for it takes the human being beyond his species. . . . Protection of the cow means protection of the whole dumb creation of God." In this era of BSE and of genetic experiments, perhaps we should stand here and reflect on how God has created all creatures and of the dangers we face when we play at being God. St Edelienta's cows and Gandhi's words should remind us that all creation is the family of God.

St Endellion to Tintagel (13 miles/21 km): *Continue on B3314, then turn L on to B3263 to Tintagel*

TINTAGEL · CORNWALL

This dramatic and haunting place is steeped in legend. The ancient church was founded *c.*500 by St Simphorian and is dedicated to St Materiana. Here you can also find the remains of a fifth-century palace as well as the spectacular castle ruins so powerfully associated with King Arthur. It is easy to see why Tintagel has become a modern pilgrimage center, part religious and part secular.

The archaeological evidence is that the first castle was built here in 1150 or so by the Earl of Cornwall, a son of Henry I born on the wrong side of the blanket. But what of Arthur? Does he have any place here? Legend asserts that this was his birthplace, though this claim is also made by sixteenth-century writers for Padstow. If Arthur existed, and if he was just a Romano-Celt in the service of Ambrosius Aurelianus trying to stop the Anglo-Saxon invaders, then he probably came from a Roman town or villa. While there are Roman milestones in the area, there is no evidence that Tintagel itself has any Roman links.

So why the story and why does it draw people today? It is because it is such a dramatic and marvelous site and because we want to believe that somewhere we can touch the greatest legend that Britain has ever produced, with its vision of honor and courage contrasted with the reality of adultery and betrayal. Here we stand on a site which claims to link us to the epic which we call the Arthurian Legend. For such an epic, you need an epic place. Tintagel is exactly that.

Here perhaps is a place to sit and read the words of the seventeenth-century metaphysical poet Thomas Traherne in "The Salutation," and so end this pilgrimage to things almost unknown and hardly discernible to the touch.

> From Dust I rise
> And out of Nothing now awake;
> These brighter Regions which salute mine Eyes
> A Gift from God I take:
> The Earth, the Seas, the Light, the lofty Skies,
> The Sun and stars are mine; if these I prize.
>
> A stranger here,
> Strange things doth meet, strange Glory see,
> Strange Treasures lodg'd in this fair World appear,
> Strange all and New to me:
> But that they mine should be who Nothing was,
> That Strangest is of all: yet brought to pass.

WALES

CHAPTER 15

-------------------- ✺ --------------------

*C*hester to Bardsey Island

And can see then
As the borderland becomes the Summerland
Where we are drawn through into the light beyond:

Ascending light, like a dream within us,
Dissolving the black ganglia that hang over Britain

In this sacred each and only moment
Where inner and outer are one

*T*HE PROBLEM with writing about Wales in a book on Sacred Britain is that virtually the whole of Wales seems sacred. Look at place-names for example. Any place which begins with the ubiquitous Llan signifies a special, usually holy, enclosure. Visit such a place and you will probably find a church of great antiquity, beside a flowing stream or well. Wales in its very fabric is sacred. Where else could you find a great chasm in a cliff and be told that this split opened up at the exact moment that Christ died upon the cross? Well, visit Abergavenny, Monmouthshire and just outside of the town you will find Skirrid Fawr and its cosmic chasm. Travel into the remoteness of the Preseli mountains, Pembrokeshire and you will find new pagans living and working around the mountains from which Stonehenge's main stone blocks came, and Christians who observe Christmas on a totally different date than the rest of Britain. Climb Plynlimon in Ceredigion and you will find a Buddhist hermit living in a cave where he

venerates the Celtic saint who first dwelled here, and hillfarmers who regularly "see" Owain Glyndwr, the last fighting prince who rose against the English and died in 1416. There are numerous saints' shrines, remains and places of special devotion. These are not just men and women of the past; like Owain Glyndwr they seem to still walk the land, shaping people's lives.

This first Welsh route leads us from two remarkable women saints to an island of twenty thousand saints. It brings us to the most complete holy well in Britain and to an ancient city which sought to mimic Constantinople. Legend, myth and history combine in this journey through the Romano-Celtic world of early Christianity.

From St Werburga at Chester to the Twenty Thousand Saints at Bardsey Island

Main Route (127 miles/203 km):
CHESTER · HOLYWELL · LLANASA · DYSERTH · ST ASAPH · LLANDEGAI · BANGOR · ANGLESEY · CAERNARFON · TUDWEILIOG · ABERDARON · BARDSEY ISLAND

CHESTER · CHESHIRE

Women saints dominate the first part of this route, drawing pilgrims into an examination of the role of women down the ages. But this is also a route into that most mysterious of elements, water. Holy wells run like a stream through the route, guiding and refreshing pilgrims today as they have done for centuries.

We start in England, just on the border at the great center of Roman and English control of Wales. Here in AD 70 the Romans built a great legionary fort and town, and from here for nearly four hundred years they ruled over the Celts of Wales. After the Romans left in the early fifth century invaders and local kings fought over the place and found it a useful ruin. Then in 907 Queen Ethelfleda of Mercia restored the town and seems to have either built or restored the main minster church of Chester.

What did Queen Ethelfleda find here? Perhaps this is an appropriate place to read the Anglo-Saxon poem "The Ruin." It probably describes Bath, but its wonderful evocation of the Roman ruins of Britain seems equally apposite here.

> Splendid this rampart is, though fate destroyed it,
> The city buildings fell apart, the works
> Of giants crumble. Tumbled are the towers,
> Ruined the roofs, and broken the barred gate,
> Frost in the plaster, all the ceilings gape,
> Torn and collapsed and eaten up by age
> . . . Often this wall
> Stained red and grey with lichen has stood by
> Surviving storms while kingdoms rose and fell.
> And now the high curved wall itself has fallen.
>
> . . . And so these halls
> Are empty, and this red curved roof now sheds
> Its tiles, decay has brought it to the ground,
> Smashed it to piles of rubble, where long since
> A host of heroes, glorious, gold-adorned,
> Gleaming in splendour, proud and flushed with wine,
> Shone in their armour, gazed on gems and treasure,
> On silver, riches, wealth and jewellery,
> On this bright city with its wide domains.

CHESTER CATHEDRAL AND ST WERBURGA

Chester's great saint, after whom the cathedral is still named, is St Werburga, and it was her cult that drew pilgrims and helped to create the wealth of what was then a great Benedictine abbey. One of the medieval pilgrims, in full traveling garb, is carved in delightful detail on a fourteenth-century bench end in front of the Dean's stall in the choir. Not long after the minster's rebuilding by Ethelfleda, nuns from St Werburga's at Threekingham in Lincolnshire (see p. 126) brought the saint's body to Chester to preserve it from the invading Danes. Her shrine can be visited

here to this day, respected and honored now as it was before the Reformation.

St Werburga was one of those remarkable Saxon women saints we have encountered earlier. A princess, born c.640, she was the daughter of another saint, St Erminilda. She entered the nunnery of St Etheldreda at Ely but was soon running her own clutch of nunneries which she founded at Threekingham, at Hanbury in Staffordshire and at Weedon Bec in Northamptonshire. The choir at Chester contains a carving depicting one of the most famous stories told about this woman, which explains why her symbol is a pair of geese.

At Weedon, a large flock of geese were causing a nuisance by eating the community's corn. St Werburga summoned the birds, gave them a strict

OGHAM — AN ANCIENT SCRIPT

The fusion between Roman and Celtic societies produced some of the earliest Christian sites and remains which still exist. Scattered across Wales are Romano-Celtic gravestones of Christians. These stones are often marked not just with Latin inscriptions but with an extraordinary written language based upon Latin that used a series of strokes rather than letters. Known as Ogham this is the earliest form of written Cymric language and seems to have been developed, perhaps by Christian missionaries, as a way of giving a script to Cymric and Gaelic in Ireland. The stone which enabled Ogham to be read is in Nevern churchyard, Pembrokeshire (11 miles east of Fishguard off A487), along with a bleeding yew which will only stop bleeding, legend has it, when all the evil has been purged from the world.

lecture about greediness and told them to leave next morning. The geese apparently agreed. However, during the night one of them was killed, cooked and eaten by some poachers, and as a result the arrangement was off. St Werburga instituted an investigation, uncovered the culprit and restored the victim to life, whereupon the geese did indeed take their leave.

Werburga considered herself – and was considered by her contemporaries – the equal of any man, king or peasant. These Saxon and Celtic women saints seem to have had this status; their role as abbesses of double communities – men and women – and as founders of religious communities is without parallel in later centuries, especially after the Conquest in 1066. Saxon law freely allowed women to possess, inherit and dispose of property and land; it was not so under subsequent legal systems. Indeed, the compilers of the Domesday Book, William's great census of post-Conquest England, found that much of the land was owned and managed by women.

Is it significant that it was a Queen who offered sanctuary and homage to a woman saint? We suspect she was expressing certain values which, sadly, the Church lost, buried or even deliberately set out to eradicate for many centuries afterward. Only now can the Anglican Church in Chester look this woman saint square in the face. For now women have ritual equality in the Church. But it has been a long hard slog and there is still much prejudice to overcome. This cathedral is a good place for both women and men to come on pilgrimage, to celebrate the coming of equality. This has been and should be a very sacred place.

ST WERBURGA'S SHRINE

The shrine, destroyed in the 1530s, has been rebuilt and now represents one of the best-preserved medieval shrines in England. To it has been added a modern carved wooden statue of St Werburga, which very appropriately shows her holding the church in her hands.

Let us leave Chester with a prayer

St Werburga's shrine in the Lady Chapel of Chester Cathedral, Cheshire

written by the great twelfth-century German abbess Hildegard of Bingen, whose life was not unlike that of the great Anglo-Saxon women saints and echoes the spiritual focus of their lives that they made manifest in their work and foundations.

"Antiphon for Divine Love"

Love
Gives herself to all things,
Most excellent in the depths,
And above the stars

Cherishing all:
For the High King
She has given
The kiss of peace.

Chester to Holywell (21 miles/34 km): *Take A483 (signposted Wrexham), go W on A55 and follow signs to Holywell*

HOLYWELL · FLINTSHIRE

ST WINIFRID'S WELL

The most visited holy well in Britain is, appropriately enough, at a place called Holywell. This is the shrine of a female saint – the well has long been associated with women's ailments. The shrine has survived intact from the Middle Ages, unlike any other holy well shrine or indeed any shrine at all. Worship, although at times discouraged, has never ceased and today the well is cared for by Roman Catholic nuns, while above it stands the Anglican parish church (see also p. 44).

The reason why this shrine has survived has to do with the power of a grandmother. It was rebuilt in 1490 by Lady Margaret Beaufort, the mother of Henry Tudor who became Henry VII in 1485. She and her son both died in 1509, when her grandson Henry VIII became king. Margaret Beaufort was a considerable

Pilgrims at St Winifrid's Well, Holywell, Flintshire

force in her lifetime and would seem to have continued to be respected after her death, which is why,
despite the Reformation, the shrine has survived to
this day.

ST WINIFRID

St Beuno, whom we shall meet throughout this pilgrimage route, built a small chapel – probably where
the Anglican parish church now stands – in the seventh century. According to some sources, Winifrid
was his niece and it was to him that she fled when
Caradoc, son of a local chieftain, made advances to
her. Caradoc followed and, when she again rebuffed
him, drew his sword in anger and struck off her
head. Instantly the ground opened up and swallowed him, and where Winifrid's head fell a spring
arose – the spring which feeds the well. Hearing her
screams as she was murdered, Beuno came running,
picked up her head and restored her to life. Winifrid
spent the rest of her days uneventfully as a nun at
Gwytherin near Aberconwy.

Today her shrine is visited by people of all faiths
who value such holy places. The water is free to
those who bring their own containers. It is still
believed to have healing powers and many homes
nearby keep a bottle for use at times of distress or
injury. There is an octagonal central well and a
bathing pool designed for the infirm. There is a pilgrims' walkway around the central well, like a small
cloister, while above the well is a beautiful chapel.

Here is a place to reflect on women whose lives
are destroyed or twisted by the violence of men and
the fear that this generates. The sacred often
emerges out of the violent and destructive, as in this
story. It never excuses the violence – indeed, it
should cast a light upon violence itself – but it is an
essential teaching of many faiths that violence can
only be overcome by love, not by returning violence.

Holywell to Llanasa (7 miles/11 km): *Leave on A5026 going W and take A5151 (signposted Dyserth) and follow local signs to N for Llanasa. (For Whitford take R turn off A5151 a mile or so W of Holywell)*

THE MAEN ACHWYNFAN CROSS

Just north of Whitford is the great Maen Achwynfan cross of the tenth or eleventh century, one of the tallest in Wales. Its simple boldness, intricate knot patterns, slightly wobbly top cross and enigmatic figure on the lower panel make this one of the most intriguing of Welsh Celtic crosses. It is unclear why it was raised here; perhaps it marked the site of some monastic cell out on the windswept flats.

LLANASA · FLINTSHIRE

The name Llanasa means "the enclosure of Asaph," whom we shall meet again at the city named after him. The church here appears to have been founded c.570 or even earlier. At Gwespyr, the next village, are the remains of a small abbey, possibly again built on a Celtic site.

Llanasa to Dyserth (4 miles/6 km): *Rejoin A5151 and continue W to Dyserth*

GOP HILL

Between Llanasa and Dyserth, to the north of the A5151, is the vast Bronze Age burial mound of Gop Hill. It is the largest such burial mound in Wales, but excavations have not revealed why it is so huge. From its position it was clearly built to dominate the surrounding landscape. It seems that this area has been a special place for thousands of years, and the scale of the Celtic Christian remains here indicates that this tradition lived on and was honored by the early Christians.

DYSERTH · DENBIGHSHIRE

The name Dyserth means "wilderness" or "desert," and indicates the dwelling place of a monk or hermit inspired by the Egyptian monastic tradition of going to the desert to live and pray. There are a number of similarly named places in Wales, all remote or hidden away.

Dyserth to St Asaph (11 miles/18 km): *Take A5151 to Rhuddlan and follow A525 to St Asaph*

ST ASAPH · DENBIGHSHIRE

The ancient sacred landscape through which we have traveled to St Asaph helps us understand why the city is here. There is little to the place beyond the cathedral, and that is how it has always been. Here we can see clearly how a monastic site would attract a small settlement around it – in this instance, between the hill on which the cathedral stands and the river crossing below. In Welsh the name captures this sacred geography exactly: Llanelwy means "the enclosure beside the River Elwy."

ST KENTIGERN AND ST ASAPH

It was to this spot, possibly the old Roman fort of Varae, that a remarkable man with three names came in 560. St Kentigern is known as Mungo in Scotland, where he is the patron saint of Glasgow; and in Wales, where he founded St Asaph, he is called Cynderyn. A twelfth-century biography of St Asaph includes a description of the building of the first monastery here:

> When Kentigern, the Saint of God, has set his mind on building a monastery, in which the scattered sons of God might, for their souls' health, come together, like bees, from the east and from the west, from the north and from the south; at the first, when these sons of God, coming under the inspiration of the Holy Spirit, had finished their prayers and divine offices, they set manfully and eagerly about their different operations; some cleared ground, some made it level and others prepared the foundations. Some too carried the timbers and others welded them together, and erected with skill and speed the church and other buildings of planed woodwork, after the British fashion.

The land appears to have been donated by Cadwallon Liu, the local lord, and his nephew, while Asaph was one of those who seem to have joined this young community. For when Kentigern was invited back to Scotland Asaph became abbot, and it is his name which has become so associated with this ancient site. Of Asaph himself we know virtually nothing except that he probably came here from his church at Llanasa (see previous page). He is described as a man "calm of manners, [with] grace of body, holiness of heart and [a] witness of miracles."

Celtic Christianity did not have cathedrals in the way that the Roman Church did: their centers were monasteries and holy shrines. St Asaph's was the main administrative monastery for this area and, when the Normans came, they created a diocese here and then rebuilt the earlier Celtic church into a small but fine cathedral. To legitimize their work they named it after the popular local saint, Asaph. The Welsh continue to call it Llanelwy.

THE WELSH BIBLE

Ironically, given the Normans' role in the story, the city of St Asaph contains a shrine for those who treasure the Welsh language. It stands right outside the cathedral and celebrates the translators of the Bible, Prayer Book and other religious texts into Welsh in the sixteenth century. The main protagonist was the then bishop, William Morgan. The complete Bible in Welsh was published in 1588 and this is what the cross monument, raised in 1888, commemorates.

Language, culture and faith are the three legs of Celtic Christianity, and the need for a Welsh Bible was succinctly put by one of the translators, William Salusbury: "Unless you wish to be worse than animals, insist in getting learning in your own language – and unless you wish to abandon utterly the faith of Christ, insist on getting the Holy Scriptures in your own tongue." It was the vigor and forethought of men such as Salusbury and Morgan that initiated the slow recovery of Celtic Christianity in Wales and the strengthening of the Welsh language at a time when it was in great danger of extinction.

St Asaph to Bangor (33 miles/53 km): *Return to A55 and turn W through Colwyn Bay, Conwy and Penmaenmawr. For Llandegai, take A5122 just before Bangor*

THE DRUIDS' CIRCLE

Between St Asaph and Bangor there is not a great deal to see apart from the Druids' Circle on the edge of the moors south of Penmaenmawr (the name is an anachronism as the place was abandoned long before the druids came this way). This is one of the most important sets of circles, tombs and standing stones in Wales. The earliest parts go back to c.3000 BC, and it seems to have been in use into the mid-Bronze Age.

It is said that the original dedicatees of the two main circles were god-

The Druids' Circle, near Conwy, Gwynedd is one of the most important sets of standing stones in Wales

desses named Andras and Ceridwen. Other legends associate the place with the ritual sacrifice of children. This, however, is a standard charge brought against people who are feared, despised or misunderstood, and should be treated with suspicion. The stone north of the main circle is known as the Stone of Sacrifice, while to the south stands the Deity Stone. It used to be said that if you blasphemed near the Deity Stone you would be struck down. One skeptic decided to spend the night here to taunt and blaspheme; next morning he was found dead at the foot of the stone. It is even said that a coven of witches meeting here one night were shouted at by the stones, resulting in two of the witches going mad.

THE HOLY LAND OF WALES

Very many places in Wales bear names, usually chosen in the nineteenth century for new developments, which come straight from the Bible: Bethesda, south of Bangor, is typical. This is another way in which Wales is consciously a sacred land even today. Such names were picked because there was a real sense that the Holy Land was to be found here as much as in Palestine. Lloyd George, the first Welsh Prime Minister of Great Britain, said that when he was negotiating with the Zionist leader Chaim Weizmann for the right of Jews to resettle Palestine in the aftermath of the First World War, Weizmann kept bringing up place-names which were more familiar to him than those of the Western Front.

LLANDEGAI · GWYNEDD

Just south of Bangor, the church here stands on the site of the hermitage of the fifth-century St Tegai. The ancient row of yews is very typical of such old sites in Wales and is thought to be over a thousand years old, perhaps planted to mark a ceremonial walkway to the shrine of the saint.

BANGOR · GWYNEDD

ST DEINIOL

Bangor owes its existence to the church which still stands at its heart. Here in 525 came St Deiniol, probably from Scotland, to found one of his two monasteries both called Bangor – the name means a fence of twigs or branches surrounding a site. The other site, at Bangor-on-Dee, Wrexham, had a huge monastery until the Saxons destroyed it in 615, massacring all the monks. The community at Bangor-on-Dee is said to have first come together in 180, making it, along with Whithorn and perhaps Winchester, one of the three oldest monasteries in Britain.

St Deiniol became Bishop of Bangor when the great administrator of Celtic Christianity in the sixth century, St Dubricius (Dyfrig), divided Wales into three bishoprics: St Deiniol had Bangor, St Padarn central Wales and St Teilo South Wales. It is clear from this that, by 540 or so, Wales was a land of many Christian communities. St Deiniol is buried not here but on Bardsey Island: the oldest pilgrimage route in Wales starts from Bangor Cathedral and heads down the Lleyn Peninsula to Aberdaron and then by boat to Bardsey Island. It is in the footsteps of St Deiniol that the pilgrims went, and this is the route we shall now follow for the rest of this pilgrimage.

Bangor to Anglesey (4 miles/6 km): *Take the A5 W to the bridge across the Menai Strait*

ANGLESEY

The Holy Island of Anglesey, known to the Romans as Mona, was a great center of druidic training which the Roman legions assaulted twice, first in 61 and then more successfully in 78 under Agricola. This invasion was recorded by the Roman historian Tacitus – the first historical record of

North Wales. Looking across the straits it is not difficult to imagine the sight that greeted Agricola and his troops when they drew up on the shore. Facing them would have been tens of thousands of druids and Celtic warriors, both men and women. The bloodcurdling battle cries of the Celts terrified the Romans, but in the end the invaders' discipline and superior weaponry proved more powerful.

Anglesey to Caernarfon (9 miles/14 km): *Return on A5 and take A487*

CAERNARFON · GWYNEDD

ST HELEN

Caernarfon is famous for the Roman town and fort of Segontium, founded in 78, and for its castle and links with the princes of Wales. There is a very ancient legend that Helen, mother of Constantine the Great who as Roman emperor in the 330s declared Christianity a state religion of the Roman Empire, was born in Wales. So strong is this tradition that the main Roman road out of Caernarfon is still called Helen's Causeway. At Caernarfon, this mythic link is even stronger, for tradition claimed that Constantine himself was born here. This is commemorated in a most unusual, but very Welsh, way.

The walls of the castle and town are made of banded masonry and have polygonal towers, which are very rare in Britain; there is also no precedent for banded masonry. However, these are very distinctive features of the great walls of Constantinople. When these Welsh walls were built, some time between 1290 and 1320, many knights had been to Constantinople during the Crusades and would have seen these architectural marvels of the medieval world. Imitating the walls of Constantinople is another way of expressing the sacredness of Wales. This masonry is saying that the holy city of Constantine stands both on the waters between Europe and Asia, and on the shore of North Wales.

Caernarfon to Tudweiliog (27 miles/43 km): *At the A487 and A499 junction take A499 to Clynnog Fawr, continue on A499, then just before Llanaelhaearn turn onto B4417 to Tudweiliog.*

THE PILGRIM CHURCH AT CLYNNOG FAWR

This is a pilgrims' church without parallel in Britain. It was designed to house, sleep and service the vast crowds of pilgrims who came here to start the official main section of the route to Bardsey Island. The route is known as the **Saints' Way** because there are so many saints' shrines en route, as well as the reputed twenty thousand saints buried on Bardsey Island.

The church here was founded, probably as a monastery, by St Beuno c.616 (see also Holywell, p. 218). Here beside a stream he built a chapel where in due course he was buried and which now contains the remains of his shrine. It is unique in being separated from the main church by a covered walkway.

The church itself was rebuilt in the sixteenth century to house the huge numbers of pilgrims who came here to start the Saints' Way, but ironically this took place only a few years before the Reformation tried to put an end to such pilgrimages. The Saints' Way was one of the most popular routes in northern Europe, and to travel this route three times was considered equivalent to making a pilgrimage to Rome. The route is lined by churches, shrines and holy wells. Some of the details of the route are also known: for example, at Pistyll Farm you could demand shelter and bread and cheese from the tenants, who in return were excused paying rent to the monastic owners of the land.

ST BEUNO'S WELL

From Clynnog Fawr the pilgrims walked to St Beuno's holy well, where healings were frequently recorded and where you can still step down into the waters from a stone platform.

LLANAELHAEARN CHURCH AND WELL

At the next village, Llanaelhaearn, there is a charming little church set in an ancient graveyard, with a fifth-century Romano-Celtic Christian grave-marker under an ancient yew. This church was founded by St Aelhaern, who sounds like a Saxon saint. It is of course possible, for the intermingling of Celts and Saxons was a feature from the seventh century, as can be seen at Deerhurst in Gloucestershire (see p. 175). The village contains St Aelhaern's Holy Well, which in common with so many others was covered over in the early twentieth century, presumably to protect the purity of the water. Unfortunately, the key has long been lost and so the well itself remains unseen, though its waters still flow down into the village.

TUDWEILIOG · GWYNEDD

ST BRIGID

The next pilgrims' church, at Tudweiliog, was much restored by the Victorians. It is jointly dedicated to St Brigid, the greatest of Irish women saints – who is also the goddess Brigid, most revered of the pre-Christian goddesses. The pre-Roman Celtic tribe which lived in the north-west of Britain, the Brigantes, took their name from her. Perhaps here we have a trace of even earlier worship, and St Bridit/Brigid is a goddess who has been matched with a saint bringing her and her powers into the fold.

Nearby is the holy well of St Cwyfan or Gwyfan, the other dedicatee of the church, where sore eyes, ague and warts were cured by throwing pins into the water.

> **Tudweiliog to Aberdaron/Bardsey Island (8 miles/13 km):** *Continue on B4417, then at crossroads turn R on to B4413 to Aberdaron. At Aberdaron boats can be hired for Bardsey. For Llangwnnadl turn R off B4417 following local signs*

LLANGWNNADL

The route becomes flat and featureless until you turn off and enter the tiny, magical, tree-lined valley in which lies the exquisite church of Llangwnnadl. Here, sometime in the sixth century, a priest or monk brought his people – quite literally his extended family – settled and built a church. His name was Gwynhoedl and he is buried here, marked by an inscription in late medieval Latin. The site is a classic Welsh *llan* – the enclosure sits on a slight rise above the stream which carves the valley.

ABERDARON · GWYNEDD

It is possible that the next church was the ruined one down by the seashore about 4 miles further on. But the main route seems to have swung along the present B4417 until the sharp bend about a mile or so on from the turning to Llangwnnadl. Where the road now turns almost south the old pilgrims' path went straight on, heading for Rhoshirwaun. From here the last pilgrim church is the twelfth-century one at Aberdaron, where the traveler is still refreshed in the fourteenth-century Pilgrims' Hall before contemplating the often rough crossing to Bardsey Island. In former times the pilgrims walked to Porth Meudwy or Braich-y-Pwll to sail to Bardsey. At Braich-y-Pwll a ruined chapel and holy well can still be seen.

BARDSEY ISLAND · GWYNEDD

THE TWENTY THOUSAND SAINTS

This is still a wild, isolated place – exactly the kind of spot to which the Celtic monks liked to retreat. Here came St Deiniol and St Dyfrig to spend their last years and be buried along with the other twenty thousand saints. The first monastery here was founded by St Cadfan, who came from Brittany, in 429. Today's remains are thirteenth-century and are of the Augustinian abbey of St Mary, built on the site of the original monastery.

Bardsey is still a sanctuary, guarded by the *Bardsey Island Trust*, which takes care that neither the twenty thousand saints nor the wildlife are unnecessarily disturbed. It is an ideal place for contemplation and prayer.

$\mathcal{L}$landaff to St David's

Stand in the presence
Though you cannot name it
By any name, or only one

Stand in the presence
Where the bread is given
Stand and sing –
Where all our names are sung

$\mathcal{S}$OUTH WALES is the heartland of saints. Here strode the greatest of the saints and the most mysterious. There are places of miracles here, and places of solitude. This is a journey into the heart of the Celtic Church and through that to the heart of the Celtic world itself, druidic as well as Christian – and in some places the two become but one.

In drawing up this pilgrimage route we were spoiled for choice. There are so many sites which could be visited, so many saints' shrines along the way, so many interesting ancient carved crosses, so many sites of prehistoric interest. In the end we opted for the route outlined below, but we would stress that this whole area is rich in sacred sites.

From St Teilo at Llandaff to St Dewi at St David's

Main Route (133 miles/213 km):
LLANDAFF (a suburb of Cardiff 2 miles/3 km northwest of·the city center) · LLANCARFAN · LLANTWIT MAJOR · MARGAM · NEATH · LLANGYFELACH · PARKMILL · CARMARTHEN · ST CLEARS · WHITLAND · HAVERFORDWEST · ST DAVID'S

LLANDAFF · CARDIFF

ST TEILO

"The enclosure by the River Taff" is the meaning of this place-name, and it was here in the sixth century that St Teilo built the first church. Here was a holy well, which now bears his name. Teilo was one of the most popular of Welsh saints: there are many churches dedicated to him and many towns which bear versions of his name. Although Llandaff does not appear to have been one of his major centers, the church grew in importance especially after the bishopric was fully established in the twelfth century. Teilo's links were exploited and his body was removed from Llandeilo to add sanctity to the new cathedral.

ST DYFRIG

This is also the final resting place of one of the Fathers of Welsh Christianity, St Dubricius or Dyfrig. He may well have been a member of a surviving Roman family that had moved from the old Roman safe lands of Herefordshire into Wales as the invading Anglo-Saxons advanced. Alternatively, he may have been sent from Rome as a missionary. His dates are c.460 to 540, and his work stretches from Herefordshire across South Wales and beyond. St Teilo was one of his disciples, and his authority seems to have been second to none.

Dyfrig's body was originally buried on Bardsey Island (see p.228) but was moved for ecclesiastical and political reasons. In 1120 Bishop Urban was establishing the Norman see at Llandaff and exerting control over much of South Wales on behalf of the thoroughly Roman Norman Church. He was, however, anxious to establish his validity by claiming to be a direct and worthy successor of the great Celtic saints, even if he was part of the very movement which was undermining the Celtic Church. Having obtained Teilo, he sent monks to dig up Dyfrig and bring him here to be reburied.

ST EUDDOGWY

Finally there is St Euddogwy or Oudoceus, supposed to be the nephew of Teilo and his successor at Llandaff. Euddogwy is the only one of the three saints of Llandaff whose life story really does center on the city. We are grateful to the Archivist of Llandaff Cathedral, Nevil James, for the following story from the twelfth-century text *Liber Landavensis*, which he included in a letter to us.

St Euddogwy being thirsty after undergoing labor, and more accustomed to drink water than any other liquor, came to a fountain in the Vale of Llandaff, not far from the Church, that he might drink, where he found women washing butter after the manner of the country; and sending to them his messengers and disciples, they requested that they would accommodate them with a vessel that their pastor might drink therefrom; who, ironically, as mischievous girls, said, "We have no other cup besides that which we hold in our hands, namely the butter." And the man of blessed memory taking it, formed one in the shape of a small bell. And he raised his hand so that he might drink therefrom, and he drank. And it remained in that form, that is a golden one, so that it appeared to those who beheld it to consist altogether of the purest gold; which by divine power is from that day reverently preserved in the Church of Llandaff, in memory of the holy man; and it is said that by touching it, health is given to the diseased.

Mr James goes on to speculate that the holy well near the cathedral known as Dairy Well relates to this story.

Today, it is to see a new wonder that many pilgrims come to Llandaff. Rising majestically above the central part of the church is a stunning figure of Christ by Jacob Epstein. It is a reminder that cathedrals are not just repositories of the past but creative centers of new expressions of faith.

Llandaff to Llancarfan (11 miles/18 km):
Take A48 toward Cowbridge. Turn S at junction with A4226, then turn R to Llancarfan following local signs

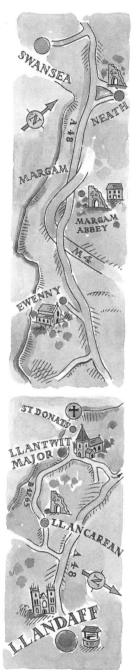

LLANCARFAN · VALE OF GLAMORGAN

THE MONASTERY OF ST CADOC

There is little to see here now, but it would have been a site of great importance for a Celtic pilgrim. Here stood the great monastic establishment founded by a local landowner, St Cadoc, in the sixth century. Llancarfan means "the enclosure of the stags" and the name recalls a miracle which explains why Cadoc is usually shown with two stags. One day he asked some monks to till the land near the monastery, but the men were not disposed to undertake the work. Suddenly two stags appeared from nearby woods, and with their antlers dug the soil ready for planting.

St Cadoc's missionary center was only really rivaled by Llantwit Major (see below). From here missionaries went to northern France and throughout Wales and the Scottish Borders. Many saints were educated here, and the place was a major center of both learning and pilgrimage. However, all this ended in 987 when the monastery was sacked by Vikings; for some reason it was never rebuilt.

> **Llancarfan to Llantwit Major (6 miles/10 km):** *Go S to B4265. Turn R and follow road to Llantwit Major*

LLANTWIT MAJOR · VALE OF GLAMORGAN

The wonderful church here is dedicated to St Illtyd, Eltut or Iltut, who c.500 founded a monastery, school and missionary center similar to that of Cadoc at Llancarfan. Illtyd was French and trained missionaries for work in Wales and France. They included St Samson, who evangelized Cornwall, the Scilly Isles, Brittany, Jersey and Guernsey; St David; the early historian St Gildas (493–570); and the Breton St Paul Aurelian.

One possible reason for the proliferation of great teaching centers in this area is that some aspects of druidic culture, such as a love of learning and knowledge of languages, had persisted, though probably underground. At this time, too, Patrick was building on druidic foundations in Ireland. Perhaps here we are witnessing the contribution which that most learned pre-Christian priesthood made to Christianity – a religion which took away the violent and human sacrifice elements of druidic faith and put the dying Christ in their place.

The two sections of the church mark the different uses of the building. The Old Church was Illtyd's original site, which then became the parish church. The New Church, built in the thirteenth century, is the monastic church. As with Llancarfan, the great monastery was destroyed in the Viking raids of 987 and never regained its former glory.

This whole area is full of saints and holy places, as any casual glance at the map will show. It is impossible to do justice to them all, but it is worth visiting places such as St Donats, 3 miles south-west of Llantwit Major, Llandough, 3 miles south of Cowbridge, and Ewenny Abbey, just south of Bridgend. This was holy ground for many centuries and something of that feeling remains today.

Llantwit Major to Margam (18 miles/29 km): *Take B4270 (signposted Cowbridge), continue on to B4268 and then left on to A48 toward Margam*

MARGAM · NEATH AND PORT TALBOT

MARGAM ABBEY

This was the site of one of the greatest monasteries in South Wales. It was founded in an area rich in very early Christian carved stones, which have been gathered together in the museum beside the ancient church. Here are inscriptions and crosses of the greatest beauty and antiquity, housed in what is believed to be the medieval building of one of the oldest schools in Britain.

The monastery was founded in 1147 on a site that already had long-standing Christian associations. Many stories about Margam are recorded by Gerald of Wales in his *Journey through Wales* of *c.*1188. They tell of terrible deaths for those who offended against the sanctuary and holiness of the abbey by acts of violence, as well as the miraculous feeding of the starving people during a famine. Not long before Gerald's visit, a severe famine had struck the area. The poor turned to the monastery for help: hundreds filled the gateways and pleaded for food. The monks sent a ship to Bristol to buy grain but it was delayed by strong winds. The famine grew worse but, on the day the last food ran out, a miracle occurred. A field of unripe wheat suddenly became ready for harvesting, and this unexpected food sustained everyone until the ship returned.

The Chapter House and part of the Abbey at Margam Park, Neath and Port Talbot

Margam to Neath (9 miles/14 km): *Continue along A48, then take A474 (signposted Neath)*

NEATH • NEATH AND PORT TALBOT

NEATH ABBEY

Here is an abbey, founded *c.*1130, which has been to the fires of Hell and back again. Neath was a major abbey in this area and had been a significant outpost during the Romanizing and later Normanizing of South Wales, but by the time of the Reformation it had fallen upon hard times. The site was bought and a family mansion built here, though the ruins of the abbey church were retained as they now are. In the eighteenth century copper smelting was an important local industry, and strong buildings were needed in which to smelt the ore. The abbey church seemed ideal, so fires of nightmare intensity turned the monks' former place of prayer into a raging inferno. Since that time a more benign attitude has been shown to these venerable remains, though traces of fire and smoke can still be clearly seen.

Neath to Llangyfelach (8 miles/13 km): *Take M4 NW from Neath, leave at J46 and follow local signs to Llangyfelach*

LLANGYFELACH • SWANSEA

This is the site of another major Celtic monastery, founded in the sixth or seventh century, and a very holy well dedicated to St David. Llangyfelach has strong links with St David/Dewi, and a fair of St David used to take place here.

Llangyfelach to Parkmill (12 miles/19 km): *Take A48 to Gorseinon, then turn S on to B4296 to Killay and join A4118 W to Parkmill*

PARKMILL • SWANSEA

To get a flavor of the history and sacred landscape that have built up here over the centuries, visit Parkmill, a restored mill. Here is the Parc le Breose Burial Chamber, and nearby are the Penmaen Burrows. The Burrows,

Neolithic burial mounds, have a Norman earthwork fort and the ruins of a thirteenth-century hermit's chapel upon them. This is a place which has been ritually sacred to different peoples at different times. It is possible that before it was a Neolithic burial mound it was sacred to the Paleolithic peoples who lived in the caves. Here we tread on ancient ground, hallowed for millennia.

Parkmill to Carmarthen (30 miles/48 km): *Retrace route to Gorseinon, then turn L on to A48 and A484 through Llanelli to Carmarthen*

CARMARTHEN

MERLIN/EMRYS

The Welsh name, Caerfyrddin, indicates that this was a Roman fort (*caer*); in fact it was the furthest west of any Roman town in South Wales. Here a monastery was established in the seventh century and here too according to legend, Merlin, known in Welsh as Emrys, was born. The stories associating this greatest of wizards with the town and area go back a very long time. In one of the earliest versions his mother was a nun who one night was ravished by some form of spirit, usually described as a devil. Forced to leave the nunnery, she came to Carmarthen where she gave

PALEOLITHIC MAN IN THE GOWER PENINSULA

A detour into the Gower Peninsula south-west of Swansea will take you into one of the loveliest places in South Wales and an area of immense antiquity. It was here, in Paviland caves, that the oldest ritual burial in Britain was found, containing the remains of a young man from about nineteen thousand years ago. The body was painted with red ochre coloring, which appears to have had religious significance. With the man was also buried, in a ritual position, an elephant skull. This area, free from ice during some of the ice ages, seems to have become home to many species driven from the rest of Wales by the advancing cold. Here too came early humanity, Paleolithic peoples, who found the caves of the seashore an ideal refuge and hunted the cave lion, elephant, rhinoceros, hippopotamus, bear, bison and other wild animals. Remains of all these have been found in the caves.

birth to Merlin. At the time Vortigern, one of the last Romano-British rulers (*c*.450), was desperately trying to hold off the invaders – though he also employed some of them, notably the notorious Hengest and Horsa (see p. 88), as mercenaries. As part of his defenses Vortigern tried to build a castle at Dinas Emrys in Gwynedd, but due to some evil force the stones kept falling down. He was advised by his seers that only by mixing with the mortar the blood of a child whose father was not human would the stones remain standing. Merlin and his mother were therefore brought to Dinas Emrys to be questioned by Vortigern.

However, Merlin was not sacrificed. He told Vortigern that if he dug deeper he would discover the real reason why it was impossible to build there: the presence of two dragons. So Vortigern's men dug and indeed found two fiery dragons, one red, the other white; they stood, Merlin said, for the Welsh and the Saxons, warring peoples. Vortigern saw the white dragon overcome the red, but Merlin stated that eventually red would again triumph – a prophecy not yet fulfilled! Merlin then delivered a whole string of prophecies which ended with one about Vortigern's own untimely death.

Merlin is a figure of immense fascination. Part druid, part seer, part saint, part wizard, he seems to contain within him all that is considered sacred in Wales. He is, if you like, the embodiment of the sacred, and this manifests itself physically in the landscape too. For centuries, Merlin's Oak has stood in the center of Carmarthen. Now so old that it is nothing more than a stump, it has been preserved partly in the local museum and partly by the town hall. It was said that if Merlin's Oak fell, so would Carmarthen.

Carmarthen to St Clears (10 miles/16 km): *Take A40 W*

ST CLEARS · CARMARTHENSHIRE

THE REBECCA RIOTS

Named after its local saint, this town contains the remains of the priory which once stood here. But St Clears is famous for much more recent events. In 1843–4 it was a center of the Rebecca Riots against removal of common rights – free passage of people and goods along the roads. Tollgates, essentially privatization of public roads, had been set up by landowners so that farmers and others had to pay to bring their goods into a market town such as St Clears. This, against the background of the

agricultural slump of the 1830s and the increasing power of the landowners is what sparked off the riots.

Their name comes from the text which, being good Nonconformists,
the leaders of the rebellion took as justifying their rebellion. Genesis 24:60
says: "And they blessed Rebecca and said unto her, Thou art our sister, be
thou the mother of thousands of millions, and let thy seed possess the gate
of those who hate them." With this text as their battle cry they struck out
and, although the riots were suppressed, tollgates disappeared from South
Wales.

The right to move, to travel, is a fundamental one that pilgrims have
been asserting for centuries. In our own day, privatization of woods and
forests, lakes and reservoirs, lands and parks, has limited access to places
where people have been walking for years. To use against those who
believe that the earth is their exclusive property we too need a good text
– these verses from Psalm 24:

> The earth is the Lord's and the fullness thereof; the world, and they who
> dwell therein.
> For He hath founded it upon the seas, and established it upon the
> floods.
> Who shall ascend into the hill of the Lord? Or who shall stand in his
> holy place?
> He who hath clean hands, and a pure heart, who hath not lifted up
> his soul unto vanity, nor sworn deceitfully.

St Clears to Whitland (5 miles/8 km): *Continue on A40 W*

WHITLAND · CARMARTHENSHIRE

Here you will find a monument to Welsh law and the ruins of an abbey
where St Cynan was abbot in the twelfth century. The monument commemorates the formal gathering which took place here in 930 at the
behest of the Welsh prince Hywel Dda, at which Welsh tribal laws and
customs were welded into a single legal system enforceable across Wales.
Whitland has very imaginatively created a small sacred landscape to celebrate and honor this achievement. A visitor center explains the significance of what happened here in 930, and a paved area represents the
arrival of the delegates. But most delightful and thoughtful are the six little gardens, each symbolizing one of the six divisions of the legal code:

society and status, crime and tort (libel and liability), women, contract, the monarchy, and property.

> **Whitland to Haverfordwest (17 miles/27 km):** *Follow A40 W*

HAVERFORDWEST · PEMBROKESHIRE

The ruins at Haverfordwest or Hwlffordd, to give it its Welsh name, are excellent – castle and abbey are both good sites to visit. As is so often the case with Christian towns, the church next to the castle is dedicated to St Martin – a reminder to the military that here was a saint who was once a soldier, but who when he converted withdrew from the army, saying, "I am Christ's soldier; I am not allowed to fight."

THE PEMBROKESHIRE COAST

This coast was loved by the saints of old and many made the caves, headlands and islands their home. Of these holy islands, Caldey, just off Tenby, is the most famous. To get to Tenby from Haverfordwest take A40 east to junction with B4313 (9 miles). There turn right to Narberth (about 1 mile along B4313). Continue south along A478 to Tenby (10 miles).

CALDEY ISLAND

The monastery on Caldey was founded in the fifth century by St Here, and St Samson was abbot. There was still a thriving Celtic Christian community here in the ninth century when the splendid Ogham and Latin inscribed stone was worked, but by the eleventh century it had been destroyed by Vikings and pirates. In 1127 the monastery was given to the Benedictines, who lived here until the Reformation, after which it was converted into a private house.

In 1906 the abbey became the home of an Anglican monastic order – much in fashion in the Anglican Church at that time. However, seven years later the community converted to Catholicism and became Benedictines.

By 1928, however, the Benedictines had outgrown the site and moved to Prinknash in Gloucestershire, where they remain to this day. In their stead came the Cistercians, who now care for the shrine and relics of St Samson, patron saint of the island. Their presence and the beauty of the island make this a very sacred place, one where the centuries seem to fall back to reveal the spirituality that drew the Celts here in the first place.

St Govan

Moving westward round the coast you will come to St Govan's Head (see right). From Tenby go west along A4139 to Pembroke (13 miles). Take B4139 south to St Petrox and follow local signs to Bosherston (5 miles). Continue south to St Govan's Chapel on coast (1 mile).

St Govan's Chapel, St Govan's Head, Pembrokeshire – a classic example of a sacred landscape

The chapel here is probably sixth-century and therefore the oldest in Wales. St Govan was an Irishman, a former abbot who late in his life, c.580, came to these parts to retire as a hermit. While walking along the cliffs he was attacked by a band of thieves. Falling to his knees in terror, he prayed for help. Instantly the cliff opened and he was swallowed up by the rocks as the thieves fled in amazement. The split in the rocks is still there, and right across it is the primitive chapel. It is a place of immense power – a devout place, a place of hardships made beautiful by age and simplicity. Here is a classic example of a sacred landscape.

St Ishmael's

The next stop lies on the opposite side of the channel leading to the port at Milford Haven. Return north to Pembroke (6 miles). Join A477 heading north and cross the water by the toll bridge, taking B4325 to Milford Haven (6 miles). Continue west following local signs via Herbrandston and Sandy Haven to St Ishmael's (about 6 miles).

St Ishmael's was founded by a disciple of St Teilo in the sixth century, and near the village is a very tall standing stone of Neolithic date. Was St Ishmael drawn here by older religious practices and a sense of the holy? Here too lived the Celtic St Caradoc, a sort of St Swithun of Wales whose stories always seem to involve heavy rain and miraculously dry saints.

ST DAVID'S · PEMBROKESHIRE

This is the end of the pilgrims' route. This remote and smallest of cathedral cities, Twyddewi in Welsh, was such a long way from anywhere that two pilgrimages here equaled a pilgrimage to Rome. Yet many kings and queens came here, for St David (St Dewi in Welsh) is of course the patron saint of Wales. To be ruler of Wales, you need his blessing.

ST DAVID

Dewi came here c.550. His mother was said to be St Non, to whom a number of churches are dedicated. St Patrick is supposed to have been told of the birth of Dewi and asked not to set up a monastery where St David's now stands, because it was reserved for a special man.

When he had taken his vows as a monk, Dewi set off on his travels. He is credited with the founding of twelve monasteries, from Crowland in Lincolnshire to Leominster in Hereford and Worcester, and of course here at St David's, known in his time as Mynyw. He also visited Bath, where he was cured of illness, and built a church at Glastonbury. In southern Wales, Devon, Cornwall and Brittany many churches of great age are dedicated to him: there are fifty in South Wales alone. His church became the center of ecclesiastical authority throughout South Wales and then further as his reputation grew. St David's and the surrounding area are full of places made sacred by his presence or those of the saints around him. From his mother's chapel and the delightful St Non's Well, just ten minutes' walk south of the city on the coast, to the chapel of St Justinian, his confessor, opposite Ramsey Island, this is the kind of sacred landscape that only Wales can produce.

A modern statue of St David, the Patron of Wales – portrayed as a bishop in eucharistic vestments

St Dewi's remains still lie in the cathedral built by the dominant Norman bishops. Beside him lie St Caradoc and many other saints. Here too is the vast medieval bishops' palace, symbol of a lifestyle which Dewi would have denounced as un-Christian, for it was built to display power and wealth, not austerity and humility. Dewi was a fine orator – hence the dove, the emblem of the eloquence of the Holy Spirit, often shown on his shoulder.

All around this area are holy wells, and the cathedral had some until the mid-nineteenth-century restoration. Like so many of the Celtic saints, Dewi chose a place beside a river where he could baptize, with wells for healing. Unfortunately, when vast cathedrals were erected to emphasize temporal power, if they were in marshy grounds they sank or toppled. To prevent such costly embarrassment the practical Victorians drained the land – and in the process finished off the holy wells.

A mighty church, buttressed against sinking on land where a saint passed his austere life! Religious history is full of such paradoxes. Stand here a while, beside the flowing stream, and think of the simplicity at the heart of all religions.

SCOTLAND

CHAPTER 17

◦◦◦◦◦◦◦◦◦◦◦◦◦◦◦◦◦◦◦◦◦ ෨ *◦◦◦◦◦◦◦◦◦◦◦◦◦◦◦◦◦◦◦◦◦*

Gretna to Lindisfarne

Stand and see
At the harvest of time,
That as we build in the light
Your Will shall be done

And in the temple between us
That is a ruin of light,
That is a man and a woman
Made of naked light

WEAVING ALONGSIDE the M6 motorway through the Cumbrian countryside is the railway, so that the modern traveler from England approaches Scotland surrounded by the clatter of machinery. A small burn delineates the Border between two ancient rivals "where Sark runs to the Solway Sands and Tweed runs to the Ocean, to mark where England's province stands," as the old song proclaimed which lamented the Union of Parliaments between Scotland and England in 1707. But for all its many inequalities the resulting alliance enabled the island to resist Napoleon, Kaiser Wilhelm and Hitler, and it brought peace to a landscape that had endured a millennium and more of war between Celt and Anglo-Saxon.

Obviously a single chapter in a book can only glance at a nation's perception of the sacred, but it should be enough to whet the appetite. It will be a journey of discovery and in many ways a journey through time. Generations before us shaped this land and held in awe all that was sacred before machinery drowned out the echo of the ages.

From Lovers at Gretna Green to Monks at Lindisfarne

Main Route (840 miles/1343 km):
GRETNA · HODDAM · RUTHWELL ·
DUMFRIES · NEW ABBEY · KIRKCUDBRIGHT ·
CAIRNHOLY · WIGTOWN · WHITHORN ·
GLASGOW · OLD KILPATRICK · IONA ·
INVERNESS · FORRES · BRECHIN ·
ARBROATH · SCONE · ST ANDREWS ·
DUNFERMLINE · STIRLING · EDINBURGH ·
LINDISFARNE

GRETNA · DUMFRIES AND GALLOWAY

The most southerly town in Scotland to fly the saltire of St Andrew, Galilean fisherman and companion of Jesus, is Gretna. It is an undistinguished huddle of brick buildings that sprouted during the First World War to house workers in the great munitions factories that were sited nearby. Before the coming of the railways Gretna had been just a village providing coaching inns and fresh horses for travelers between Scotland and England.

GRETNA GREEN

One of the clauses in the Treaty of Union insisted that Scotland retain its own legal system, which differed substantially from English law. Under Scots law, for instance, people could get married at a younger age without parental consent than was possible in England. As a result Gretna Green, the first settlement over the border, gained a certain notoriety as regular stagecoaches brought eloping couples from the south to be married. The traditional Gretna marriage ceremony was conducted by the village blacksmith in between shoeing horses, the clang of hammer on anvil being the sign that the exchange of simple vows before witnesses had bound the man and woman in marriage.

Gretna today is not a peaceful spot. The roar of the M74 fills the air and buses bring tourists in the hundreds to tramp around the modern marriage factories. The road to the west follows the northern Solway shore into the wide lands of Dumfries and Galloway, but to the north is a strange flat-topped hill – and to find that hill the traveler has to persist with a few more miles on the motorway.

Gretna to Hoddam (12 miles/19 km): *Take M74 N to Ecclefechan, then B725 W*

HODDAM · DUMFRIES AND GALLOWAY

ST MUNGO

Wooded hills rise above the river and enclose a meadow which was once home to an early Christian community whose sixth-century bishop was Mungo of Glasgow. Hoddam was renowned for centuries until the Vikings silenced its litanies in the ninth century. An early baptistry with Roman-style plaster, brick and mosaic was recently excavated here.

Behind Hoddam bridge is Repentance Hill, dominated by a strong

THE ROMAN OCCUPATION OF BRITAIN

The legions of Rome did not find the pacification of Britain an easy task. Only in the south and east did they establish civilian government. In Wales, west of the Pennines and southern Scotland the countryside remained under military rule. In the second century AD the Emperor Hadrian ordered a defensive wall to be built from the Tyne to the Solway in an attempt to control and monitor the movements of the northern tribes. The Emperor Antonine ordered a similar enterprise to span and control central Scotland between the Firths of Clyde and Forth. Occasional campaigns brought the legions into the Highland fringes, but by the third century they had been forced back to Hadrian's Wall. However, the influence of Rome on the people of southern Scotland remained considerable.

square tower which served as an outlier for Hoddam Castle in the valley. Small towers like this are scattered throughout the Scottish countryside as a legacy from those centuries which endured incessant brutal incursions from the south.

Ancient stories give an interesting origin for Repentance Hill. In the fifth century AD the Roman occupiers were overwhelmed by barbarian invaders from northern Germany and Denmark. However, in the western and northern districts under military administration the native tribes had maintained their warlike instincts. From Cornwall, Wales and west along the Pennines into southern Scotland the Roman-influenced Celts delivered hammer blows against the newcomers. These leaders continued the successful defense of the west and north against the new and growing power of the east and south and kept Christianity alive.

King Roderick of Strathclyde was one of these leaders. In the second half of the sixth century he ruled a kingdom which stretched from Glasgow into the Cumbrian mountains, and maintained a powerful alliance with the princes of Wales. When King Roderick came to visit his friend Mungo at Hoddam, so great was the crowd of people gathered to witness this momentous event that the ground swelled beneath the two men's feet to raise them up so that the people could see and hear them. This, goes the legend, is how Repentance Hill came to be.

Here is an old place of faith. Stand a while and recall those who, in a dark hour of invasion and destruction, bore witness to the life and love which the Christian gospels bring and the civilization which springs from such faith.

Hoddam to Ruthwell (9 miles/14 km): *Go back E along B725 to junction with B723, go S to Annan and join B724 W*

RUTHWELL · DUMFRIES AND GALLOWAY

RUTHWELL CROSS

Near the Brow Well (see p. 248) in the little village of Ruthwell is one of the most remarkable survivals from the early Christian centuries. Ruthwell Cross is now sheltered under the roof of the parish kirk, but it once stood sentinel over the Solway marshlands. It was placed there in the Golden Age of the kingdom of Northumbria during the eighth century, the time when the Venerable Bede wrote his history of the English people. Mungo of Hoddam and Bede of Northumbria were separated by two centuries that had transformed the life of Britain: the invaders of northern England confronted by Roderick in the sixth century had gradually been converted to Christianity by Celtic missionaries.

Ruthwell Cross is a stylistic hybrid incorporating Celtic and Germanic motifs, and on it is inscribed the oldest fragment of written English from the saga of the "Dream of the Cross," an eighth-century mystic poem:

I was reared up a rood
I raised the great King,
liege-lord of the heavens . . .
They drove me through with dark nails:
On me the deep wounds manifest,
wide-mouthed hate-dents . . .
I was all moist with blood
sprung from the Man's side
after he sent forth his soul.

Stand here and reflect on how much blood has been shed by those frightened of the other, of those who were not the same. And think of how men and women of faith have gone into the violence and terror of warfare in order to bring enemies together by recognizing their common humanity. Today the same witness by Christians, Buddhists, Jews, Hindus, Muslims and others continues. Pray for them and for all peacemakers.

Northumbrian overlordship over south-western Scotland was short-lived and ended in the ninth century when the Vikings brought their terror to end the generations of peace which Bede recorded. The Ruthwell Cross stands as a reminder that Scotland and England were not always at

each other's throats, and that times of peace rebuilt what wars destroyed.

THE BROW WELL

A mile to the east of Ruthwell is the Brow Well, whose reputation as a place of healing pre-dates the Christian era. Much of the region round about is pastoral and gentle, the landscape which Robert Burns described and cherished. During his last month of life the poet visited the Solway shore to drink from the waters of the Brow Well.

> **Ruthwell to Dumfries (11 miles/18 km):**
> *Take B724 N and join A75 to Dumfries*

DUMFRIES · DUMFRIES AND GALLOWAY

The warm red sandstone buildings of the town cluster around the bridges over the River Nith. In previous centuries Dumfries grew on a hog back of dry ground surrounded by impenetrable marshlands. These natural defenses and the moated walls of Caerlaverock Castle at the estuary of the Nith with the Solway enabled Dumfries to remain a safe refuge.

Just upstream from the town, Nithsdale narrows as steep hills draw closer. At Newbridge is one of the most spectacular stone circles in Scotland, and beyond it the wild district of Holywood, reputed to have been an important center of druid learning that rivaled the famous community on the Isle of Man. The Isle of Man is named after the Celtic aspect of deity which personified the majesty of the oceans: Manannan was the equivalent of the Mediterranean Neptune. The northern flanks of Snaefell, the highest mountain on the island, open to reveal an oak-filled valley called Druidale. The wisdom of the druids of Manannan was famed through Britain, and dialogue along the tideways of the Solway was continual between Holywood and Druidale.

The patron saint of Dumfries is St Michael. His dedication was usually given to Christian communities which evolved at places which had been of importance to pre-Christian cults.

Dumfries to New Abbey (7 miles/11 km): *Take A710 S*

NEW ABBEY · DUMFRIES AND GALLOWAY

SWEETHEART ABBEY

Following the coast south and west from Dumfries around the flanks of Criffel a traveler comes on the beautiful red sandstone ruins of Sweetheart Abbey. The name records a political marriage of convenience which blossomed into a romance whose fame has survived the centuries. Devorgilla was a princess of the long and illustrious line of semi-independent Celtic lords of Galloway. In the thirteenth century the Scottish kings were determined to impose their authority on Galloway, and insisted that Devorgilla marry a Norman baron called John Balliol. The lovers, as they became, were buried at Sweetheart Abbey with Devorgilla clutching the embalmed heart of her husband. For friendship to blossom out of enmity is sweet, and

THE ORIGIN OF THE CELTS

The stone circles, standing stones and burial mounds which dot the landscape of Britain are the legacy of the Neolithic farmers from long before Egypt raised the pyramids. Clouds of volcanic dust or some other disaster then emptied the land of the people who built them. When the climate improved again the north was repopulated. Alongside the people of the Atlantic coastlines who again moved north appeared newcomers who had traveled west along the Danube and the Rhine. These were the forefathers of the Celts, who were noted for their reckless bravery. The Greeks record meeting a band of roving Celts and asking them what they feared most. Without hesitation the foreigners replied that they were most afraid of the sky falling on their heads. Was this a folk memory of a volcanic disaster which had forced people to move to the Scottish Borders from the Caspian Sea?

to reinforce this memory of happiness and laughter every gargoyle at the abbey wears a smile. In the words of the poet George MacLeod:

> Patient lover give us love:
> till every shower of rain speaks of
>   Thy forgiveness
> till every storm assures us that we
>   company with Thee:
> and every move of light and shadow speaks
>   of grave and resurrection:
> to assure us that we cannot die:
> Thou creating, redeeming and sustaining God.

Beyond Criffel the shore of the Solway changes from sand to rugged cliffs that drive the roads inland to offer only occasional glimpses of the sea. However, proposals are under way to develop coastal footpaths for travelers on foot. The law on trespass differs between England and Scotland. In England trespass is a criminal offense, but as a result every parish has a network of recognized footpaths and bridleways. In Scotland trespass is a civil matter and the right to wander the hills is a cherished freedom. However, unlike England there are few signposted and maintained rights of way. So when farmers put up wire fences across the Lowlands, access is severely limited. To remedy this situation, with the encouragement of WWF, UK and inspired by the earlier traditions of pilgrimage, the *Whithorn Pilgrim Way* was opened in 1993 and further extensions are planned. From the ruined abbey at Glenluce, the route crosses open countryside to Whithorn. From Whithorn, the route goes in a circle to the Isle of Whithorn and to St Ninian's Cave, 3¹/₂ miles south of Whithorn (see p. 252).

New Abbey to Kirkcudbright (36 miles/58 km): *Follow A710 to Dalbeattie, then continue on A711*

KIRKCUDBRIGHT · DUMFRIES AND GALLOWAY

The name Kirkcudbright means "church of Cuthbert" and commemorates the great Bishop of Lindisfarne from seventh-century Northumbria. There are few visible remains of early Christianity in Kirkcudbright, though "an ancient church of rock and stone" is referred to in a twelfth-century document on the life of St Cuthbert. In 793, the *Anglo-Saxon Chronicle* recorded, "the ravaging of heathen men destroyed God's Church at Lindisfarne through brutal robbery and slaughter." Northumbrian monks fled the eastern coastlands and brought with them Cuthbert's remains, which for a while found refuge in Kirkcudbright.

Scattered offshore are the Isles of Fleet. Ardwall island is the largest and can be reached on foot at low tide. Celtic clerics loved the isolation of islands, and the earliest Christian community of Whithorn maintained dwellings and a church here when Mungo was at Hoddam.

Kirkcudbright to Cairnholy (15 miles/24 km): *Take A755 W, then A75 to Kirkdale. Cairnholy is to N*

CAIRNHOLY · DUMFRIES AND GALLOWAY

The Galloway mountains sweep down to the shore between Gatehouse and Creetown, and on a high bluff between sea and mountains stands Cairnholy. This was a communal burial place and hallowed sanctuary in the Neolithic and Bronze Ages. It is well worth the visit today for the spectacular views to the south and west. On a clear day the Cumbrian mountains and the ridges of the Isle of Man are both visible, while to the west a long finger of gently undulating hills stretches south – the Machars of Wigtownshire.

Cairnholy to Wigtown (17 miles/27 km): *Continue on A75 and turn S on to A714 outside Newton Stewart*

WIGTOWN · DUMFRIES AND GALLOWAY

On a round hill at the head of Wigtown Bay is the royal burgh of Wigtown, sister to Whithorn (see next page). In the seventeenth century Royalist officials here attempted to terrorize Scottish country people into abandoning their Presbyterian convictions. Many were tortured and executed, while others were sent to the Caribbean to work as slaves on the sugar plantations.

The Machars are the cradle of literacy for all Scotland. In many ways this quiet, seagirt finger of land can claim also to be the cradle of liberty because of the bravery of Galloway's stubborn Presbyterians.

In so many parts of the world people are suffering for their beliefs. Hold these people in your thoughts and prayers. Stand here and be still. Stand alongside those whose faith is costly and reach out to them in their hour of need, through silence, prayer and perhaps – through Amnesty International – by action.

Wigtown to Whithorn (10 miles/16 km): *Take A714 S, then A746*

WHITHORN · DUMFRIES AND GALLOWAY

ST NINIAN

At the tip of the long peninsula of the Machars is the royal and ancient burgh of Whithorn. In the fourth and fifth centuries, when Roman civilization faltered elsewhere, Ninian established here the first Christian community in the north. Here the knowledge of the past, Hebrew, Greek and Latin, fused with a new vision of how to live in a community, fed by the spirituality of the Celts and of Christianity. Learning and literacy survived and spread out to the rest of the north. Whithorn was called the Shining Place, and missionaries educated here traveled to the north of Scotland, the east of Ireland, Wales and Brittany.

The cave that was home to St Ninian near Whithorn, Dumfries and Galloway

At a time when civilized life throughout Europe was collapsing amid the chaos of barbarian invasions, Ninian preached love, mercy and forgiveness. He rejected the concepts of vengeance and bloody vendetta for, as Gandhi notably said, "an eye for an eye makes the whole world blind." In the late twentieth and early twenty-first centuries, with environmental collapse confronting us as it did England at the end of the Roman period, the future holds unknown terrors. The example of Ninian and his followers at this earliest Christian center in northern Europe should give us the courage and hope to face that future.

The shingle shore beside Ninian's cave is worn smooth by the continual attentions of tide and wave. As you approach the lonely hermitage of the saint, look for a pebble or rock with veins of silica forming a cross. It is a good tradition to take such a stone to the cave and leave it as a memory of a murmured prayer.

> **Whithorn to Glasgow (coast route 105 miles/170 km; inland route 95 miles/150 km):** *For coast route, take A746 and A747 NW to Glenluce, then turn on to A75 W toward Stranraer. Just before Stranraer follow signs for A77 and continue up coast via Girvan, Maybole and Kilmarnock to Glasgow. For inland route, retrace road to Wigtown, take A714 to Newton Stewart, then A714 to Girvan and pick up coast route*

GALLOWAY'S FORESTS

Inland Galloway has the highest concentration of forest in Britain. North from Newton Stewart the road runs alongside the River Cree. The Wood of Cree on the eastern bank is one of the last survivors of the ancient oak forests, now a nature reserve that abounds in wildlife. From its freshwater source to the salt of Wigtown Bay the Cree flows through one of the least spoiled landscapes in Europe.

During the centuries before Ninian and Columba of Iona, the druids had no difficulty in finding their oak groves of thoughtfulness. Natural forests of oak, ash, birch and pine clothed the land, but as early as the fifteenth century the Scots Parliament was passing legislation to protect the remaining Lowland woodlands. Even so, by the seventeenth century much of the countryside was bereft of trees because of the demands of shipbuilding and the effects of sheep farming. The naked hills were exposed to the Atlantic storms, and unfenced cattle and sheep devoured any seedlings. In the 1690s famine came to a land stripped of its trees when fields of barley and oats were flattened. It has been estimated that the population of Lowland Scotland was reduced by a third, and it was this context of famine which ushered in the Union with England and Wales of 1707.

CROSSRAGUEL ABBEY
From Turnberry take A77 and follow local signs

The teaching of Jesus emphasized the needs of the poor, and the early

Church taught the same. However, inland from Culzean stand the ruins of Crossraguel Abbey, founded in 1244. Kennedys from Culzean roasted a sixteenth-century abbot of Crossraguel on an iron grid until he consented to sign away the abbey lands to his rapacious neighbors.

Offshore lies the island of Arran with its adjoining Holy Island, now a base for Tibetan Buddhist teaching (see p. 290).

GLASGOW

Beyond Fenwick Moor, Clydesdale opens out to reveal the panorama of Glasgow with its Highland backdrop. In 1707 it was a university town of ten thousand inhabitants who clustered around the fine medieval cathedral dedicated to St Mungo. By 1807 Glasgow had grown into a city of one hundred thousand that traded with America for sugar and tobacco. By

1907 it was the second city of the Empire, with a population of a million who smelted iron and steel to build steam locomotives and ships for every ocean on the planet.

When Burns was a boy nine out of ten Scots lived in the "fermtouns" of the countryside. By 1907 the ratio had been reversed. The industrial revolution that caused Glasgow to grow a hundredfold changed the face not just of Scot-land but of the world.

Mungo called Glasgow his "dear green place." In the age of steam the city was black with coal grime. A new city has emerged that is brighter and washed clean, but a generation of unemployment has blighted too many lives.

Glasgow Cathedral, photographed from the necropolis, the town's ancient burial place

GLASGOW CATHEDRAL
Off Castle St

The present structure, with its original tower and spire intact, dates back to the thirteenth century and houses the tomb of St Mungo in the Lower Church. (The cathedral is in fact made up of two churches. The Lower Church, under the east end, is the second church.) The cathedral towered over the small city of 1707, but today it is dwarfed by the plate glass, steel and concrete of the world of commerce. After the Reformation many of Scotland's great medieval churches were left to molder, a handy source of building materials. But this was not the case in Glasgow, whose citizens cherished their cathedral. This hallowed site, chosen so legend says by a miracle, offers architectural and religious imagery which captures Scotland's turbulent history from Catholicism to Reform and beyond.

A steep hill rises above the Clyde beside the great survivor: this is the necropolis, the ancient burial place of Glasgow. Merchants and industrialists in the eighteenth and nineteenth centuries built grandiose monuments for themselves that were considerably more lavish than the huddled tenements of their workers.

Beside Mungo's cathedral there is a magnificent museum of religion (see also p. 291). Artifacts from every part of the globe and from every religious tradition speak of the yearning of the human soul for understanding. "What is truth?" asked Pilate of Jesus. It is a perennial question.

Glasgow to Old Kilpatrick (10 miles/16 km): *Go NW on A82*

OLD KILPATRICK · WEST DUMBARTONSHIRE

Downstream the Clyde widens into its firth, and the road for the Atlantic coast of Argyll passes the old town of Kilpatrick before the great rock of Dumbarton. Kilpatrick is reputed to have been the childhood home of Patrick, the apostle of Ireland. Dumbarton was the fortress of the Britons and the heart of the kingdom of Strathclyde, where the Celtic people of southern Scotland spoke a form of Welsh and not the more sibilant Gaelic of Ireland.

Old Kilpatrick to Iona (97 miles/155 km): *Take A82 N from Kilpatrick through Tarbet to Crianlarich. Take A85 W to Oban. From Oban take ferry to Craignure (Mull) and follow signs to Iona ferry*

LOCH LOMOND

"The bonnie bonnie banks of Loch Lomond" have been made famous in song. The road for Iona soon brings you to the loch, and from there to Crianlarich and past Loch Awe and Loch Etive to the ferry at Oban. Off Mull's western extremity is the island of Iona, which has had as great an influence on the life of Scotland as the Shining Place of Ninian. Iona was the ecclesiastical heart of the western Highlands, but the contemporary kings of Argyll had their headquarters at the hill fort of Dunadd.

From Tarbert on Loch Lomond the road for Crinan and Dunadd (A83) rises up a pass whose summit is well-named "Rest and Be Thankful." It then follows the sheltered fjord of Loch Fyne. From Inverary Castle the great Dukes of Argyll dominated the south-western Highlands: the name of Campbell carried as much authority as that of Kennedy in southern Ayrshire. At the Reformation the Campbells embraced Protestantism. As a consequence, the earliest printed as opposed to manuscript example of the Gaelic language consists of the Psalms and New Testaments which the Duke of Argyll commissioned at the instigation of the Reformers.

THE IRISH IN SCOTLAND

Across the waters is Ireland, whose inhabitants have had no less turbulent a history than that of their Celtic cousins in Scotland. Cymric (Welsh-speaking) and Gaelic Celts struggled for supremacy in both countries. By the sixth century, the time of Columba, the Gaels were in the ascendant in Ireland, and only in Down and Antrim, facing Galloway, was Cymric still heard among the Irish Picts.

From the fourth century AD, when Irish immigrants began to colonize the west coast, until 845 when Kenneth MacAlpine moved to Scone to rule the Picts also, the mighty hill fort of Dunadd had been the heart of the kingdom of the Scots. It wielded great authority and could summon warriors and fleets of swift boats, but another authority grew to rival that of the warlords of Dunadd.

IONA · ARGYLL AND BUTE

Straddling the tideways of the Hebrides, Iona can seem remote from mainland life; but before the days of metaled roads people traveled by sea, and Iona was central to life on the entire western seaboard of Scotland. Druids came here to escape the persecutions of Imperial Rome and founded a

THE STONE OF DESTINY

Eastern Ulster is separated from the rest of Ireland by Lough Neagh and the wide River Bann. Ancient legends have it that in the sixth century BC two princesses from Jerusalem arrived on the shore of the lough with Phoenician traders. An army from Babylon had captured their city and the princesses had fled west and north to preserve the royal line. They brought with them one of the great talismans of their people, a stone called Jacob's Pillow on which the old patriarch of the Jews had dreamed of angels descending and ascending. This legend insists that Jacob's Pillow became the Stone of Destiny upon which kings of a line originating with David and Solomon were inaugurated to rule over the lands around Lough Neagh.

The pressures of war in Ireland caused this dynasty to establish a colony over the narrow waters in the peninsulas, islands and fjords of Argyll. So it was that the Stone of Destiny eventually came to Scotland.

In 1296 the English took the stone south, a symbol of their suppression of the Scots. For many centuries it rested beneath the coronation chair in Westminster Abbey and was known as the Stone of Scone. Recently it has been returned to Scotland and is now in Edinburgh Castle.

library. A Christian cemetery was also established on Iona before 540 and used as a royal burial ground.

In 563 a boatload of refugees arrived here from Ireland. Their leader, Columba, was a descendant of the High Kings of Ireland. Through his actions, a terrible civil war had broken out in Ireland. Columba was banished and accepted this as his punishment. He came to Iona to start a new life and to make amends for the deaths he had caused in Ireland. A Christian priest, he founded a community whose influence reverberated throughout the north of Scotland for generations. Columba called Christ his "archdruid." He loved the world of nature and saw it as a parable for the majesty and love of God the Creator. The tangible atmosphere of God's presence rings out today in every acre of Iona, from shimmering white sand beaches to flower-strewn pasture and rocky promontories and hills.

Columba died in 597, and the achievements of his lifetime ensured that the Gaelic colony of Argyll was not destroyed by the Picts of the north or the people of Strathclyde. As the Christian message of mercy, not vengeance, and peace, not war, spread among the tribes a common heritage and culture began to emerge. This was the legacy which Ninian, Mungo, Columba and countless unnamed others bequeathed to Scotland's future. Even the savage Vikings were tamed by Iona: their descendants mingled with the Celts and spoke the Gaelic language.

Once Kenneth MacAlpine had got the upper hand over the Scandinavian invaders he laid the foundations of a new Scotland, moving his headquarters from the vulnerable west coast to Scone in Perthshire. With him he took the Stone of Destiny, but the central role of Iona in establishing his dynasty resulted in generations of kings from Scotland, Ireland and Norway being taken to the small island at the heart of the Celtic Church for burial.

A little inland from the cathedral is the mound of Columba's cell. To the south are the site of his tomb and the ancient burial place of Scottish, Norse and Irish kings. Behind that is the hill of Dun I, the highest point on the island, which has a beautiful view of silver sand and translucent green sea pinpointed with a scattering of rocks and small islands. From here you can make your way south-west through the steep rocks of Cnoc Druidean, where druidic rituals were performed, to reach the Bay of the Coracle, where Columba first landed and above which he raised the Cairn-of-the-Back-to-Ireland when he decided to stay. Today, in solitude and quietness, explore the delight and awe of this place, knowing that on your pilgrimage you walk in the footsteps of the saints and sinners, plowmen and kings who came here before you.

THE NEW COMMUNITY

Only the residents of Iona are allowed motor vehicles on the island; visitors' cars have to be left on Mull before the half-mile trip over crystal waters to the island of kings. A small village clusters around the white beaches beside the jetty. A ruined nunnery stands beside the road to the abbey, founded as a Benedictine house in the twelfth century by St Margaret, and the nearby Cathedral of the Isles. A century ago the abbey was as ruined as the nunnery: the cathedral was restored by a Duke of Argyll at the beginning of this century, and the rebuilt abbey was the result of the life work of one of Scotland's most significant churchmen this century.

Inspired by the traditions of the earliest Celtic Church and depressed by the legacy of Calvinism and Roman Catholicism, the Very Rev Lord MacLeod of Fuinary established the renewed Iona Community in 1938. His avowed aim was to rebuild the abbey with the skills of unemployed people from Glasgow. This was to be in fulfillment of a prophecy by Columba that "where once there was the singing of monks there shall only be the lowing of cattle, but before the world comes to its end things shall be as they were." Lord MacLeod lived to a grand old age and the prophecy has been fulfilled. The Iona Community has worked since its inception to bridge the gulf between Protestant and Catholic. A vibrant life of worship is sustained, and a theology of social concern and environmental aware-ness has brought new life to waters that were becoming stagnant.

Both abbey and cathedral have quiet chapels, but perhaps the loveliest spot is the tiny chapel associated with St Columba at the west door to the cathedral. It is shadowed by the St John's Cross and the St Martin's Cross, which stand as tall as that at Ruthwell. The tiny late eighth-century inte-rior has an atmosphere that has brought blessing to countless thousands. Inside are the echoes of the ancestors and the message of grace from Nazareth. Echoes from infinity abound and, in Oscar Wilde's words, "Love can read the writing on the furthest star."

Every Wednesday there is a pilgrimage around the island, but no trav-eler who is fit enough should leave without climbing to the top of Dun I and surveying the Hebrides. Just below the summit is the Well of Youth. Drink from it and remember the traditions which attributed healing and renewal to these waters. Iona was considered a holy place where the veil between the mortal and the eternal was gossamer-thin, even before Columba and his companions arrived.

> Deep peace of the running wave
> Deep peace of the flowing air
> Deep peace of the shining stars
> Deep peace of the quiet earth
> Deep peace of the Prince of Peace
>   to you and yours.

Kneel here, or stand, alongside the saints who still fill this place. Iona came to be because of pride and foolishness. Columba arrived here in dis-grace from Ireland after a bloody battle which he precipitated. From this, and from his remorse, rose the wonder that was and is Iona. In your own life you will have things of which you are not proud. Here God meets you, and takes from you the burdens you carry. Let holy Columba take your hand and lead you to a new start, a new way forward. Allow yourself, in this sacred place, to be touched by forgiveness.

Iona to Inverness (128 miles/206 km): *Return to Oban by ferry. Out of Oban follow signs to Crianlarich on A85, then take A828 and A82 to Fort William and continue on A82 to Inverness*

LISMORE

The ferry from Mull to Oban passes the low green island of Lismore, which was once a powerful center of Celtic spirituality where the earliest bishops of Argyll lived. In the middle of the island stands a modest rough-cast, slate-roofed church whose stones were laid on foundations that survived the Vikings of the ninth and tenth centuries. Columba was Abbot of Iona, but he was never consecrated a bishop and could not ordain priests. That honor fell to his friend Moluag, and Lismore, sheltered in the Firth of Lorne, was the Bishop's Isle.

NEOLITHIC REMAINS IN A STERN LANDSCAPE

The mainland ranges rise higher than Ben More on Mull and include the mountains of Glencoe and Ben Nevis, the tallest peak in Britain. Another great geological fault line drives north-east from Ben Nevis to Inverness. The land to the north of the Great Glen which formed along the fault is quite distinct from the rest of Scotland. It is even more thinly populated than the southern Highlands, and lunar ranges of rocky mountains rise up out of wide miles of peat and marsh with plantations of conifers in more sheltered locations. Ferries from Ullapool and Thurso link the archipelagoes of the Outer Hebrides and Orkneys with the mainland. Ships for distant Shetland sail from the more southerly docks of Aberdeen.

Four thousand years ago the climate of northern Britain was more benign, and during the Neolithic and Bronze Ages there were considerable communities of farmers in the coastlands and the islands. At Callanish in Lewis and Brodgar in Orkney they built magnificent stone circles to rival Stonehenge (see Chapter 2).

In these northern latitudes the Aurora Borealis – the Northern Lights in the sky – is often seen. Despite the rational explanations of science, the handiwork of God can still astonish the soul as the fire of the heavens reaches out over the huge landscape and the tiny lives of humans.

INVERNESS · HIGHLAND

Swift new roads lead from the west to Inverness at the head of the Great Glen. Little of any antiquity remains of the town's religious past. Perhaps the lone pillar of the friars' Burying Ground, site of the Dominican priory

THE HIGHLAND CLEARANCES

After the defeat of Bonnie Prince Charlie, the Stuart claimant to the British throne, at the bloody battle of Culloden in 1746, the British embarked on a deliberate policy of clearing the Highlands of his supporters. The introduction of sheep further depleted the native forests, and eventually the new sheep ranches were bought up by wealthy Victorians for sporting estates. So began a diaspora of the Scottish people as thorough as any endured by the Jews.

The peasants of the Lowlands endured the famine that drove so many to the new industrial cities such as Glasgow and many more to America, Canada, Australia and elsewhere. The peasants of Ireland suffered the same after their Potato Famine, but the Highlanders suffered first military defeat and then forced evictions. The unnatural emptiness of the Highlands is history's rebuke to the present.

of 1233 which later became a burial ground, speaks of the changes the Reformation brought. North of Inverness is the Black Isle, so called because when winter brings snow to blanket the mountains the lowlands of the Black Isle often remained free of whiteness.

THE ORKNEY ISLANDS

Further north still, the Orkneys came under the domination of Norway in the ninth century and Scandinavian emigrants settled there in great numbers. Their initial interest in Christianity was limited to the loot they took from the defenseless monasteries and unarmed monks. However, just like their Anglo-Saxon cousins who had earlier settled in England, the faith and gentle courage that they encountered among Celtic clerics began the long process of conversion.

Magnus, Earl of Orkney, shared power with his cousin Earl Hakon. However, Magnus was no Viking war leader but a devout Christian who loved peace and scholarship. Hakon wanted to wield sole power in Orkney, and on Easter Sunday 1116 Magnus was murdered. In the centuries that followed he became patron saint of the islands in the eyes of the people. This prayer to the saint illustrated the devotion in which he was held: "O Magnus of my love, thou it is who would guide us. Remember us, thou saint of power who did encompass and protect the people. . . . Lift our flocks to the hills, quell the wolf and the fox, ward from us, specter, giant, fury and oppression."

At Dornoch, Fortrose, Tain and Portmahomack there were great ecclesiastical centers which had their origin when the Picts were free of Gaelic overlords and Inverness was capital of a powerful Pictish kingdom. The influence of Gaelic Iona never grew in the far north until Kenneth MacAlpine united the Picts and Scots in the ninth century in an attempt to drive back the Vikings. Dedications to Ninian of Whithorn in the far north-east illustrate that the earliest evangelists were from the south and not the Hebrides.

The great Christian site is Kirkwall Cathedral, a powerful building of Norman design. But it is the pre-historic sites – see Chapter 2 – which are the greatest treasures of the Orkneys.

TAIN
On Dornoch Firth, reached via A9 N from Inverness

At Tain, some 30 miles north of Inverness, another saintly life made that burgh a center for pilgrimage. In 1065 a man called Duthac, whom the Irish called "primus Anamchara" or "the first among soul friends," died in Armagh. Duthac had been born in Tain and had a reputation as a great healer. After his death the church dedicated to his name became a place of pilgrimage.

Inverness to Forres (26 miles/42 km): *Take A96 E*

FORRES · MORAY

There is a tradition that the three witches whom Macbeth encountered met on the "blasted heath" outside this town. A more tangible survival from the past is the massive Sueno Stone, which dates from the time when the Gaels of Argyll imposed their dominance on the Picts in the late ninth century. A Christian cross is carved on it, chillingly accompanied by headless corpses and armed men. Sadly, the history of the Christian centuries is also that of the Church being appropriated by the powerful, who used Christian symbolism as a cloak to justify their brutality and to give respectability to the authority which they gained by force of arms.

Pictish stone,
The Manse,
Glamis, Angus

North-east Scotland contains hundreds of engraved Pictish standing stones. Deciphering their symbolism has exercised the minds of scholars but no consensus has emerged. One plausible theory insists that the stones tell the story of the rise of an indigenous Pictish Church that had developed independently of Iona. Outstanding examples are the Glamis Stone in Angus, the Rhynie Stone in Aberdeen and one at Abernethy on the Firth of Tay.

Forres to Brechin (114 miles/180 km): *Take A96 and A92 to Aberdeen, then continue S on A92 and at Stonehaven take A94 for Brechin*

BRECHIN · ANGUS

The city of Brechin was the center of the medieval diocese which embraced Angus and the eastern Grampians. Beside the restored cathedral rises a much older round tower, dating from the tenth century. There is only one other like it on mainland Scotland – at Abernethy on the Tay, once capital of the southern Picts. Round towers abound in Ireland, however, as a legacy from the centuries of their Celtic Church. When the Vikings attacked in order to loot monasteries the monks retreated to these round pencil towers.

Brechin to Arbroath (15 miles/24 km): *Take A933*

ARBROATH · ANGUS

In 1320 on the Angus coast at the great abbey of Arbroath a convocation of the Three Estates of Scotland was held. Gentry, churchmen and representatives of the people formulated the Declaration of Arbroath, which explained to the Pope why Scotland resisted English domination. Of paramount importance in the context of the feudal Middle Ages was the astonishing claim that sovereignty ultimately depends on the wishes of the people:

> The Divine Providence, the right of Succession by the Laws and Customs of the Kingdom of the Scots . . . which we will defend till death . . . and the due and lawful consent and assent of all the People, made Robert Bruce our King. To him we are obliged and resolved to

adhere in all things, both on account of his right and his own merit, as being the People's safety in defense of their Liberties.

But after all, if this Prince shall leave these principles he hath so nobly pursued, and consent that we or our Kingdom be subjected to the King or People of England, we will immediately endeavor to expel him as our enemy and as the subverter both of his own and our rights, and we will make another king, who will defend our Liberties; for so long as there remain but one hundred of us alive we will never subject ourselves to the domination of the English. For it is not glory, it is not riches, neither is it honors, but it is Liberty alone that we fight and contend for which no honest man will lose but with his life.

The Declaration of Arbroath was a forerunner of one of the foundation stones of modern international understanding, which insists that the self-determination of small nations against the imperial ambitions of large neighbors is a right upheld by the United Nations.

The battle of Bannockburn in 1314 left Scotland free of the English and made the Declaration of Arbroath more than empty words. There was an equivalent victory during an earlier epoch of Scotland's history. In 685 the English of Northumbria invaded the lands of the Picts but were decisively beaten at Nechtansmere in Angus. It was six centuries before English armies again threatened the north after this defeat, though sporadic warfare in the borderlands continued.

The Northumbrians had been converted to Christianity by Celtic missionaries, but in 664, at the Synod of Whitby, the Northumbrian Church decided to conform to the Roman Catholic understanding and practice of the faith. Had the English won at Nechtansmere the Roman Catholic Church would have been imposed on the people of the north. One of the results of Nechtansmere was the continuance of Celtic individuality.

The ruins of Arbroath Abbey are one of the wonders of Scotland – especially the magnificent circular window of the south side. St Vigean's Museum, just off the A92 in the north-west of the city, houses a superb collection of Pictish and Celtic sculptural stones.

Arbroath to Scone (40 miles/65 km): *Take A92 SW to Dundee, then A972 W and continue SW along A85 to Perth. Scone is on A93 just N of Perth*

FORTINGALL AND PONTIUS PILATE

N orth of Loch Tay and west of Aberfeldy is the village of Fortingall. Beside a venerable yew, one of the most ancient living things in all Europe (see p. 61), is a complete archaeological record of the inhabitants of Britain. Neolithic burial mounds and Bronze Age tumuli accompany stone circles, standing stones and Iron Age and medieval fortifications. The unusual Celtic rectangular site (circular defenses were more usual in those times) has long been known as the Praetorium, and lends credence to a strange and enigmatic legend.

Fortingall, according to the story, was the birthplace of Pontius Pilate: his mother was a Menzies from Balquidder and his father a Roman ambassador to northern Britain. Rome maintained diplomatic and trading links with peoples beyond the frontiers of the Empire, so it is possible that a diplomatic mission wintered at Fortingall where a Roman caught the eye of a local lady. Many associated legends claim that Pilate studied with the druids in Britain, and his question to Jesus, "What is truth?," was the core conundrum of druidic wisdom. The oldest regiment of the line in the British Army is the Royal Scots, who claim to be descended from Pontius Pilate's bodyguard. On that fateful day in Jerusalem was it men from distant Perthshire who scourged and mocked Jesus?

SCONE · PERTHSHIRE AND KINROSS

This was the first capital of the united Picts and Scots and the place where the Stone of Destiny was kept for centuries. Scone Abbey was one of the great ecclesiastical buildings of medieval Scotland, but in 1559 it was destroyed by Protestant revolutionaries who had been roused by the impassioned oratory of John Knox (see p. 267) against the Church of Rome. Little remains of the abbey, many of whose stones were used to build the neighboring Scone Palace. A small church built in 1624 stands beside the low mound of the Hill of Credulity, on which the ancient kings of Scotland were crowned sitting upon the Stone of Destiny (see p. 257).

Scone to St Andrews (35 miles/40 km): *Retrace route to Perth, then take A912 and A913 to Cupar and join A91 to St Andrews*

ST ANDREWS · FIFE

This ecclesiastical center grew to prominence after the Vikings had been tamed in the eleventh century, deriving its authority from relics thought to be those of St Andrew. It developed into a prosperous city with a huge cathedral and ancient university, and became the major pilgrimage center in north-western Europe (see also p. 58).

Saintly relics were thought to be a key which opened up the possibility of heavenly dialogue, and no key was more powerful than the remains of the apostles who had known the living Jesus of Nazareth. In the early Middle Ages the story was circulated that relics of St Andrew had been carried to the shores of Fife. It is possible that wandering monks, perhaps fleeing the advance of Islam in Egypt, arrived in Scotland with precious relics of the apostle, but another interpretation for the growth of the cult of St Andrew in Scotland is that it was linked to the gradual Romanizing of Celtic Christianity. Andrew, the brother of Peter whose authority was appropriated by the bishops of Rome, was to eclipse the authority of native saints like Columba and Duthac who had been wayward in conforming to continental Christian practice.

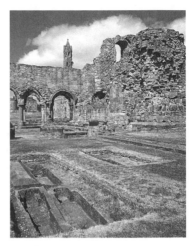

The ruins of the Chapter House at St Andrews, Fife – once a major pilgrimage center

Reformers such as Martin Luther and John Calvin in the sixteenth century denounced the cult of saints and the veneration of bodily remains which were often of doubtful authenticity. They urged their followers to cleanse church buildings of the entire paraphernalia of these cults. After decades of brutal suppression the Protestant Reformation in Scotland burst out in fury. The cathedral of St Andrew was sacked in 1559 and left to crumble into dereliction. On a promontory above a small harbor which once received pilgrim ships from Scandinavia, Germany and the Low Countries stand the roofless remains of the cathedral whose nave was as large as that of Canterbury.

Stand here and reflect on how easily violence can destroy beauty but also how easily religion can become nothing but empty gestures.

JOHN KNOX

Ninian, Mungo, Patrick and Columba have been encountered on this journey, but several centuries later John Knox changed the religious life of Scotland as profoundly as any of them. He was one of a band of Protestant revolutionaries who in 1546 assassinated the Archbishop of St Andrews, who had been responsible for burning many Protestant "heretics" – those who had preached on the need for vernacular scripture and worship. Knox and his friends retreated to St Andrew's Castle where, after a long siege, they were handed over to the French. Most of Knox's friends died as slaves on the French galleys. Knox himself survived, though severely traumatized. He later spearheaded a popular movement in Lowland Scotland which ended the alliance with Catholic France and forged links with the embattled Protestant regime of Elizabeth Tudor in Wales and England. In so doing he laid the foundations for the Union of Crowns in 1603.

The Reformation in Scotland was a kinder process than it was in England. Monks were allowed to grow old in peace and were awarded pensions. Many clerics of the old order adapted to circumstances and abandoned Latin liturgies for worship in the vernacular. Above all there was a thirst for learning, so that ordinary men, women and children could become literate and read for themselves scripture translated into the vernacular. John Knox may have urged his followers to "cast doon" the relics of saints and destroy monastic buildings, but he and his friends aimed to give every parish a maintained school and every burgh an academy; Scotland had universities in Glasgow, Edinburgh, St Andrews and Aberdeen when much larger England had only two. The world of the intellect was opened to countless Scots as a result of the Reformation; it is a proud legacy and one which has changed the world for the better.

St Andrews to Dunfermline (34 miles/54 km): *Take A915 and join A92 N of Dysart. Take A907 into Dunfermline*

DUNFERMLINE · FIFE

Standing above the shores of the Firth of Forth, Dunfermline was home to a woman who in her day changed the religious life of Scotland as much as Knox did in his.

QUEEN MARGARET

Margaret, descended from King Alfred of England and raised in Hungary, married Malcolm Canmore, the vanquisher of Macbeth, in the second half of the eleventh century. She made it her life's work to bring the native Christian traditions of Scottish Christianity into conformity with the Roman Catholic continental mainstream. For this she was canonized as the blessed St Margaret. Her children continued this process, and wide lands were granted to Benedictine and later Cistercian monastic orders. There was no Norman Conquest in Scotland such as England had to suffer, but Margaret and her husband invited Norman gentry to settle in Scotland under royal patronage as the secular arm of this "civilizing" of Scotland.

In many ways Macbeth was the last truly Celtic king of Scots. He had maintained Scotland's independence by juggling the rivalries of Viking Denmark, Viking Norway and the might of England. During his reign the native Celtic Church enjoyed its last flowering before Queen Margaret lavished royal patronage on Roman Catholic incomers. The greatest symbol of her work can be found at Dunfermline Abbey, where a massive new church was built at her command some time after 1070.

Dunfermline to Stirling (21 miles/34 km): *Take A907 W*

STIRLING

Ancient traditions insist that Ninian established a church here, the former capital of Scotland, but on the morning of the battle of Bannockburn in 1314 an event occurred outside the walls of Stirling which illustrated ancient continuity despite Queen Margaret's reforms. The Monymusk Reliquary, containing the remains of Columba, the Patriarch of the Celtic Church, was carried along the ranks of the Scottish army. When the English saw their enemies kneel they thought they were surrendering. They were mistaken.

Stirling to Edinburgh (36 miles/58 km): *Leave Stirling on A9, then join M9 and follow signs for Edinburgh*

EDINBURGH

Rising out of the Lothian plain, Edinburgh has played a central role in Scotland's history. The Protestant Reformation in Scotland created, as explained earlier, a thirst for knowledge and education. In the eighteenth century the Scottish Enlightenment established principles of liberty which were emulated in the infant republics of France and the USA. Edinburgh well merits its title "Athens of the North," for it nourished minds like those of the philosophers David Hume and Adam Smith. The architectural crown of the city is the castle but Queen Margaret's chapel inside the castle is the oldest building, constructed between 1080 and 1120. One of the newest is the National War Memorial in the castle courtyard, built after the First World War. Great open books contain the names of those who died. In the whole of the British Empire no people lost a greater proportion of their population than did the Scots. It was to be the same in the Second World War.

The Kingdom of the North has had an influence on world events way beyond its size. The message of Ninian, Mungo, Patrick, Columba, Margaret and even irascible John Knox has established international dialogue. Equally, the Scottish Protestant drive for democracy and for full and equal participation of all has laid the foundations for political involvement. Even the much mocked Wee Free Church arose as a democratic protest against clergy seeking too much power. Today the Scottish churches are one of the main groups working for a Scottish Assembly or Parliament. In Scotland, the democratic voice of the people is part of its Christian heritage.

> **Edinburgh to Lindisfarne (81 miles/130 km):** *Take A7 S to Galashiels, then A6091 through Melrose. Just before Dryburgh join A68 and follow to junction with A698 toward Coldstream. Take A698 through Kelso to Berwick-on-Tweed, then A1 and turn off to Beal, following signs to Lindisfarne*

THE LANDS OF THE TWEED

South of Edinburgh are the lands of the Tweed and their ruined monasteries that were destroyed not by the reformers' zeal but by marauding English armies. Melrose, Dryburgh, Kelso and Jedburgh are small market towns with magnificent but roofless abbeys that ordered life throughout the eastern borderlands until the armies of King Henry VIII of England destroyed them in the 1540s. The invaders paid for their plundering when a Scots army cornered them on Ancrum Moor in 1545.

In the graveyard at nearby St Boswells is the memorial of a young woman who joined in the fray when her lover was killed. The headstone reads:

> Fair maiden Lilliard lies under the stane
> Little was her stature but muckle was her fame
> Upon the English loons she laid many thumps
> And when her legs were cuttit off
> She fought upon her stumps.

Dividing the Lothian shores from the Tweed are the Lammermuir Hills. In the seventh century a young shepherd boy called Cuthbert was reared on this moorland. He was later to be abbot and bishop of the Christian community of Lindisfarne, the center from which missionaries from Iona converted the Anglo-Saxon people of Northumbria and far to the south. In so doing common cultural ties were established between the two great rivals of Britain and a future other than merciless conflict was possible.

LINDISFARNE · NORTHUMBERLAND

Leave your car at Berwick-on-Tweed and set out on foot along the clifftops and wide beaches of England to walk the 10 miles to Holy Island, where Aidan of Iona established the community which Cuthbert enlarged.

As a monk Cuthbert was first at Melrose Abbey, then at Ripon, where he entertained an angel (see p. 142). But it is with Lindisfarne that he is most associated. Cuthbert is recalled for his love not just for all people, but also for animals and birds that he protected. His gentleness and humility made him the most loved saint in Britain, and his cult was the most widespread before Thomas à Becket's death.

Missionaries from Iona established a community here in the 630s when King Oswald of Northumbria invited them to teach his people the Christian faith. The memory of Aidan, the first abbot, who died in 651, was revered by the northern English. At the Synod of Whitby in 664 the Northumbrians chose to adhere to Roman Catholic practice, but Cuthbert ensured that the legacy of Aidan and Iona was not forgotten or despised and friendship grew on both sides of the Tweed. In 1999, a new Scottish Parliament was elected – the first for nearly three hundred years. It is

Lindisfarne has been occupied and fortified since the Stone Age but the first Christian community was established here c.630

unclear how this will affect relationships with England in the long run. Whatever the future holds, let that friendship be the gift which Ninian, Mungo, Columba, Duthac, Margaret, John Knox and countless unnamed others gave to our futures. In the words of Mahatma Gandhi: "I do not want my home to be walled in on all sides and its windows blocked. I want cultures of all lands to be blown about my house as freely as possible. But I refuse to be blown off my feet by any."

꧁

CHAPTER 18

A Multi-faith Pilgrimage

As the veil is lifted –
We shall see the beginning
That lies hidden in the end:

That we are all a part
Of each other in ourselves –
Everyone, everything, everywhere sacred
Living on this pilgrim star

Then we will find each other
In the Glory.

THIS ROUTE shows what a pilgrimage might look like if it were to reflect the full picture of religion in Britain today. It is comprehensive, but not exhaustive – bearing in mind the enormous variety of faiths being practiced, it cannot cover every place, either geographically or in terms of different religious traditions. Locations of the sites listed and other useful pieces of information are given on pp. 294-296.

The route represents each of the major traditions in rough proportion to their numerical strength, although Buddhism is slightly over-represented because of its widespread influence beyond its immediate following. Also, we have included only a few key Christian holy places as a reminder of the religious background among which the "new" faiths have found a home.

From a mosque in the English stockbroker belt to a universalist community in the Scottish Highlands

Main Route (734 miles/1176 km):
WOKING · LONDON · LETCHMORE HEATH · GREAT GADDES-
DEN · MILTON KEYNES · LEICESTER · BRADFORD · BRIGFLATTS ·
ULVERSTON · ESKDALEMUIR · GLASGOW · IONA · FINDHORN

WOKING · SURREY

SHAH JAHAN MOSQUE

Beside the railway line in Woking is a faded signboard announcing in bold letters to passing commuters: "Shah Jahan Mosque, Woking." Behind it travelers may catch an unexpected glimpse of minarets and a crescent moon among tall trees. This mosque is the oldest in Britain yet the only clue to its existence is Oriental Road, named after the Oriental Institute in whose grounds it was constructed in the mid-nineteenth century. Until the 1920s it was the only mosque in Britain. Then in the 1970s a new working-class Muslim community grew up in Woking, attracted by jobs and the mosque. A school was opened, and other social amenities have been developed. There is now a mixed Muslim community of around twelve thousand, mainly from Pakistan and India, who worship here.

After removing your shoes and washing your feet you enter a small, immaculately kept prayer hall with lofty proportions, decorated in cool greens with Arabic inscriptions painted around the inside of the dome. This is a place to reflect on the building's unusual history, so different from that of many of Britain's inner city mosques. The community here has been sheltered from many of the stresses experienced by its city counterparts and has had time to establish itself gradually, which is reflected in the open, relaxed atmosphere.

MUSLIM GRAVEYARD

Before leaving Woking there is one other place to visit. Hidden among pine trees on a small patch of heathland north of the Wey Canal near the A320 is the remains of the Muslim graveyard. Walled and gated in Islamic style, it was once the resting place for some twenty-five Indian Muslim soldiers killed in the First World War. In the 1920s their bodies were removed to nearby Brookwood Cemetery, where they joined other fallen Muslim comrades. This little patch of Islam in a foreign land now lies abandoned and overgrown, a curious footnote in history. A place to stand quietly and to respect the fact that this land has always been a place of many cultures – and the better for that.

Woking to West London (20 miles/32 km): *Take A320 N to junction with A319, follow motorway signs along A319 and join M25 at J11. Head NW and join M3 at J12, heading E. M3 becomes A316. Ultimately cross Chiswick Bridge to Chiswick*

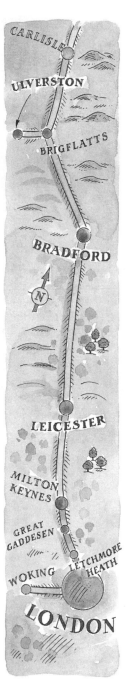

LONDON

WESTMINSTER CATHEDRAL
SW1

Situated on a recently created piazza off Victoria Street in the heart of Westminster, the Metropolitan Cathedral of the Most Precious Blood, to give the cathedral its full name, is a staggering piece of late Victorian architecture and one of the last great cathedrals built in Britain. It marks a radical departure from the traditional English cathedrals of the past, being designed in the Byzantine style by John Francis Bentley. It was completed in 1903 to be the mother church of Roman Catholicism in Britain. Its distinctive exterior is made up of alternating bands of red brick and white Portland stone and topped with a 284-foot campanile, a landmark on the London skyline.

The construction of the cathedral marked the coming of age of the newly revived Roman Catholic Church at the end of the nineteenth century. In 1829 laws restricting Roman Catholicism were repealed and the Roman Catholic Diocese of Westminster was created in 1850. Calls for a cathedral were put off for thirty years to allow resources to be channeled toward much-needed schools and facilities for the predominantly poor Catholic community. The site of the cathedral, a former correction house for paupers, was eventually purchased by Cardinal Manning in 1884. The Byzantine style was chosen because it allowed room for a large congregation to all have a view of the high altar, and was relatively cheap and quick to build, allowing the decorations to be added later. The work of building the cathedral was completed by Cardinal Vaughan whose funeral was its first major service.

A special feature of the interior is the series of Stations of the Cross, fourteen large stone panels carved by Eric Gill, and the ten side-chapels, each of which has its own style of artistic decorations. The cathedral is a sanctuary to the religious arts and crafts of the twentieth century.

Despite its status as a national monument much visited by tourists, the cathedral has retained the atmosphere of a genuine place of worship, a place where the working people of the surrounding city come to pray and worship.The cathedral runs its own busy parish and has a large staff of working priests, and a full-time choir school whose musical outpourings impart a distinctive flavor to its daily round of worship.

Westminster Cathedral, Ambrosden Avenue, London SW1. tel: (times of service) 020 7798 9097 (main office) 020 7798 9055. The cathedral is open daily from 7a.m. until 8p.m. It has a well-stocked bookshop next door and a gift shop at the rear of the nave. Personal help is always available from the Clergy House at 42 Francis Street, London SW1. Tower tour (magnificent views across London) Wed-Sun 11a.m.-4p.m.

LONDON BUDDHIST VIHARA
W4

This beautifully maintained shrine and monastery are under the charge of the Venerable Pandith Vajiragnana, who came from Sri Lanka over thirty years ago to the London mission of the Maha Bodhi Society. He was following in the footsteps of Anagarika Dharmapala, a monk who first visited London from Sri Lanka in 1893 and in 1925 was invited back to set up what would be the first Theravada Buddhist institution in Europe.

Venerable Pandith Vajiragnana describes the vihara's three functions as to be a center of devotion, principally for the more orthodox Sri Lankan Buddhists; to offer information to Westerners who wish to investigate the Dhamma – Buddhist teachings; and to be a cultural center for Sri Lankan expatriates. He says that these three aims are sometimes at odds with each other but that his ambition is to harmonize all three, as he is sure the founder intended.

LONDON CENTRAL SIKH GURDWARA
W11

This, the first gurdwara to open in Britain, was bought by the London Sikh community known as the Khalsa Jatha in 1972. The story began in 1908, when Sikh students living in London needed somewhere to meet and worship and were given a house in west London by the Maharaja of Patiala. With a much larger Sikh population to support, some sixty years later the gurdwara moved to the present building. Its brick and glass exterior is embellished with three golden domes, and at the foot of the steps outside stands the traditional Sikh flagpole wrapped in saffron cloth. The gurdwara was the first to be established outside Asia or East Africa, and attracts Sikhs from all over London. It produces a monthly newsletter and runs an Internet service for Sikhs worldwide.

The high point of Sikh worship is their music. The hymns of the Guru Granth (the Sikh holy scriptures, viewed as a living guru or teacher) are sung to thirty-one different traditional ragas, or melodic patterns, with consummate skill and spontaneity. In the gurdwara's music school the ragas are passed on to the next generation. To sit in the hall and hear these beautiful songs is a wonderfully soothing experience which speaks more eloquently than anything else of Sikh devotion to God. Afterward you will be invited downstairs to the langar and offered delicious sacred food.

BAHA'I CENTRE
SW7

This elegant terraced mansion on the south side of Hyde Park was bought by the Baha'i Community of the United Kingdom in 1955. The first Baha'is arrived in Britain in 1899, and now around six thousand attend meetings in some four hundred groups and Local Spiritual Assemblies. A Local Spiritual Assembly is formed where there are at least nine Baha'is over the age of twenty-one; there are at the time of writing 177 of them in the British Isles, and Rutland Gate is their headquarters.

Baha'is are named after a young Persian who in 1863 took the name Baha'u'llah (Glory of God) and proclaimed himself to be the Messenger of God foretold by an earlier venerated figure, the Bab (meaning Gate or Door), who had been put to death in 1850 for heresy against Islam. Baha'u'llah's teachings owe much to Islam, but soon became accepted as a new faith. He saw divine revelation as an unfolding process involving Moses, Krishna, Zarathustra, Buddha, Christ and Muhammad. The central tenet of Baha'i is the oneness of God, religion and humanity.

BEVIS MARKS SYNAGOGUE
EC3

Hidden away in a back street in the City of London, this is the oldest continuously used synagogue in Britain. Jews have a far longer history in Britain than any other non-Christian community, having first come here with the Romans. But relations between Jews and Christians began to deteriorate at the end of the twelfth century (see p. 120). By the thirteenth century the Jews were frequently persecuted, and in 1290 they were expelled. First to return, at the time of Cromwell's Commonwealth, were the Jews of the Sephardi or Spanish and Portuguese tradition, from Amsterdam. The first house of worship after their resettlement was opened in 1656 in a house in Creechurch Lane, near Bevis Marks.

The present synagogue was built in 1701. The architect, a Quaker, is said to have returned his fee rather than profit from a house of God. Queen Anne presented an oak beam for the roof from one of the Royal Navy's ships. These examples of inter-religious solidarity must have pleased the small community of newcomers. The focus of attention is the classically designed Ark decorated with the Ten Commandments, above which is inscribed in Hebrew: "Know before Whom thou standest." In the center of the synagogue hang seven many-branched candelabra representing the seven days of the week. The twelve supporting columns of the gallery are said to represent the Twelve Tribes of Israel.

The congregation at Bevis Marks are mostly descended from the original Sephardi Jews from the Netherlands. Their numbers are now much diminished since most of them have moved away from the City, but on the Sabbath around fifty worshipers still attend. The community are justly proud of their traditions and established their own welfare service, which still offers free medical facilities, 250 years before the National Health Service was set up.

LONDON CENTRAL MOSQUE
NW8

With its golden dome and 140-foot minaret on the edge of Regent's Park, this is one of London's landmarks and a far cry from the hidden rustic charm of Woking (see p. 273). The idea of such a mosque was conceived during the Second World War, when troops from many parts of the Islamic world were fighting for the Allies and it was felt that the substantial Muslim presence in the Empire should be given official recognition.

The building dates from 1969 and draws on traditional Islamic designs despite its modern appearance. Mosque, offices, library and other parts of the complex are united by the large Islamic arches. Inside, everything is austere but beautifully proportioned. The main prayer hall, with its vast central dome decorated with mosaics, stained glass windows and a huge central chandelier, holds fourteen hundred worshipers at prayer times, but can be extended outside to hold up to four thousand for festivals. On most

Friday lunchtimes the mosque is full to overflowing with worshipers from all over London and beyond.

Whereas the mosque at Woking looks toward Pakistan and India, this one has benefited from the prosperity of the Middle Eastern states and the substantial London Arab population.

SWAMINARAYAN HINDU TEMPLE
NW10

Opened in 1995, the temple has quickly established itself as north London's Hindu equivalent of the Regent's Park Mosque. The Swaminarayan sect to which it is devoted was founded by Sahajanand Swami, a saint and religious reformer born in Gujarat, India, in 1781. He belonged to the Vaishnava tradition, which worships Vishnu or Narayan as the supreme form of God. However, he himself was revered in his own lifetime as an incarnation of God, and was therefore given the title Swaminarayan. He had a huge following including three thousand ordained monks called sadhus. His immediate successor was Gunatitanand, also revered as a divine incarnation. The followers of Swaminarayan are now divided into six branches. Worship of Swaminarayan and Gunatitanand is the essential feature of this branch and their images are installed on the central altars of all their temples, taking precedence over more traditional images such as those of Krishna, Ram and Shiva.

The Neasden temple is built of stone and hand-carved marble and has been compared to the Taj Mahal. The result, as described in the *Guardian*, is "a cathedral of our times." The *Sunday Telegraph* called it "an alliance of craftsmanship and spirituality that had its parallel in medieval England . . . the most remarkable London monument of the late twentieth century."

The Swaminarayan Hindu Mission arrived in London in 1959. Meetings were held in private houses until 1970, when a former Baptist church was bought. Numbers swelled with the arrival of thousands of refugees from Idi Amin's Uganda, and the temple moved to a converted factory in Neasden in 1980. Plans were put in hand for a purpose-built marble temple, and a suitable site was sought. After planning permission for a temple on open land beside Northwick Park was refused, a site adjacent to the Neasden factory was taken. One of London's most spectacular buildings this century has therefore been relegated to a backwater of a built-up suburb. The devotees of Swaminarayan, however, will have their own impact on the railway sidings, factories and council housing which surround them. In time more and more of them will probably choose to live near the temple, and the whole landscape will be transformed. Followers say that because it has no steel in its construction – only solid stone on concrete foundations – it will last a thousand years.

ST MARY'S CHURCH, WILLESDEN
NW10

Close to the Hindu temple is the ancient church of St Mary, built on the site of the sacred well which gives Willesden its name ("the spring or well at the foot of the hill"). Here there was once a thriving pilgrimage center which was suppressed during the Reformation. Now it has come to life again, and offers a good example of a Christian holy place which has found new relevance in the twentieth century.

It is believed that this was the site of a Celtic community ruled by druids before the arrival of the Romans, and there is evidence of a Saxon wooden church. The parish church of St Mary was founded in 938. A shrine grew up dedicated to the Black Virgin of Willesden, who was believed to possess miraculous healing powers; the waters of the well were particularly renowned for healing the eyes. The shrine reached the height of its popularity during the Black Death in 1349.

The Reformation brought a drastic change of fortune for the Willesden shrine. The sacred image of the Black Virgin was ordered to be destroyed, along with similar images from elsewhere. Richard Mores, who carried out the task, gave this account of what he found: "An image of Our Ladye in robes sarcanet and with stones with a vale withal of lace embroidered with pearles and other precious jewelles and gold and silver. We did strip the image which we found to be of woode in color like ebon of ancient workmanschip onli save the upper part is throughly playted over with silver." However, no faith was ever destroyed by persecution. The "idolatrous church" lived on to pay an annual fine, originally imposed by Henry VIII, of £1 6s 0d – which incredibly continued until 1902.

In 1972 the present striking image of Mother Mary with the Child Jesus, carved in black limewood, was dedicated by the Bishop of Willesden at the now reinstated annual pilgrimage. The vicar keeps the ancient font replenished with water from the sacred well beneath the church. The presence of the feminine energy of the Mother seems strong, and the newly restored shrine to the Black Virgin dominates the church. Her church has survived over a thousand years of stormy history, and is ready to weather the next thousand. But now there is a new presence in Willesden – the little Saxon church has a grand Hindu neighbor. What surprises will the future hold? Here, where the religious impulse has continued to beat through the centuries, is a place to reflect upon that impulse. Upon the need to worship and to create places that are magnificent and places that are simple, the better to be touched by God.

STERNBERG CENTER
FOR JUDAISM AND LEO BAECK COLLEGE
N3

This is the headquarters of the Jewish Reform Movement, which sees itself as the voice of informed, questioning, compassionate and egalitarian Judaism in Great Britain. It has forty-one synagogues and forty-two thousand members, and is based in a Georgian house in grounds of about 6 acres.

The Sternberg Centre describes itself as Europe's largest Jewish religious, educational and cultural center, a shop window for Reform Judaism and an open door for all who would come and learn. The Jewish Museum tells the story of Jews in Britain, with special attention to the London area, the Holocaust and the Jewish experience in the Second World War. The Leo Baeck College trains rabbis. The center is a committed supporter of interfaith dialogue, and has its own Jewish-Christian-Muslim Dialogue Group.

Of particular interest is the Biblical Garden in the grounds. Planted with trees, shrubs, herbs, flowers and bulbs mentioned in the Bible, accompanied by appropriate quotations, it offers an oasis of peace and beauty.

North London to Letchmore Heath (15 miles/24 km): *Take A4 W to A406 (North Circular) going N. Take A5 NW to Elstree, continue along A5183 to Letchmore Heath*

LETCHMORE HEATH · HERTFORDSHIRE

BHAKTIVEDANTA MANOR

The house was a gift to the Hare Krishna Movement from former Beatle George Harrison in 1973. It became a monastic community and a training college for priests and was soon the most popular Hindu shrine in Britain, with up to twenty-five thousand worshipers a weekend at festival times. This caused it to be caught up in a long-running dispute with the local authority, which tried to restrict the number of worshipers and even to close the place down. But after a protracted battle in British and European courts, supported by MPs and leaders of many faiths, in 1996 it was declared a public place of worship without restriction. All this has made Bhaktivedanta Manor a symbol of religious freedom in multi-faith Britain.

The Manor is owned by the International Society for Krishna Consciousness, known as ISKCON, which was established in Britain in 1969 and is named after its founder, A.C. Bhaktivedanta Swami Prabhupad. Born in Calcutta in 1896, as a young man Prabhupad became a follower of Shri Chaitanya, the fifteenth-century Hindu saint and reformer who campaigned against the restrictions of the caste system and initiated a movement of devotion to Krishna which was open to all. In 1965, on the orders of his guru, Prabhupad traveled to America where he taught Krishna Consciousness and founded ISKCON, which has its headquarters at the birthplace of Shri Chaitanya in West Bengal and has since expanded to over a hundred countries.

Bhaktivedanta Manor has a resident community of about fifty and a further fifty full- or part-time workers, with an extended community of thousands. It runs a series of training programs and a nursery and primary school. Organic farming is practiced in the 70 acres of grounds. The community committed to an ecological approach to the land, taking inspiration from the life of Krishna who lived as a cowherd in the forest of Vrindavan.

Letchmore Heath to Great Gaddesden (17 miles/27 km): *Continue along A5183 to Church End. At roundabout take B487 W, which becomes A4147. Continue, turning R along A4146 to Great Gaddesden*

GREAT GADDESDEN · HERTFORDSHIRE

AMARAVATI BUDDHIST MONASTERY

Near Hemel Hempstead is a monastery in the Theravada tradition of the Thai Forest. *Amaravati* in Pali (along with Sanskrit, the ancient language of Buddhism) means "deathless realm."

In 1956 a group of lay Buddhists formed the English Sangha Trust, and subsequently established a monastery in London. In 1978 the Trust was given Hammer Wood in West Sussex, and soon afterward purchased nearby Chithurst House. The house and grounds had been abandoned and the Sangha spent many years restoring them. The community then set about the long-term project of restocking Hammer Wood with native species and preserving it as a wildlife sanctuary. Their interest in the forest, as a conservation project and a place for solitary retreats, reflects their own roots in the forests of northern Thailand. Here the monk Ajahn Pongsak and other Buddhists campaigned for many years, confronting the authorities and other vested interests and putting themselves at risk to protect the forests which were being destroyed by logging.

In 1984 the Trust acquired a former school near Hemel Hempstead and renamed it Amaravati. Once again the place was in poor condition, but since then gardens have been created and the playing fields transformed with great sensitivity into traditional English woodland laid out as a wonderful meditation space.

The community consists of a core of about thirty people including monks, nuns and novices, with short-term and long-term lay residents. As Buddhist monks and nuns, the monastics have given up the use of money and cannot cultivate the land. This obliges them to have an interdependent relationship with lay people and discourages any tendency for the monastery to become isolated from the outside world. Monks are not allowed to beg, but are dependent on the food, robes, medicine and shelter offered by lay people.

Great Gaddesden to Milton Keynes (22 miles/35 km): *Rejoin A4146 heading N. At Bletchley take A5 NW to Milton Keynes*

MILTON KEYNES · BEDFORDSHIRE

CHURCH OF CHRIST THE CORNERSTONE

The ecumenical "city church" of Milton Keynes, the last and most ambitious of Britain's postwar planned cities, makes an interesting comparison with some of the newly established religious centers of worship already described. Like them, it is a completely new place of worship formed among a community only recently established. Like them, it is seeking to establish an identity for itself as a pioneer in a new field. Unlike them, it has behind it the full experience and support of the five main established Christian Churches in Britain – the Church of England, the Baptist Union, the Methodist Church, the United Reformed Church and the Roman Catholic Church – and of the local authority. This background has helped the church to become a brilliant example of what can be achieved in a new religious center.

The church's story began in 1979, early in the life of the new city, when

Milton Keynes Christian Council formally inaugurated the City Center Parish. In keeping with the innovatory spirit of the place it was decided to make the parish fully ecumenical, which had never been done before in England. Because it is a brand-new environment with a newly gathered community, many of the barriers to change experienced elsewhere are absent.

A congregation began to form, worshiping in a temporary space which became known as the Church-in-the-Library. Ten years later a magnificent new church was dedicated in the presence of the Queen, the Archbishop of Canterbury, the Archbishop of Westminster and leading representatives of the Methodist, Baptist and United Reformed Churches.

Among the features of the church are its octagonal dome, reminiscent of the Duomo in Florence, surmounted by a cupola and an 8-foot six-sided cross. The dome stands out in the city center as the only non-rectangular, non-functional shape in sight. The ground plan of the church resembles a Greek cross, but the central worship space is again octagonal. Behind the altar stone of Spanish rose granite is another unique feature – the sunken baptistry, continuously filled by a small waterfall which ripples unceasingly down the wall as a constant reminder of the sanctity of baptism and its mystical significance. The chapel at the north-west corner is a small round space lined with American oak, centered on a round altar table. Set into the far wall is a niche containing a slender bronze cross. The peace of this chapel makes it a welcome place for quiet contemplation.

The church has a lively community life at the center of a thriving new city. All in all, the church of Christ the Cornerstone is a clear demonstration that the religious instinct which inspired countless past generations of faithful people and their architects to create sacred spaces is still alive.

PEACE PAGODA

Also in Milton Keynes is the Peace Pagoda, which stands beside the lake in Willen Park. This beautifully constructed 70-foot-high Buddhist shrine is a gift to the people of Milton Keynes from the Nipponzan Myohoji, a Buddhist order dedicated to prayer and world

The Peace Pagoda, Milton Keynes, Bedfordshire

peace which was founded in Japan after Hiroshima. Nearby is a monastery housing a small community which cares for the shrine and an exquisite little Japanese garden. Both buildings look as if they have been transported straight from Japan. They are, however, quite appropriate here, and their presence reinforces the impression that Milton Keynes is not without a sense of the sacred.

Milton Keynes to Leicester (50 miles/80 km): *Take A509 NE to M1, joining at J14. Head N, leaving at J21*

LEICESTER

This is a city with a sense of pride in its long history as well as its modern multi-cultural character. It has gone to some lengths to inform and educate both visitors and local people about its various communities, which include Muslims, Hindus, Sikhs and Jains. The old city center contains the cathedral, the castle, the Guildhall, the remains of the Roman baths, the Jain Centre and the town's first Sikh gurdwara, creating a sense of continuity from old to new communities settling and living here.

JAIN CENTRE

This is the only fully operational Jain temple outside India, which presented its founders with a unique problem: how to cater to the needs of all Jains in the community, since they normally worship in separate temples according to their affiliations to one of the four Jain traditions. The solution, to combine shrines for all four traditions under one roof, is typical of the Jain virtue of tolerance, and makes the center unique in the world.

The word "Jain" derives from the term "Jina," which describes the twenty-four original teachers of Jainism and means one who has conquered the lower nature of greed and hatred and achieved the state of supreme being. The two principal traditions are the Svetambara (whose monks are "clad in white") and the Digambara (whose monks are "sky-clad" – that is, without clothes).

The white marble facade and pillared porch of the Leicester Jain Centre create an impressive spectacle on busy Oxford St. Inside is a cool marble-floored lobby with stairs leading up to the main worship hall. The upper floor contains the four principal shrines, belonging to the Svetambara,

Digambara, Sthanakvasi and Gautamswami traditions respectively. The main hall is dominated by the inner temple of fifty-two elaborately carved red sandstone pillars which support a domed ceiling covered in figurative carvings, which were executed in India and then shipped to Britain. The style is modeled on the famous Jain temples of Mount Abu in India, and the effect is quite breathtaking.

The Digambara shrine is dedicated to the first Jinas, headed by Rishabdev, who lived countless aeons ago and to whom many famous temples in India are dedicated. It also contains a hauntingly beautiful life-size statue of a naked standing Jina named Bharavnar. The Svetambara shrine, the main one in the temple, is dedicated to the last three Jinas, among whom special attention is paid to the very last Jina, a royal prince called Mahavira (599 BC–527 BC), whose life story is told in ten large stained-glass panels.

His teachings are summed up in the declarations which appear over the main entrance to the temple:

> *Non-violence – Live and let live – Reverence for life*
> *Right Faith, Right Knowledge, Right Conduct – together these*
> *constitute*
> *the path to salvation.*

GURU NANAK SIKH GURDWARA

This gurdwara is situated in a street called Holy Bones – it would be interesting to know just how it got its name! Sikhs first settled in Leicester after the Second World War; they were mostly the families of former soldiers from the British Army in India, who after Indian independence were given British passports.

Leicester's first Sikh temple opened in the 1960s and moved in 1989 to the present site, a converted textile factory; a new purpose-built gurdwara is proposed.

Inside is a museum of Sikh history, bearing witness to the pride of the Sikh community in its military past and its loyalty to the former British Empire. Many people are unaware of this side of Sikh history, and a visit here makes one aware that Sikhs remember this aspect of their past more than the British themselves do.

Three essential principles followed by Sikhs are to honor God, to work hard and to share with others. The spirit of sharing is particularly evident in the gurdwara and there is a wonderful sense of hospitality.

SHREE JALARAM PRATHNA MANDAL

Before leaving Leicester visit one of its many Hindu temples. We chose this beautiful example because it is the result of the work of women. In the early seventies a ladies' prayer group was started in Leicester among Hindu women newly arrived from East Africa, who held their meetings in one another's houses. Later they opened a prayer hall, and have recently moved to a new purpose-built temple which was opened in 1995.

The main hall contains a marble shrine dedicated to Shree Jalaram Bapa, behind whom are a range of Hindu deities: Lord Rama, Lord Shiva, Goddess Amba, Ganesh and Hanuman. Beside the entrance is a diorama of Vishnu being cared for by the Goddess Laxmi.

Shree Jalaram Bapa was born in 1900 in Gujarat in India, and at an early age decided to dedicate his life to the service of sadhus and saints. India has a long tradition of wandering pilgrims who rely on the generosity of householders to support them as they travel from village to village giving teachings or journey to holy places. Helped by his wife, he set up a welfare center where any needy person could go and be fed. From the age of twenty he was famous as a saint whose blessings were sought by people from far and wide. In the famine of 1934 he worked hard to feed those who were suffering. Three years later he died.

"We must help each other," Shree Jalaram Bapa said. "The whole world is my family – let us love each other." It is said that the saint would pray constantly, while his wife would feed any guest who came. His followers are gentle people who, like him, spend their time at the temple singing bhajans (devotional songs), listening to invited sadhus and sharing prasadam, consecrated food, with their guests.

Leicester should remind us that anywhere is sacred – we just have to realize it. Think of where you live and of how special that is – or how special it could be.

> **Leicester to Bradford (100 miles/160 km):** *Take A50 NW to join M1 at J22, heading N. Continue to J42, turning W on to M62. At J26 take M606 N to Bradford*

BRADFORD · WEST YORKSHIRE

BRADFORD INTERFAITH EDUCATION CENTRE

Perched above the city center on the busy Listerhills Road, the Interfaith

Centre prominently displays its insignia – a circular emblem bearing the signs of six faiths grouped about the planet Earth. This emblem very much represents the modern city of Bradford, which has become one of the most thriving multi-faith communities of Britain, and the center provides education on other religions to those who deal with the public, such as nurses, social workers and bank staff. The existence of such a center is a vivid indication of the changes that have taken place in urban society in Britain over the last three decades. There was a time when the presence of minority communities of Muslims or Hindus was something to be overlooked or worried about. Now such a multiplicity of faiths has become a distinctive and enriching feature of life in cities such as Leicester, Birmingham and Bradford.

JAMIA MASJID HANFIA MOSQUE

Among the places of worship to which the Interfaith Centre can direct you is this purpose-built mosque. It lies on the north side of Bradford's inner ring road, the latest of over thirty mosques in the city. This new one is two stories high, with a golden dome and distinctive minaret. The main prayer hall is big enough to hold four hundred men; above is a balcony for women, with additional space for men. A large community hall is used for prayer at special festivals and for social occasions or funerals. The mosque has its own madrassah or Islamic school where children from the age of five are taught the Qur'an, a vital concern to all Muslim communities.

Bradford to Brigflatts (65 miles/104 km): *Take A650 NW to Keighley, then A629 to Skipton. Join A65 W to Kirkby Lonsdale, then take A683 to Sedbergh and follow local signposts*

BRIGFLATTS · CUMBRIA

FRIENDS' MEETING HOUSE

The little hamlet of Brigflatts lies a mile or so south-west of the small town of Sedbergh in Cumbria, just off the A683. At the bottom of the lane the Friends' meeting house has stood for over three hundred years. It is a plain stone building set in a little garden, surrounded by fields. The poet Basil Bunting, sitting here in 1975, wrote these lines:

Stones indeed sift to sand, oak blends with saints' bone.
Yet for a little longer here stone and oak shelter
Silence while we ask nothing but silence. Look how clouds dance
Under the wind's wing, and leaves delight in transience.

It was in 1652 that George Fox, founder of the Quakers, arrived among the Westmoreland Seekers, a Non-Conformist group who rejected conventional forms of Christianity, and preached an open air sermon to a gathering of over a thousand beside the chapel on Firbank Fell near Sedbergh. This meeting is generally regarded as the beginning of Quakerism. A plaque is fixed to the rock where Fox stood to deliver his message that June day, and this site – known locally as Fox's Pulpit – has become a place of pilgrimage for Friends from many countries.

In 1660 over five hundred Friends, many from the Sedbergh district, were imprisoned for such offenses as non-attendance of church and non-payment of church dues. Some died in prison, while others had their belongings confiscated. By 1674, although the Conventicle Act forbidding meetings was still in force, the Friends around Sedburgh purchased a piece of land at Brigflatts and built this meeting house, now the second oldest in England. Designed by no architect and built by those who meant to use it, the meeting house at first consisted of four walls and a roof with a trodden earth floor. The benches were just one plank wide with no backs. Each winter two Friends were paid to stuff moss into the crevices between the roofing slates to stop the rain and snow falling on the heads of the worshipers. Around 1711 the gallery was extended and a dog pen added for sheepdogs accompanying their masters. After that nothing changed until 1905, when the meeting house was restored and some of the roof timbers replaced.

This place is now a quiet backwater. But once, passions ran deep and many would have viewed the group meeting here as

The simple interior of the Friends' meeting house, Brigflatts, Cumbria

a strange sect. Today the Quakers are one of the most respected of religious traditions. We do well to reflect here that we should be slow to condemn what we do not understand or like. God moves in mysterious ways.

> **Brigflatts to Ulverston (37 miles/60 km):** *Go W along A684 to M6, joining at J37. Head S and leave at J36. Take A591, then A590 W to Ulverston*

ULVERSTON · CUMBRIA

MANJUSHRI MAHAYANA BUDDHIST CENTRE

After delivering his historic sermon in 1652 George Fox travelled on to Ulverston at the southern end of the Lake District, where he stayed with Judge Fell (see p. 163). Our journey too takes us here, to the peaceful shores of Morecambe Bay and Conishead Priory, home of the Manjushri Mahayana Buddhist Centre since 1976.

The name "priory" commemorates the original Augustinian house which stood here from the twelfth to the sixteenth century under a charter granted by Edward II in 1338. In 1538 the priory was suppressed and its buildings dismantled, after which the estate passed through a succession of wealthy families. In 1821 the surviving house was entirely rebuilt in Gothic Revival style as the present Conishead Priory for the Bradyll family, who soon went bankrupt. Over the last hundred years it served first as a health spa and then as a convalescent home for miners. It was sold again in 1976 to the Manjushri Mahayana Buddhist Centre. So the wheel of history has turned full circle and once again the ancient site has become the home of a spiritual community.

The community is also the home of Venerable Geshe Kelsang Gyatso, who has thousands of disciples and over 250 centers internationally, of which Conishead Priory is the "mother center." The New Kadampa Tradition, or NKT, as his movement is called, is said to be the fastest-growing religious community in Britain. It is a branch of the Gelug, one of the four schools of Tibetan Buddhism, and is in open theological and political dispute with the Dalai Lama. The NKT's success has attracted controversy, both for its disagreements with the Dalai Lama and for its recruiting activities in the West, which are felt by some not to be in the traditional spirit of Buddhism.

The main activity of the center is to teach Buddhism in a way suited to the modern Western temperament. Three basic courses are offered: the General Program, the four-year Foundation Program and the seven-year Teacher Training Program. The resident community has nearly one hundred lay and ordained members, while others live in the locality. A new meditation hall is being constructed; it will include an authentic temple for the Buddhist tradition of Je Tsongkhapa, which the community follows.

Ulverston to Eskdalemuir (111 miles/178 km): *Return to J36 of M6 and head N to Carlisle, leaving at J44. Take A7 N to Langholm, then B709 to Eskdalemuir*

ESKDALEMUIR · DUMFRIES AND GALLOWAY

KAGYU SAMYE LING BUDDHIST MONASTERY

At Eskdalemuir is another Tibetan Buddhist center, Kagyu Samye Ling Buddhist Monastery. In 1968 two young Tibetan refugee monks were offered Johnstone House as a place to start their own Tibetan monastery. They named it Samye Ling, "a place that defies the imagination." They must have felt at home in the rugged, windswept environment, where the winters are long and cold. In contrast with the austerity of the surroundings, though, the monastery is a warm and welcoming place.

Samye Ling has a community of around one hundred. In addition a wide group of supporters make regular visits, participating in the many courses on offer. The displays of Tibetan art in the purpose-built temple which dominates the life of the community are unique in Britain. Regular services with all the bells and smells of traditional Tibet are held in the temple, the only difference being that most of the monks and nuns are from Britain.

The spiritual head of the monastery is the seventeenth Gyalwang Karmapa, a reincarnated Tibetan lama who lives in Tibet. The new lama's identity was confirmed by the Dalai Lama and in 1992, at the age of seven, he was enthroned at Tsurphu, his traditional seat in central Tibet, as the head of the Karma Kagyu tradition which includes Samye Ling.

One of the special features of Samye Ling is its long retreats. Groups of monks and nuns are taken in for periods of four years at a time to the retreat house near the main community. Once inside they do not leave until the four years are up. The director of Samye Ling, Lama Yeshe Losal, has himself completed twelve years of such retreat, as have some other members of the community.

Lama Yeshe is particularly enthusiastic about the Holy Island project run by the monastery. The island off Arran was offered to the community in 1991 and is being developed as a center for the long retreat and as a nature sanctuary. It is an ancient place of spirituality, having been the home of the sixth-century Christian saint Molaise, who after being educated at the monastery of Iona and that of St Finbar in southern Ireland came to Holy Island to live a hermit's life in a cave.

> **Eskdalemuir to Glasgow (86 miles/138 km):** *Head SW along B723 to join A74 at Lockerbie. Go N on A74 which becomes M74, then A74 again on outskirts of Glasgow*

GLASGOW

From the seclusion of Samye Ling move on to the heart of industrial Glasgow (see also p. 254) to visit a multi-faith museum and an impressive mosque.

ST MUNGO MUSEUM OF RELIGIOUS LIFE AND ART

The museum, next to the cathedral, is named after the sixth-century saint who founded Glasgow, which may seem to imply that the museum is predominantly Christian. It is in fact a genuine attempt to represent all religious traditions equally through beautiful works of art, and to show something of the life and practices of different religions.

The museum has three galleries: an art gallery,

a religious life gallery and a Scottish gallery which tells the story of religion in Scotland, starting from the present multi-cultural city of Glasgow and working backward to show how it evolved. The most impressive work on display in the art gallery includes the famous Salvador Dali painting *Christ of St John of the Cross*, and a very large and exquisitely rendered nineteenth-century south Indian bronze statue of Shiva performing the dance of destruction of the universe. The gallery of religious life takes visitors on a tour of the world's religions through imaginative displays involving objects, pictures and words.

Before leaving, pause for a moment in the museum's Zen meditation garden, the only permanent one in Britain.

GLASGOW CENTRAL MOSQUE AND ISLAMIC CENTRE

This group of buildings beside the Clyde in central Glasgow shows how much the Muslim community can contribute to the city environment once it has had the time to settle and develop its own resources. The community here had its beginnings in the 1920s when Muslim sailors used to visit the city regularly on cargo vessels. Some made friends ashore and decided to stay on. In 1942 Scotland's first mosque was set up, and in 1974 a second was opened.

Eventually, in 1979, the community acquired the present site, on the banks of the Clyde. With assistance from the city of Glasgow, the President of Pakistan and wealthy donors in Saudi Arabia, a magnificent new mosque complex was opened for worship in 1984. The impression created is of a community which has come of age, and has had the sensitivity and cultural awareness to create an environment which is pleasing to the eye and uplifting to the spirit.

There are now about thirty thousand Muslims in Glasgow, and ten mosques. The Central Mosque serves the entire community and its activities include care of the elderly and the teaching of Islamic studies.

> **Glasgow to Iona (75 miles/120 km):** *Take A82 N to Tyndrum, then A85 W to Oban and catch ferry to Iona*

IONA · ARGYLL AND BUTE

This pilgrimage ends with visits to two important communities of faith on opposite sides of Scotland: Iona (see pp. 256-259 for a full description of

St Columba's sacred island as part of the Gretna to Lindisfarne pilgrimage) and Findhorn.

Iona to Findhorn (136 miles/218 km): *Return to Oban on ferry. Head NE on A85 to Connel, take A828 N to Fort William and join A82 NE to Inverness. Then take A96 NE to Forres, and B9011 to Findhorn*

FINDHORN · MORAY

A visit to the Findhorn Foundation Community, 20 miles east of Inverness near Forres, is an experience of a unique social and religious experiment. Two things are never far away: religious life and care for nature. However, religion is practiced in a way quite different from that in any of the other places visited on this pilgrimage: this is a community which attempts to make religion central, but leaves its expression open to the individual. Wherever you are in the community – and it is spread widely around Forres – you are never far from a sanctuary where regular gatherings for prayer and meditation take place. There is a Christian leaning to some of these meetings, and chanting from the ecumenical Christian community of Taizé in France is popular, but they are essentially universalist, incorporating aspects of all religions in response to the rhythms of equinoxes, solstices and full moons, with an emphasis on silent meditation.

The community was founded in 1962 by Peter and Eileen Caddy and Dorothy Maclean when they came to live in what was then a featureless caravan park of sand dunes and rubbish tips. They did not intend to start a community, but were brought together by "a commitment to follow God's will" and a desire to "love who you are, love who you're with, and love what you're doing." The original caravan with its now famous gardens is still preserved as a place of quiet meditation.

Pioneer work is going on at Findhorn to find ways of living in harmony with nature, and to this end the community's electricity is partly wind-powered. The nature sanctuary is an imaginative and mystical little building, hidden among trees and half submerged into the earth. Built entirely from recycled materials, it is a wonderful place for quiet contemplation.

Sitting in the lovingly tended gardens of Findhorn, watching the sun slide over the north-eastern horizon of the sea at the end of the day, reflect on all the places visited – churches, temples, mosques, monasteries, converted factories or country houses, places which have been holy for thousands of years or places which are just beginning to be seen as sacred. All this shows how much of the sacred there is to experience in this small island – how much more than we can ever find time to see. Those of us who contributed to this book are comforted to know that the tradition of making and finding the sacred in this land is still very much alive and will continue to inspire its peoples, of all faiths or none, far into the future.

MULTI-FAITH PILGRIMAGE ADDRESS LIST

Shah Jahan Mosque, 149 Oriental Rd, Woking, Surrey, GU22 7BA (Tel. 01483 760679). Visitors are made very welcome. Each day at 1.30p.m. the mosque is opened and attended, and this is the best time to visit.

London Buddhist Vihara, The Avenue, London W4 1UD (Tel. 0181 995 9493). The vihara is open daily, except Saturday and Sunday, for classes 7–9p.m.

London Central Sikh Gurdwara, 62 Queensdale Rd, London W11 4SG (Tel. 0171 402 4696/0181 904 4191). The main services are on Sunday and Wednesday evenings, from 7p.m. (participants must cover their head and take off their shoes).

Baha'i Centre, 27 Rutland Gate, London SW7 1PD (Tel. 0171 584 2566). Visitors are most welcome, especially to the informal evenings held each Thursday.

Bevis Marks Synagogue, Bevis Marks, off St Mary Axe, London EC3 5DQ (Tel. 0171 289 2573). By appointment only: 0171 626 1274.

London Central Mosque, 146 Park Rd, London NW8 7RG (Tel. 0171 724 3363/7). On Sunday afternoons Western converts to Islam run a special question-and-answer session for non-Muslims. Non-Muslims are welcome to attend prayers most days and evenings, provided they respect the sanctity of the house of God by removing their shoes, dressing modestly and covering their heads.

Swaminarayan Hindu Temple, Meadow Garth, London NW10 8HD (Tel. 0181 965 2651). The temple and cultural center are open daily 9a.m.–12 noon and 4–6p.m.

St Mary's Church, Willesden, High Rd, Willesden, London NW10 2TT (Tel. 0181 1459 2167).

Sternberg Centre for Judaism and Leo Baeck College, The Manor House, 80 East End Rd, London N3 2SY (Tel. 0181 346 2288).

Bhaktivedanta Manor, Letchmore Heath, Herts WD2 8EP (Tel. 01923 857244). The best time to visit is on a Sunday afternoon, but visitors are warmly welcome at any time.

Amaravati Buddhist Monastery, *Great Gaddesden, Hemel Hempstead, Herts, HP1 3BZ (Tel. 01442 842455).* The monastery organizes formal meditation retreats for periods ranging from a weekend to a month. Lay guests may come for just a few hours – to hear a public lecture, attend a meditation class, visit the library, or join in the daily evening meditation with the Sangha.

Church of Christ the Cornerstone, *300 Saxon Gate West, Central Milton Keynes, MK9 2ES (Tel. 01908 237777).*

Jain Centre, *32 Oxford St, Leicester, LE1 5XU (Tel. 0116 254 3091).* Visitors to the temple are very welcome each afternoon between 2p.m. and 5p.m., Monday to Friday. Groups should make an appointment so that they can be shown round.

Guru Nanak Sikh Gurdwara, *9 Holy Bones, Leicester, LE1 5LJ (Tel. 0116 251 7460).* Visitors are always welcome. The museum is open to visitors on Thursday afternoons between 1p.m. and 4p.m., and this is the best time to visit the gurdwara.

Shree Jalaram Prathna Mandal, *85 Narborough Road, Leicester, LE3 0LF (Tel. 0116 254 0117).* All guests are welcomed at any time. The temple is open daily from 9a.m. to 8:30p.m., but closed on weekday lunchtimes from 1p.m. to 3p.m..

Bradford Interfaith Education Centre, *Listerhills Rd, Bradford, BD1 1HD (Tel. 01274 731674).* Staff at the center are happy to organize your visit to places of worship in Bradford, or even to take you there themselves.

Jamia Masjid Hanfia Mosque, *Carlisle Rd, Bradford, BD8 8AD (Tel. 01274 492539).* The community is sensitive to visitors entering the mosque and request that an appointment should be made first. A visit can be arranged through the Bradford Interfaith Centre.

Quaker Meeting House, *Brigflatts, Sedbergh, Cumbria.*

Manjushri Mahayana Buddhist Centre, *Conishead Priory, Ulverston, Cumbria, LA12 9QQ (Tel. 01229 584029).* Visitors are always welcome, whether to attend a course (there is a retreat or course most weekends), participate in the daily program, or just relax and enjoy the atmosphere. One way to sample the life of the community is on a working visit: you receive a week's vegetarian meals and accommodation in return for thirty hours of work.

Kagyu Samye Ling Buddhist Monastery, *Eskdalemuir, Langholm, Dumfries and Galloway, DF13 0QL (Tel. 013873 73232).* Accommodation can be booked in one of their guest rooms at standard rates. The shop is open in the afternoons and a café is open in the afternoons and evenings at weekends. Lunch is served daily 12:30–1:30.

St Mungo Museum of Religious Life and Art, *Cathedral Precinct, Glasgow, G4 0RH (Tel. 0141 553 2557).* The galleries are open daily 10a.m.–5p.m. (Sundays 11a.m.–5p.m.).

Glasgow Central Mosque and Islamic Centre, *1 Mosque Avenue,* *off Ballater St, Glasgow, G5 9TX (Tel. 0141 429 3132)*. Opening times are 9a.m.–5p.m., Monday to Thursday. Visitors should telephone beforehand and someone from the office will show them round. The office is also open on Fridays, but the mosque is very busy for Friday prayers and visitors are requested to avoid visiting during this time.

Iona Abbey, *Isle of Iona, PA76 6SN (Tel. 01681 700404)*. For a visitor with little time to spend on Iona, the best way of seeing the island is to join the weekly pilgrimage tour on Wednesdays. In summer there are regular groups in residence. The island has two general shops, a post office, a restaurant and the Abbey Shop and Coffee House.

Findhorn Foundation Community, *The Park, Findhorn, Forres, IV36 0TZ (Tel. 01309 690311)*. The visitors' center welcomes visitors and supplies information about the community. Accommodation can be booked in the caravan park (Tel. 01309 690203). Check in advance to make sure no special activities such as conferences are on, when the normal programs are disrupted. Bed and breakfast with one of the open-community members can be arranged.

$\mathscr{P}$laces to Stay Along the Way

This list suggests two sorts of accommodation: Retreat Houses (RH), including monasteries, abbeys and other spiritual centers, most of which offer one-night stays, and Bed and Breakfast stops (B&B) with special character.

Where retreat houses advertise that they accommodate overnight guests we have said so; otherwise you are advised to inquire. In any case, make sure you book ahead, as many retreat houses are booked well in advance.

The Canterbury Pilgrimage

Mays Farmhouse, B&B
Near Winchester
Longwood Dean, Hampshire SO21 1JS
Tel 01962 777486, Fax 01962 777747
3 bedrooms and large garden.

This sixteenth-century thatched house, with its oak beams and open log fire, is right in character with nearby Winchester. The owner runs craft workshops and cares for white goats in her garden.

Old Alresford Place, RH
Near Winchester
Alresford, Hampshire SO24 9DH
Tel/Fax 01962 732518
50 bedspaces in 25 rooms.

In the heart of Hampshire. A house for retreats, workshops, conferences for self-development and spiritual growth. Protestant orientation, but welcomes all to drop in for quiet and reflection. Home cooking, friendly staff, specializes in counseling, meditation and prayer.

Bulmer Farm, B&B
Near Dorking
Holmbury St Mary, Surrey, RH5 6LG
Tel 01306 730210
8 comfortable rooms, large garden.

In the folds of Surrey's high North Downs a number of picturesque villages lie hidden, and Holmbury is one. Near the center stands Bulmer Farm, built around 1680. Inside are oak beams and a log fire. Some of the rooms are in outer buildings, offering a tranquil place to contemplate amid the varied wildlife attracted to the garden's lake: heron, kingfishers, Canada geese, snipe and other wildfowl. The lake received a conservation award.

High Edser, B&B
Near Guildford
Shere Rd, Ewhurst, Surrey GU6 7PQ
Tel 01483 278214, Fax 01483
278200
3 bedrooms, large garden.

*Ewhurst means "yew wood" and the
great stump of an ancient yew tree
dominating the garden is a reminder
of the past surroundings of this large,
handsome sixteenth century house.
Inside can be seen the wattle and daub
construction, winding staircase, lattice-
paned windows and stone floors of the
original construction.*

The Friars, RH
Aylesford
Kent ME20 7BX
Tel 01622 717272, Fax 01622 715575
100 bedspaces in 62 rooms.

*Home of a community of Carmelite
Friars running a program of retreats in
this ancient restored friary. Its revival,
and its large open-air church, has made
it an important Catholic pilgrimage center. Beautifully situated on the banks of
the River Medway, with lovely gardens
maintained by the friars, which include
a unique rosary meditation walk under
the trees. Specializes in counseling and
prayer. Individuals welcomed for
overnight stays.*

Cathedral Gate Hotel, B&B
36 Burgate
Canterbury, Kent CT1 2HA
Tel 01227 464381, Fax 01227 462800
24 bedrooms.

*In the heart of old Canterbury tucked
beside the ancient gateway to the cathedral. The bedrooms, retaining ancient
beams and bow windows, are reached
through a maze of corridors and creak-*

*ing stairways. Direct access to the cathe-
dral grounds, and a magnificent view of
the cathedral's floodlit towers at night.*

Ely to Walsingham

Bishop Woodford House, RH
Barton Rd, Ely,
Cambridgeshire CB7 4DX
Tel 01353 6630339
32 single rooms and 2 double rooms.

*In the cathedral town of Ely. Chapel,
conferences, garden and library.
Anglican orientation. Individuals
welcomed for overnight stays.*

Spinney Abbey, B&B
Near Ely
Wicken, Cambridgeshire CB7 5XQ
Tel 01353 720971
3 spacious and comfortable rooms.

*Stands on the site of the original
Spinney Abbey, dissolved under Henry
VIII. The abbey's stones were used to
build the present house in 1775. Views
from the farmlands to Wicken Fen, a
National Trust nature reserve.*

Old Stable House Centre, RH
3 Sussex Lodge, Fordham Rd,
Newmarket, Suffolk CB8 7AF
Tel/Fax 01638 667190
14 bedspaces in 9 rooms
(includes 4 singles).

*Old stable building converted to a small
retreat and spirituality center with an
attractive and restful environment.
Individuals welcomed for informal time
out and reflection or retreat. Supports
spiritual growth with workshops and
retreats with a holistic creation-centered
focus. Arts & crafts, bodywork &
breathwork, counseling, health & heal-*

ing, meditation and prayer. Individuals welcomed for overnight stays.

Wood Norton Hall, RH
Near North Elmham
Hall Lane, Wood Norton, Norfolk
NR20 5BE
Tel 01362 683804
22 bedspaces in 8 rooms.

A fine Georgian house with spacious and comfortable rooms set in 4 acres of tranquil private grounds. A varied program of residential courses is offered, with a New Age orientation. Arts & crafts, bodywork & breathwork, health & healing, meditation and self-expression. All Vegetarian. Individuals welcomed for overnight stays.

Berry Hall, B&B
Great Walsingham
Norfolk, NR22 6DZ
Tel 01328 820267
5 bedrooms and a sitting room with an open fire in large grounds.

This fine Tudor house, built in 1532, was once home to the poet Rupert Brooke's family. Flagstone floor, great staircase, fine paneling and impressive oak ceiling. Beyond the gardens with their rose beds and magnificent copper beech tree lies a moat with ducks.

Sue Ryder Retreat House, RH
Walsingham
Norfolk NR22 6AA
Tel 01328 820622, Fax 01328 820505
8 single rooms and 9 doubles.
Chapel, small garden and guest lounge.

Inter-denominational, offering private retreats and conferences. Traditional food, situated in the quiet country. Individuals welcomed for overnight stays.

Lincoln to Crowland

Edward King House, RH
The Old Palace, Lincoln LN2 1PU
Tel 01522 528778
5 single and 12 double rooms.
Garden, library and guest lounge.

This historic Anglican house was once the residence of the Bishops of Lincoln and stands in the cathedral precincts next to the Old Palace. Programs include a "journey of the senses" and a pilgrimage round the cathedral as a "path of holiness."

Guy Wells, B&B
North-east of Crowland
Eastgate Rd, Whaplode,
Lincolnshire PE12 6TZ
Tel 01406 422239
3 bedrooms.

This beautifully located Queen Anne house gets its name from the springs welling up among the traditional gardens and trees which surround it. Beyond these are spread the Fens, the East Anglian wetlands which teem with wildlife. Delicious whole foods using home-grown vegetables, honey and eggs.

The Mill, B&B
Near Market Deeping (and east of Stamford)
Mill Lane, Tallington, Lincolnshire
PE9 4RR
Tel 01780 740815, Fax 01780 740280
6 bedrooms.

The medieval town of Stamford, just off the pilgrimage route, is rich with old inns and churches, on the River Welland. As the river flows eastward, it passes Tallington village where it flows beneath this eighteenth-century water-

mill, which still retains its original gears, shafts, winches and millstones.

Lichfield to Mam Tor

New House Farm, RH
Ashbourne
Kniveton, Derbyshire DE6 IJL
Tel 01335 342429
15 bedspaces in 6 rooms.

Traditional organically managed family farm. Bronze age burials, quarry, wild-flower area, free-range livestock and beautiful gardens. Converted hayloft is a library and study. Retreats are self-directed. Herbalism, conservation work and horticulture, with a Celtic Christian orientation. Individuals welcomed for overnight stays.

Atlow Mill Centre, RH
Near Ashbourne
Hognaston, Derbyshire DE6 1PX
Tel 01335 370494
23 beds in 7 rooms
(4 singles included).

A beautifully converted old mill nestling in its own secluded valley, surrounded by pasture and woodlands with a brook running nearby. Has many courses for mind, body and spirit including art therapy, the inner child, relationships and one-to-one counseling. The orientation is New Age. Vegetarian food only. Individuals welcomed for overnight stays.

Well Head Farm, B&B
Near Buxton
Wormhill, Derbyshire SK17 8SL
Tel 01298 871023
4 cottage-style bedrooms.
Adjoining teahouse.

A 400 year old oak-beamed limestone farmhouse with stone slabbed roof in the midst of the Peak District of the Pennines, Britain's ancient backbone. As its name suggests, the house stands upon an old well, which supplies its water. A nearby footpath leads down to the Wye River in Miller's Dale.

Ripon to Jarrow

Bay Tree Farm, B&B
Near Ripon
Aldfield, Ripon, Yorkshire HG4 3BE
Tel 01765 620394
6 bedrooms.

Close to the spectacular ruins of Fountains Abbey. Converted seven-teenth-century stone barn.

Crofts, B&B
Near Thirsk
Carlton Husthwaite
North Yorkshire, YO7 2BJ
Tel 01845 501325
2 bedrooms, garden.

Two typical, warm-yellow-bricked Yorkshire cottages converted into one. A pony and free-range hens live out-side, and three dogs and a cat are included in the household.

Grove House, B&B
Near Bishop Auckland
Hamsterley Forest, County Durham, DL13 3NL
Tel 01388 488203
3 bedrooms.

Fairy-tale house buried deep amid 5000 acres of forest managed by the Forestry Commission. Birdsong is the loudest sound.

Cartmel to Aspatria

Rydal House, RH

Carlisle Diocesan Retreat
& Conference Centre,
Ambleside, Cumbria LA22 9LX
Tel 01539 632050
10 single rooms and 15 doubles.
Garden, library.

A relaxed atmosphere in this big Georgian house set in the heart of the peaceful Lake District among waterfalls and many gardens. Personal talks, meditation and directed study. Individuals welcomed for overnight stays.

Fell Edge, B&B

High Ireby, Cumbria CA5 1HF
Tel 016973 71397
2 bedrooms. Garden, open fireplace, piano.

In the tiny hamlet of High Ireby, Fell Edge was built in the eighteenth century as a chapel. Quiet and peaceful location with glorious views of the northern fells and gardens. Near Holm Cultram Abbey and the western end of Hadrian's Wall.

Riggs Cottage, B&B

Routenbeck, Bassenthwaite,
Cumbria, CA13 9YN
Tel/Fax 017687 76580
3 bedrooms, large garden.

Riggs Cottage is a sixteenth century house hidden at the foot of a private lane. Home-cooked food. Friendly and peaceful atmosphere. Near Cockermouth, birthplace of William Wordsworth.

Low Hall, B&B

Brandlingill,
Near Cockermouth
Cumbria CA13 0RE
Tel 01900 826654
3 double rooms, garden.

Low Hall stands by itself in a beautiful valley on the quieter side of the Lake District National Park. The 300-year old house has a relaxing family atmosphere.

Worcester to Dorchester-on-Thames

Prinknash Abbey, RH

Near Cheltenham
Cranham, Gloucester GL4 8EX
Tel 01452 812455
6 single rooms. Chapel, library.
Men only.

The monastery sitting on the hill looks from the outside rather stark and modern but inside it is warm, comfortable and reassuringly modest and simple. St Peter's Grange is the guest house, a mellow pile of stone set against a hill with a quiet garden entrance. It is a distinguished place of mainly Tudor buildings originally connected with Gloucester Cathedral, which was used as a monastery until the new abbey was built in the 1970s. Most of the original paneling and antique features have been retained, including a beautifully decorated chapel and choir.

The Abbey, RH

Near Abingdon
Sutton Courtenay, Oxfordshire
OX14 4AF
Tel 01235 847401
7 single rooms and 6 doubles in the Abbey and modern guest house. Garden, library, meditation room and shrine room.

The small Abbey community seeks to offer rest and support for all looking for peace and spirituality. There are events to encourage personal, social and ecological change. Many courses on offer. Individuals welcomed for overnight stays.

Priory of Our Lady, RH
Burford
Oxfordshire OX8 4SQ
Tel 01993 823605
4 single and 4 double rooms.
Chapel, gardens, library.

Situated in picturesque Burford, this is the home of an Anglican community of monks and nuns. The guesthouse is a late sixteenth century house with its own gardens in the Priory grounds. Warm and welcome atmosphere, perfect for prayer, study and reflection.

Rectory Farm, B&B
Near Oxford
Northmoor, Oxfordshire OX8 1SX
Tel 01865 300207, Fax 01865 300559
2 bedrooms, large garden.

This fifteenth century stone farmhouse has views of fields, animals, farms and gardens; 400 acres of land with crops, cattle and sheep.

Cherwell Centre, RH
14 -16 Northam Gardens
Oxford OX2 6QB
Tel 01865 52106, Fax 01865 58183
29 bedspaces in 21 rooms.

The Cherwell Centre is run by a group of Catholic women, the Society of the Holy Child, who work hard to create an atmosphere that is peaceful and free from distraction. Situated in North Oxford near some beautiful parks. Specializes in counseling, inner process,

meditation and prayer. Individuals welcomed for overnight stays.

Stonehenge to Glastonbury

Tordown Healing Centre, RH
5 Ashwell Lane
Glastonbury, Somerset BA6 8BG
Tel 01458 832287, Fax 01458 831100
2 single, 3 double and 2 family rooms. Garden & park. All vegetarian food.

On the southern slopes of the Tor overlooking the Vale of Avalon. Activities include Reiki teaching, healing, personal talks, group sharing and meditation. Quiet surroundings. Glorious views of waterfalls and ponds. Welcoming, friendly, peaceful and spiritual atmosphere. Individuals welcomed for overnight stays.

Yew Tree Cottage, RH and B&B
Near Salisbury
Grove Lane, Redlynch, Salisbury, Wiltshire SP5 2NR
Tel 01725 511730
5 bedspaces in 3 rooms.

The spacious cottage is in a large garden overlooking a grazing paddock in the beautiful New Forest. Superb for quiet walks and exploring the countryside. Peaceful and quiet. Hands-on healing and massage available. Individuals welcomed for overnight stays.

Little Langford Farmhouse, B&B
Wilton
Little Langford, Wiltshire SP3 4NR
Tel 01722 790205, Fax 01722 790086
3 bedrooms, large garden.

The farmhouse is a fine example of

Victorian Gothic architecture. The house is situated in the rolling downs of the Wyle Valley where you can see as far as the Marlborough White Horse. Quiet and peaceful.

Farthings, B&B
9 Swaynes Close
Salisbury, Wiltshire SP1 3AE
Tel/Fax 01722 330749
4 bedrooms, small garden.

Though in the city, Farthings is very quiet, with views of Salisbury Cathedral, the tallest spire in England, in the distance. It has a garden brimming with flower beds.

Melbury Hill, B&B
Shaftesbury
Melbury Abbas, Dorset SP7 0DB
Tel 01747 852163
3 bedrooms, large garden.

Melbury Hill was built in the eighteenth century. Views of beautiful garden and millpond. Many beautiful places to go for a quiet country walk. Very peaceful.

St. Michael's Mount to Tintagel

Tregeraint House, B&B
Near St Ives
Zennor, St Ives, Cornwall TR26 3DB
Tel 01736 797061
8 beds in 4 rooms (1 single).

A roomy and traditional granite cottage in a magnificent location overlooking sea and hills. Warm and friendly.

Boswednack Manor, RH
Near St Ives
Zennor, St Ives, Cornwall TR26 3DD
Tel 01736 794183
10 beds in 5 rooms.

Overlooking sea and moors. Organic garden and meditation room. Buddhist spiritual orientation. Individuals welcomed for overnight stays.

CAER, RH
Rosemerryn, Lamorn, Penzance, Cornwall TR19 6BN
Tel 01736 810530
24 beds in 10 rooms (4 singles).

On the site of an Iron-Age settlement near the sea, with 7 acres of woodland, gardens and streams. In the grounds is a 2500-year-old temple. The surrounding area is said to have more ancient sites than anywhere else in Europe. Individuals welcomed for overnight stays.

Old Mill, B&B
Near Padstow
Little Petherick, Cornwall PL27 7QT
Tel 01841 540388
7 bedrooms, 3 sitting rooms.

A sixteenth-century watermill with working waterwheel in a picturesque village. The house is full of interesting antique objects and has exposed beams and white stone walls. The paved terrace by the stream is a sun-trap.

Chester to Bardsey Island

Plas Penucha, B&B
Near Holywell
Caerwys, Clwyd CH7 5BH
Tel 01352 720210
4 bedrooms, large garden.

Ancestral home originally built by one of Elizabeth I's buccaneers with gold from the Spanish Armada, and still occupied by his descendants. Oak-beamed interior with Elizabethan paneling. Views outside toward the Clwydian Mountains.

Christian Retreat and Holiday Centre, RH
South of Colwyn Bay
Pencraig Arthur, Llanddoged,
Llanwrst, Gwynedd LL26 0DZ
Tel 01492 640959
2 singles, 5 doubles.

On the edge of Snowdonia National Park in the Conwy Valley with excellent walks and the famous Bodnant Gardens 5 miles away. Spiritual breaks and guided retreats offered by the resident Methodist minister. Inter-denominational. Individuals welcomed for overnight stays.

Trigonos Centre, RH
Near Caernarfon
Nantlle, Gwynedd LL54 6BW
Tel 01286 882388
28 beds in 14 rooms (4 singles).

The site is of spectacular beauty, sheltered in 18 acres of woodlands overlooking a lake and through the foothills to Mount Snowdon. Arts center, large library, organic food. Group work and community development a speciality. Individuals welcomed for overnight stays.

Loreto Centre, RH
Near Llandudno
Abbey Road, Llandudno, Gwynedd LL30 2EL
Tel 01492 877031
24 singles, 10 doubles.

Spectacular views from the foot of Great Ormes Head over the West Shore. A comfortable place to stay, it is run by the Roman Catholic Loreto Sisters who are on hand for personal help or guidance.

Bronant, B&B
Near Caernarfon
Bontnewydd, Gwynedd LL54 7YF
Tel 01286 830451
3 bedrooms.

Looking out over the Menai Straits to Anglesey is this handsome Victorian house, which includes a public tea-room serving traditional Welsh teas with prize-winning Welsh cakes. Spacious rooms with views of sheep, pine trees and mountains.

Llandaff to St. David's

West Usk Lighthouse, RH
Near Cardiff
St Brides, Wentloog, Newport,
Gwent NP1 9SF
Tel 01633 810126
2 singles, 4 doubles.

The lighthouse was built in 1821 and designed to house two lighthouse-keeper families. It overlooks the Bristol Channel and Severn Estuary as well as Welsh hills and valleys. An ideal place to unwind. Brilliant coastal walks. The lighthouse is on the crossing point of two leylines and has a special atmosphere about it. Individuals welcomed for overnight stays.

Graig Fach Workshops, RH
Near Llanelli
Llangennech, Llanelli,
Dyfed SA14 8PX
Tel 01554 759944
2 double rooms.

Family small-holding and studio in the woods above a river, a world away from the nearest highway. From the door, walks lead to lakes, castles and a sandy beach. Arts & crafts, writing and meditation are offered.

Tregynon, B&B
Near Fishguard
Gwaun Valley, Dyfed SA65 9TU
Tel 01239 820531
6 bedrooms, 2 sitting rooms.
Large grounds.

*Surrounded by spectacular scenery.
Across the River Gwaun (pronounced
"Gwine") rises the peak of Carningli
Mountain — "Mountain of Angels" —
where St Brynech was regularly attended
by angels when he prayed. The sixteenth-
century farmhouse is carefully restored
and offers spacious accommodation,
with a restaurant for those who do not
wish to cater for themselves.*

Gretna to Lindisfarne

**Kagyu Samye Ling Tibetan
Centre, RH**
Near Eskdalemuir
Langholm, Dumfries DG13 0QL
Tel 01387 373232
58 singles, 6 doubles.

*This might well be Britain's best-
known Tibetan Buddhist center.
Accommodation can be booked in one
of their guest rooms. Individuals are
welcomed for overnight stays.*

Isle of Iona

*There are three options at Iona, all of
which offer overnight stays in a retreat
environment:*

Duncraig, RH
Isle of Iona, Argyll PA76 6SP
Tel 01681 700202
Bishop's House, RH
Isle of Iona, Argyll PA76 6SJ
Tel 01681 700306

Iona Community, RH
The Abbey and MacLeod Centre
Isle of Iona, Argyll PA76 6SN
Tel 01681 700404

Centre of Light, RH
Near Inverness
Tighnabruaich, Struy, By Beauly,
Inverness IV4 7JU
Tel 01463 761254

*Situated in 5 acres of grounds surround-
ed by mountains, rivers, forests and
waterfalls, and overlooking Beauly
Firth. Meditation and personal therapy.
Organic vegetarian food. Individuals
welcomed for overnight stays.*

Minton House, RH
Near Forres
Findhorn Bay, Forres,
Moray IV36 0TZ
Tel 01309 690819
7 bedrooms.

*A retreat house linked to the Findhorn
Foundation. The large pink mansion
stands on the shoreline of Findhorn Bay
in 7 acres of grounds with lovely views.*

Letterfourie House, RH
Buckie, Banffshire AB56 2JP
Tel 01309 690311

*A magnificent eighteenth-century
mansion on a historic estate offering
great walking. An ideal place for peace
and relaxation. Individuals welcomed
for overnight stays.*

BIBLIOGRAPHY

Antiquities of Roman Britain, British Museum, 1964

Asser, *Alfred the Great*, Penguin Books, London, 1983

Brodie, Ian O., *Cistercian Way*, Carnegie Press, Cadley, Preston, 1989

Burl, Aubrey, *A Guide to Stone Circles of Britain, Ireland and Brittany*, Yale University Press, New Haven, USA, 1995

Carlisle Diocesian Board of Education, *Christian Heritage Trails*, Carlisle, 1993

Chetan, Arnand and Brueton, Diana, *The Sacred Yew*, Penguin Arkana, 1994

Clarke, David, *A Guide to Britain's Pagan Heritage*, Robert Hale, London, 1995

Diocese of Carlisle Resource's Centre, *Outstanding Cumbrian Christians*, West Walls, Carlisle

Doble, G.H., *Lives of the Welsh Saints*, University of Wales Press, Cardiff, 1971

Eden Tourism, *Eden Church Trails*, Eden District Council, Penrith

Houlder, Christopher, *Wales: An Archaeological Guide*, Faber & Faber, London, 1978

Jeffrey, P.H., *Ghosts, Legends and Lore of Wales*, Old Orchard Press, Cambridge, 1990

Jones, Francis, *The Holy Wells of Wales*, University of Wales Press, Cardiff, 1992

Julian of Norwich, *Revelations of Divine Love*, Penguin Books, London, 1966

Lloyd, David W., *The Making of English Towns*, Gollanz, London, 1992

Mackay, Sheila, *Lindisfarne Landscapes*, Saint Andrew Press, Edinburgh, 1996

O'Malley, Brenda, *A Welsh Pilgrim's Manual*, Gomer, Llandysul, 1989

O'Malley, Brian Brendan (compiler), *A Pilgrim's Manual – St. David's*, Paulinus Press, Marlborough, 1985

Ordnance Survey – *Roman and Medieval Canterbury*, *Ancient Britain* and *Roman Britain*

Palmer, Martin, *Travels through Sacred China*, Thorsons, London, 1996

Pearson, Michael Parker, *Bronze Age Britain*, Batsford/English Heritage, London, 1993

Pennick, Nigel, *Celtic Sacred Landscapes*, Thames and Hudson, London, 1996

Pevsner, Nikolaus, *The Buildings of England: North Somerset and Bristol*, Penguin Books, London, 1958

Ponting, Clive, *A Green History of the World*, Sinclair-Stevenson, London, 1991

Ramsay, Jay (editor), *Earth Ascending*, Stride Publications, Exeter, 1997

Rattue, James, *The Living Stream*, Boydell Press, Suffolk, 1995

Salter, Mike, *The Old Parish Churches of Mid-Wales*, Folly Publishing, Malvern, 1991

Thomas, Patrick, *Candle in the Darkness*, Gomer, Llandysul, 1993

Tomes, John, *Blue Guide: Scotland*, A & C Black, London, 1992

Tomes, John, *Blue Guide: Wales*, A & C Black, London, 1992

Webb, J.F. (translator), *The Age of Bede: Bede – Life of Cuthbert; Eddius Stephanus – Life of Wilfred; Bede – Lives of Abbots of Wearmouth and Jarrow with the Voyage of St. Brendan*, Penguin Books, 1965

Westwood, Jennifer, *Albion – A Guide to Legendary Britain*, Grafton, London, 1992

Wood, Eri. S., *Collins Field Guide to Archaeology in Britain*, Collins, London, 1979

GENERAL INDEX

Bold indicates illustrations.

Whitby Abbey, North Yorkshire

INDEX OF PLACES

~~~~~~~~~~~~~~~~~~~~~~~~~~~~~~~~~~ 〽〜 ~~~~~~~~~~~~~~~~~~~~~~~~~~~~~~~~

Bold indicates illustrations.

Callanish, Isle of Lewis, Western Isles

CREDITS

⸎

Photographs: book cover © Spectrum Colour Library; p. IX © Woodmansterne; p. 5 © Janet and Colin Bord/Fortean Picture Library; p. 10 © Collections/Michael Allen; p. 23 © Collections/Esther James; p. 24 © Collections/Fay Godwin; p. 30 © CircaPhoto Library/John Smith; p. 33 © the Ancient Art and Architecture Collection Ltd./Charles Tait; p. 37 © Spectrum Colour Library; p. 42 © Homer Sykes; p. 44 © Janet and Colin Bord/ Fortean Picture Library; p. 61 © Jean Williamson/Mick Sharp; p. 65 © the Ancient Art and Architecture Collection Ltd./Cheryl Hogue; p. 72 © Viewfinder Colour Photo Library; p. 86 © Mick Sharp; p. 92 from A Book of the Prospects of the Remarkable Places in and about the City of London by Bob Morden, © O'Shea Gallery, London/Bridgeman Art Library, London; p. 98 © Sonia Halliday Photographs; p. 101 © Spectrum Colour Library; p. 109 © Dorset County Museum/Bridgeman Art Library, London; p. 111 © Heather Angel; p. 123 © Collections/Liz Stares; p. 137 © Collections/Robin Weaver; p. 140 © Collections/Robin Weaver; p. 147 © Robert Harding Picture Library Ltd.; p. 148 © Viewfinder Colour Photo Library/Barry Davies; p. 152 © the Ancient Art and Architecture Collection Ltd.; p. 153 © Jean Williamson/Mick Sharp; p. 165 © Robert Harding Picture Library Ltd./M. Jenner; p. 177 © Viewfinder Colour Photo Library; p. 179 © Viewfinder Colour Photo Library; p. 183 © Mick Sharp; p. 200 © Viewfinder Colour Photo Library; p. 202 Roy 10 A XIII f.2v St. Dunstan writing "Commentary of Smaragdus" (c. 1200), © British Library, London/Bridgeman Art Library, London; p. 203 © Viewfinder Colour Photo Library; p. 210 © Viewfinder Colour Photo Library; p.

217 © Mick Sharp; p. 218 © Janet and Colin Bord/Fortean Picture Library; p. 223 © Homer Sykes; p. 234 © Collections/Collier's; p. 240 © Janet and Colin Bord/Fortean Picture Library; p. 252 © Jean Williamson/Mick Sharp; p. 254 © Robert Harding Picture Library Ltd./C. Bowman; p. 266 © J. Allen Cash Ltd.; p. 271 © Robert Harding Picture Library Ltd./Roy Rainford; p. 288 © J. Allen Cash Ltd.; four-color insert, page A, top left © Sonia Halliday and Laura Lushington; top right © Robert Harding Picture Library Ltd./Ellen Rooney; bottom © Viewfinder Colour Photo Library; page B, top left © Mirror Syndication International (BTA)/Barry Hicks; top right © Collections/Gary R. Smith; bottom left © the Ancient Art and Architecture Collection Ltd./Charles Tait; bottom right © Viewfinder Colour Photo Library/Barry Davies; page C © Robert Harding Picture Library Ltd./Roy Rainford; page D top left © the Ancient Art and Architecture Collection Ltd./Cheryl Hogue; top right © Viewfinder Colour Photo Library/Christopher Nicholson; bottom left © Janet and Colin Bord/Fortean Picture Library; bottom right © Mick Sharp.

Text: chapter opening verses, Jay Ramsay, "The Sacred Way," 1996; p. IX T. S. Eliot, excerpt from 'Little Gidding', Four Quartets, reprinted by permission of Faber & Faber Ltd.; p. 38 Bronwen Griffiths, Sacred Sites, unpublished report for the Women's Environmental Network, 1995; pp. 90/91 Keith Douglas, 'Vergissmeinnicht,' from The Complete Poems of Keith Douglas, edited by Desmond Graham, by permission Oxford University Press, 1978; pp. 94 and 98 extracts from Medieval English Verse, translated by Brian Stone (Penguin Classics, 1964, © Brian Stone) — no. 22 (p. 56, 16 lines) and 6 lines (p. 67) from no. 32 — and reproduced by permission of Penguin Books; pp. 111/112 William Cowper, 'The Poplar Fields' (1784), taken from The New Oxford Book of English Verse, edited by Helen Gardner, Oxford University Press, 1972; p. 123 Jacob

Glatstein, 'The Dead Do Not Praise God,' taken from *Judaism*, edited and interpreted by Arthur Hertzberg, Touchstone Books, a division of Simon and Schuster, New York, 1991; pp. 129/130 'Wish of Manchan of Liath,' from *Celtic Fire* by Robert van de Weyer, by permission of Darton, Longman and Todd, London, 1990; p. 135 Sydney Carter, 'George Fox,' reproduced by kind permission of Stainer & Bell Ltd., London; p. 138 Aubrey Burl *A Guide to Stone Circles of Britain, Ireland and Brittany*, Yale University Press, New Haven, 1995; p. 150 Prue Fitzgerald, 'Dream III' taken from *Earth Ascending*, Stride Publications, Exeter, 1997, sponsored by the Sacred Land project; p. 168 Alfred, Lord Tennyson, 'Morte d'Arthur,' Penguin Books, London, 1975; p. 181 Robert Crowley, 1551, 'Pleasure and Payne, Heaven and Hell,' taken from *The English Bible and the Seventeenth-Century Revolution* by Christopher Hill, Penguin Books, London, 1993; p. 188 John F. X. Harriot, *The Tablet*, vol. 235, no. 7409, 10 July 1982; p. 198 James Rattue, *The Living Stream*, Boydell Press, Suffolk, 1995 and reproduced by permission of Boydell and Brewer Ltd.; p. 209 *Tao Te Ching*, translated by Man-Ho Kwok, Martin Palmer, Jay Ramsay, Element Books, Longmead, 1993; p. 212 Thomas Traherne, from 'The Salutation,' *Penguin Book of English Verse*, Penguin Books, London, 1956; p. 215 *A Choice of Anglo-Saxon Verse*, translated by Richard Hamer, Faber & Faber, London 1970 (pp. 27-29) and reproduced by permission of Faber & Faber Ltd.; p. 218 Hildegard of Bingen, 'Antiphon for Divine Love,' taken from *Hildegard of Bingen — An Anthology*, edited by Fiona Bowie and Oliver Davies, translation by Robert Carver, SPCK, London 1990 and quoted by permission of the publishers; p. 231 *Liber Landavensis*, twelfth-century text provided by Nevil James of Llandaff Cathedral; p. 250 Very Rev. Lord MacLeod of Fuinary, 'The Whole Earth Shall Cry Glory,' Wild Goose Publications, the Iona Community, 1985; p. 259 'Deep Peace,' taken from *The Iona Community Worship Book*, Wild Goose Publications, 1984; and p. 288 Basil Bunting 'At Brigflatts Meeting House,' copy on display at the meeting house.

Whitby Abbey, North Yorkshire

KEY TO MAP SYMBOLS

Abbey		Multi-faith site
Castle		Municipal building
Cathedral		Omphalos
Cave		Pilgrim Fathers (home)
Cemetery		Place of interest
Church		Ruined abbey
Friend's meeting house		Shrine
Folly		Standing stone
Hadrian's Wall		Stately home
Hill fort		Stone circle
Megalithic tomb		Well
Monastery		Yew tree over 1500 years old
Mountain/hill		Tower

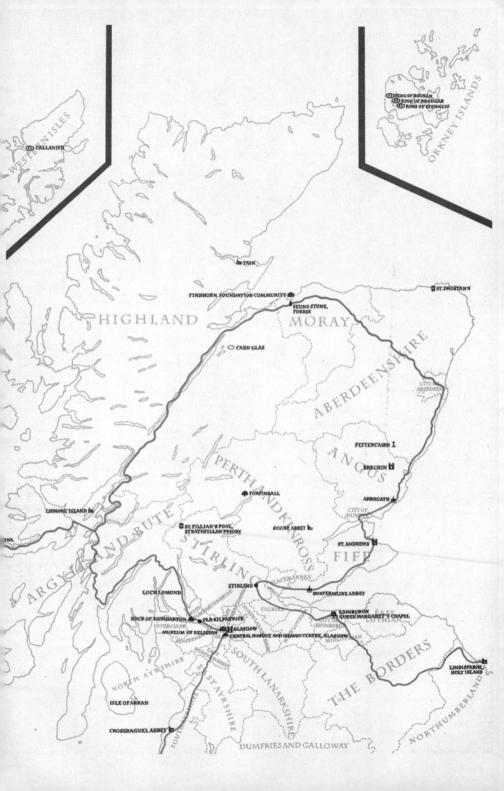

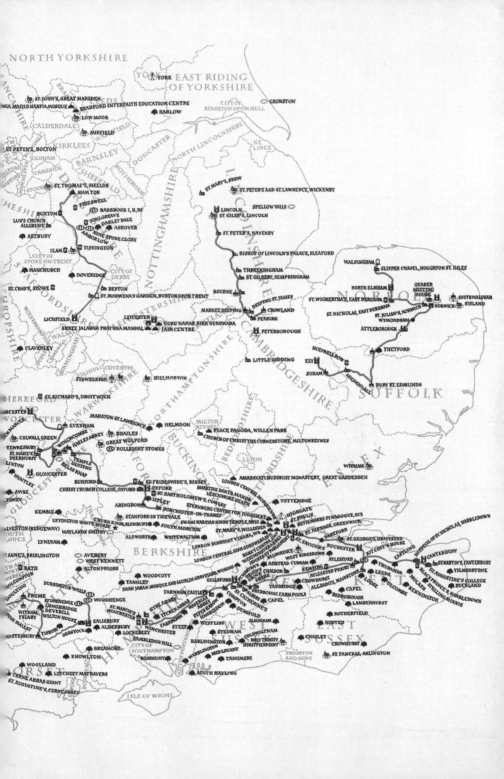